MY **9** INNINGS

MY 9 INNINGS

An Autobiography
of 50 Years in Baseball

Lee MacPhail

Meckler Books

C.1

B
MACPHAIL, L.

FIRST EDITION

Library of Congress Cataloging-in-Publication Data

MacPhail, Lee.
  My nine innings.

  Includes index.
  1. MacPhail, Lee.   2. Baseball—United States—
Managers—Biography.   3. New York Yankees (Baseball
team)   4. Baseball—United States—History.
I. Title.
GV865.M23A3   1989   796.357′092′4 [B]   89-2773
ISBN 0-88736-387-3 (alk. paper)

British Library Cataloguing in Publication Data

MacPhail, Lee
  My nine innings : an autobiography of 50 years in
  baseball.
  1. United States, Baseball — Biographies
  I. Title
  769.357′092′4

  ISBN 0-88736-387-3

Meckler Books, the Trade Division of Meckler Corporation,
  11 Ferry Lane West, Westport, CT 06880.
Meckler Ltd., Grosvenor Gardens House, Grosvenor Gardens,
  London SW1W 0BS, U.K.

Printed on acid free paper.
Printed and bound in the United States of America.

92 91 90 89   4 3 2 1

Dedication

This book is dedicated to Jane and Gwen, who suffered the absences and shared the hopes and worries of these years. It is also dedicated to the other members of my family, all of whom were very much a part of my life during these decades.

Contents

Preface

When I went into baseball in 1941, my father was president and general manager of the Brooklyn Dodgers. He had previously been president of the Cincinnati Reds and after the war would become president and part owner of the New York Yankees. Everywhere he went, he was very visible and made a major impact. Throughout my early years in the game, I was known as "Larry MacPhail's son."

More than four decades later, the year after I retired, my 34-year-old son, in his first year as executive vice president of the Minnesota Twins, helped guide that team to the pennant and World Championship. Suddenly, I became "Andy MacPhail's father."

This book is primarily concerned with the forty-some years between Larry and Andy—my own nine innings.

1

Pre-Game—Life Until Baseball

April 2, 1987 was about as perfect a day as I could imagine. Outside of the fact that my wife had a cold and an earache and couldn't participate, it would be hard to fill twelve hours more pleasantly. The weather in Delray Beach, Florida, was ideal—blue skies, a few puffy, white clouds, a little wind, no humidity. My son Andy, who is executive vice president of the Minnesota Twins, had come down from Orlando the night before, as the Twins were playing the New York Yankees in Fort Lauderdale in the afternoon. We got to play golf on our little course at St. Andrew's Club in the morning. It is only a par three course, but there are eighteen beautiful holes with sand, water, and flowers. (If your golf is bad you can check out the many species of birds in the ponds.) Fortunately, we were both playing pretty well and had a good match. Then after a shower and a quick lunch we took in the game in Fort Lauderdale.

I love that little ballpark. The playing field was the right shade of green and was in tip-top shape, with evergreens and palm trees behind the fences. The stands were close to full and the spring training crowd enthusiastic. Both teams had close to their opening day lineups on the field. Joe Niekro was starting for the Yankees, Bert Blyleven for the Twins. Minnesota looked good. Their fourteen hits earned them an 8–3 victory and made the afternoon most pleasant for Andy and me. After the game we took a quick tour of our old Fort Lauderdale haunts along Sunrise Boulevard and A1A, including the hotels where we had stayed while I was with the Yankees and the boys had come down for spring training. Then we had an early dinner at the Charcoal Pit restaurant, one of our old favorites. We shared a good bottle of wine and toasted Joe Iglehart (the owner of the Baltimore Orioles while I was there), who loved that restaurant, plus others in our family who could not be with us. We located the exact table and laughed over remembrances of my father holding his nose and grimacing as he downed a double martini. The food was good and we enjoyed ourselves. Spring training is that kind of time for baseball people. Optimism abounds. It is usually possible to dwell on good developments and encouraging signs. Losses don't yet count against you.

I dropped Andy at the Fort Lauderdale Airport for his flight back to Orlando and drove back to Delray Beach. The pleasant day started me thinking about how fortunate my life has been—how lucky I was to spend my working years in baseball. As I covered the thirty or so miles of I-95 between Fort Lauderdale and Delray, many poignant memories came flooding in. Ballparks in Columbus, Cincinnati, and New York. Ebbets Field with its happy memories (and some not so happy—Mickey Owen missing the third strike in the 1941 World Series when my father was with the Dodgers and Cookie Lavagetto doubling to ruin Floyd Bevens's no-hitter and beat the Yankees in the 1947 World Series when my father was with the Yankees). And the time in Kansas City in 1947 when I was running the Kansas City Blues; we had a full ballpark and the Toledo Mud Hens train was three hours late. (We held every kind of field event you could think of to try to keep the fans entertained.) The finish of the 1949 pennant race after I had moved to New York as Yankee farm director when the Yankees beat the Boston Red Sox in the last two games of the season to finish one game ahead. I can still see the Red Sox right fielder diving for and missing Jerry Coleman's sinking line drive with the bases full late in the game. And Moose Skowron's long home run to left to clinch the seventh game of the 1958 World Series for the Yankees, after we had trailed Milwaukee three games to one.

There were my years with the Baltimore Orioles—the agility and grace of Brooks Robinson and Luis Aparicio in the field; the awesome power of Boog Powell at the plate; all the good, young pitching arms—plus the baffling styles of Stu Miller and Dick Hall in relief. A come-from-behind win over the Yankees in the 1964 pennant race, with seven runs after two were out in the eighth.

And then there were the Yankees, this time as general manager. Sparky Lyle riding in from the bull pen to the strains of "Pomp and Circumstance" on the stadium organ; Mickey Mantle's towering drive that almost got all the way out of Yankee Stadium; the quiet dependability of Mel Stottlemyre. The scores of minor league cities and towns I saw games in throughout my career in various capacities.*

---

*An incomplete list would include Rochester, Syracuse, Elmira, Binghamton, Olean, Bradford, Oneonta, West Haven, Manchester, Pittsfield, Norfolk, Richmond, Salem, Johnson City, Bristol, Charlestown, Bluefield,

The scouts and minor league managers. Watching prospects in high school and college games. Signing Thurman Munson at his home in Canton, Ohio. The countless baseball meetings and the camaraderie with people such as Jim Campbell, John McHale, Haywood Sullivan, Buzzie Bavasi, Gabe Paul, Hank Peters, Joe Brown, Bing Devine, Chub Feeney, Joe Burke, Bob Howsam, and scores of others. Worrying about whether or not to call a game for rain. My years as American League president. Being booed by 55,000 fans in Baltimore when I tried to make a presentation to Brooks on Brooks Robinson Day. Defending the umpires. Anguishing over American League All-Star losses. Arguing with the Players' Association during negotiations for a new Basic Agreement in 1985 and our great relief when an understanding was reached.

And 5,001 baseball games, each one capable of producing something you had never seen happen in a game before. Great, great memories. I still cannot quite accept that I am retired, for I feel as though I am fifty years old instead of seventy. The important thing is that, retired or not, one can still anguish over and exult in this wonderful pastime called baseball. It has been my world.

Life started for me on October 25, 1917, in Nashville, Tennessee. My sister Marian was already on the scene. Nashville was an unlikely birthplace for a member of our family, for my father came from Michigan, my mother from Illinois, and all of our time before and after has been spent largely in the Midwest or the East. My father was a young lawyer working in Chicago when he was sent to resuscitate a department store in Nashville. That is where he was when World War I finally engulfed the United States in April of 1917 and he enlisted in the 114th Field Artillery, a volunteer Tennessee unit. When he went off to war, my mother took my sister and me to Florida to live near relatives, and when the war was finally over, business opportunities took my father to Columbus, Ohio.

Greensboro, Winston-Salem, Kinston, Columbia, Augusta, Tampa, St. Petersburg, Orlando, Thomasville, New Orleans, Nashville, Memphis, Louisville, Newark, Toledo, Muskegon, Eau Claire, Aberdeen, Fargo, Grand Forks, Quincy, Peoria, Evansville, Springfield, Joplin, Muskogee, Independence, McAlester, Lawton, Beaumont, Little Rock, Amarillo, Longview, Salt Lake City, Boise, Helena, Portland, San Jose, Stockton, Modesto, and Santa Barbara. I can count forty-one states in which I have seen professional games.

Columbus is where our roots are. The same house on Woodland Avenue on Columbus's east side was our home for fifteen years. Woodland Avenue was a pleasant, elm-lined street in a middle-class neighborhood. It was a nice place in which to grow up.

My brother Bill was born in 1920, and we had a very normal and happy childhood. My father's father had some small-town banks in Michigan and a cottage at a Methodist resort north of Ludington. As a result, my family built a cottage there and we were fortunate enough to spend every summer vacation there, from the early 1920s to the time I graduated from college. Our cottage was directly on a glorious, Lake Michigan beach (eroded to nothing today) and we spent our summers swimming, sailing, and playing tennis and golf. Dad was a college football official and he took me on a few fall trips with him, mostly to small colleges in Ohio, but on one occasion to Washington, DC. We went to the Smithsonian, the Capitol, and the top of the Washington Monument.

My mother was a great lady and a friend to her children. She took part in all our family games, taught us bridge, and followed the baseball team with emotion. Her favorite pursuits were reading detective stories, talking with her friends on the telephone, driving her Auburn electric car, doing volunteer work for a hospital, and going to bridge parties. I remember once, when she was leaving the cottage in Michigan to go to a luncheon or some afternoon function and was dressed in a white linen suit, suddenly realizing that she was prettier than any of the young girls.

We were slightly afraid of our father. When angry, he was formidable, but I only remember being punished twice. During Prohibition, when I was quite young, I was punished for making mudpies out of the ale he had stored in the garage; the sentence for that would have been either to sit on a chair for an hour or stand with my nose in the corner. The second time was when one of my friends, in the presence of my parents, started innocently recounting how much fun we were having hopping freight trains for rides on the Norfolk and Western trains, whose tracks ran a mile from our house.

Life could not have proceeded more happily. My father started in the glass business in Columbus and switched to automobile agencies (Franklin, Willys-Knight, Overland, etc.). As far as I am aware, he was doing just fine. "Just fine" was never good enough for him, however, and he took everything he and my mother had and invested it in constructing a medical office building next door to the University Hospital on Columbus's north side. The idea was good, the timing disastrous. It was 1929 and he lost everything they had.

The Depression cast its pall on everything in Columbus in the early 30s, including the Columbus Senators baseball team, the city's representative in the American Association. The team was owned by Sid Weil, who also owned the Cincinnati Reds; he was close to bankruptcy. The team in Columbus was not going to be able to operate in 1931. At this point, a group of Columbus businessmen decided that, with morale at an all-time low, the area needed its baseball team more than ever, and they banded together to take it over. Then they looked for someone to run it, and their attention focused on one of their own group—a golfing partner, a Big Ten football official, and a fellow member of the Columbus Club (a top downtown business and social club), who happened to have time on his hands. Who better than Larry MacPhail?* My father thus became president of the Columbus Senators and, as a result, the entire MacPhail family became a part of the baseball world.

I was thirteen. Until that time I thought that the biggest sporting event in the world was the Ohio State-Michigan football game. Baseball had hardly existed for me. But from that moment until this, it has been a central and a very important part of my life. Except for my family and our country, it has been the most important thing in my life (two wives on isolated occasions have disputed which ranked first—baseball or family). We used to run home from school, jump in the car along with a couple of our friends, and our mother would drive us all to Neil Park, a not-too-modern wood ballpark where the team played. Next door was a bakery and when we approached the park there was often the smell of freshly baked bread, an aroma that is still associated in my mind with baseball. Across the street was a military encampment and whenever a Columbus player (usually the first baseman, Pat Crawford) would hit a ball over the right-field fence, the crowd would shout: "To the soldiers."

One spring Saturday, my father took me to the park with him and said he would take me down on the bench to meet some of the players. It was probably the first big thrill of my life. After my father had left me in the dugout during pregame batting practice however, I overheard veteran outfielder Pid Purdy (called "First Bounce Purdy" by the fans because of his knack for playing fly balls so safely he fielded them on the first hop) make a side remark to a fellow player. Pid said, "To hell with the kid, how about introducing us to the

---

*My father's name was Leland Stanford MacPhail. Leland Stanford (California railroad man, governor, "Robber Baron") was a friend of my father's parents. When Stanford lost a son named Leland, my grandmother said that she would name her first son in his memory. The name Larry attached to my father when his name was erroneously carried in an Ohio State football program (as an official) as Lawrence MacPhail. His friends thereafter called him Larry in fun and it stuck.

daughter?" meaning my eighteen-year-old sister, who was just entering the park down the first base aisle.

That group of Columbus businessmen wanted to save the team but they really did not want to remain in the baseball business. Therefore, my father made the rounds of the major league teams trying to get one to take over the franchise. He succeeded with the St. Louis Cardinals, agreeing to continue as the Columbus team's president. Thus began a love-hate relationship between Dad and Branch Rickey, the vice president and general manager of the Cardinals, which lasted until Rickey's death in 1965.

Branch Rickey was a strict Methodist (he did not attend games on Sunday); his personal habits were disciplined; he was dramatic; he was perhaps more egocentric than most people; and he continually and carefully planned ahead. My father was brilliant and impulsive, and his habits sometimes got him into trouble. It is no wonder that they clashed. But the clash did not come until after the Red Birds (as they had been renamed) had rekindled baseball interest in Columbus and created a great deal of excitement.

A new modern park with adjoining parking was constructed for the 1932 season. Lights were installed and the Cardinal farm system channeled talented young prospects to its new farm team (Burgess Whitehead, Lou Riggs, Bill Delancey, Bill Lee, Bud Parmelee, Daffy Dean, and others who would play in the majors), plus some Triple-A stars acquired from other teams, such as Nick Cullop, Art Shires, and Bevo LeBourveau (purchased from Toledo, my father boasted, for the largest sum ever paid for a minor league player). Bud Parmelee was my favorite and because he had an unusual way of walking on his toes, I went around for a year walking on mine. The team finished second in 1932 and drew more than 300,000 people—more than their parent Cardinals—an unbelievable figure then for Columbus, and rare for minor league baseball anywhere.

Early in the 1933 season, the clash occurred. There were several causes: my father fought with Rickey over the recall of a young player by the Cardinals; there was a fracas on the road when my father, after a heated exchange with the hotel manager, took the team out of the hotel in the middle of the night; and finally, a Columbus sportswriter wrote, "Branch objected to all the headlines Larry MacPhail was getting on the Columbus sports pages." So in mid-season of 1933, Dad refused the suggestion that he resign, but his relationship with the Red Birds was brought to an end. My father went fishing in Michigan, and Columbus went on to win the pennant.

He was not out of baseball for long. The depression had finally caught up to Sidney Weil in Cincinnati. Underfinanced, the team was finishing last and not drawing (under 200,000 in 1933), and ownership reverted to the Central Trust Company. Tom Conroy, the bank's top official, aware of the Columbus turnaround and of Larry MacPhail's availability, lost no time in hiring him and giving him complete charge of the team. As usual, my father jumped in with both feet; made a rash of player trades; appointed a new player-manager; refurbished the park; and beat the drum loudly.

More important, knowing that it would take capital to rebuild the Cincinnati Reds, he convinced Powell Crosley, Jr., owner of the Crosley Corporation (manufacturer of radios, refrigerators and, for a short spell, small automobiles), to take controlling interest in the club. He was now assured of the financing needed to set up a farm system, hire scouts, and buy players. Moreover, Crosley owned the powerful WLW radio station which, coincidentally, had just hired a young announcer from Florida named Red Barber. Barber became the team's announcer and he and my father became fast friends. To assist with promotion and publicity Dad employed a young Ohio State graduate, whom he had met at top amateur golf tournaments, by the name of Scotty Reston. Reston went on to become an editor of the *New York Times*.

Another important move was the hiring of a man with whom he had officiated football games, Frank Lane. Lane was just my father's type—aggressive, hardworking, willing to take chances, but unwilling to lose. But despite the multiple trades, the new playing manager (catcher, Bob O'Farrell), and all the publicity, the team continued to flounder, finished last, and drew barely more than 200,000. The only first the Reds managed in 1934 was to be the first baseball team to use air transportation, flying from Cincinnati to Chicago in an American Airlines Ford Tri-Motor plane. But after mid-season, Dad made another key move hiring Charlie Dressen as manager. With both Dressen and Lane as well as Barber, relationships were formed that continued throughout all of their careers.

Regardless of how things were going on the field, these were exciting days for our family. At first we used to drive down from Columbus (by now I was driving) for weekend games. At one game, our little group from Columbus included Mother, my sister Marian, a boyfriend of hers from college, Bill, and myself. We had front row box seats and with Cincinnati in the field, the batter hit a high pop foul right over our heads. The Cincinnati catcher was just about to catch it when Marian's friend, standing up, caught it right out of his glove. We were all slightly flabbergasted as it cost the Reds an out. I was embarrassed and had no chance to explain when Charlie Dressen came over later and told me that I was right in catching that ball and protecting my mother and sister.

By 1935 the Reds were beginning to be a reputable major league club. There were some solid veterans (Jim Bottomley, first baseman; Ernie Lombardi, catcher); some good acquisitions from other organizations (Billy Meyers, at short; Lou Riggs at third base; Ival Goodman, right field); and some youngsters from the new farm system (Alex Kampouris, Al Hollingsworth, Gene Schott). And to build up the attendance, my father put in lights. Although night games had been successful where tried in the minors, both major leagues had rules against the use of lights in major league games. It was scorned as a circus tactic not conducive to good major league play. Although almost everyone, including Landis, Frick, and most of the owners, were opposed to lights, my father talked the National League owners into letting him play one night game against each of the other seven teams. He then contracted with General Electric to put in the finest lighting plant the technology of the day could supply (borrowing the money to pay for it). The first game was played against Philadelphia on May 24th with well over 20,000 in the stands. Dad got Franklin Delano Roosevelt to throw a switch in Washington that lighted the field and the Reds won 2–1. Night games were an immediate and unqualified success; so much so that the railroads ran special trains from a four-state area to Cincinnati on game nights.

For the Cardinal game an overflow crowd got out of hand and rimmed the playing field. (When a young lady, in accord with the festive mood, grabbed a bat and ran up to the plate, Paul Dean tossed her a pitch.) The season was upbeat. The club moved up two notches in 1935, and in 1936 with youngsters starting to mature in the farm system (Frank McCormick, Les Scarsela, Lee Grissom), challenged for the first division, finishing fifth, only a few games under .500.

After the 1936 season, on November 1st, my father made another dramatic move, a habit he was to pursue throughout his working career. He resigned. No public explanations were given. There were no adverse pronouncements by either side: Crosley was regretful, my father highly complimentary of the treatment he had received. Obviously, there had to have been reasons—most likely linked to habits and style. Powell Crosley was a very conservative and proper person. I have heard all the rumors, but have never known exactly what the facts were. In any event, my father returned to Michigan to help his father and brother in their banking business. I was isolated from it all to some extent because, by now, in the fall of 1936, I was away at college.

I was rather immature when I entered college. I had never been away from home for any extended period. The college I attended was Swarthmore—a small, coeducational, liberal arts, Quaker college fifteen miles southwest of Philadelphia. I could not have made a more fortunate choice. Luck played a large role in the selection. I wanted a small liberal arts college (for some reason, I hoped in the South).

Though nothing could have been farther from that, I had looked at the University of Michigan, because my father went there, one of my best friends was there, and I always pulled for the Wolverines in football. Dad also took me to see Beloit, where he had started college, and I saw Ohio Wesleyan, which my sister Marian attended. We then—all of us but Dad—took a trip the summer preceding my freshman year and looked at William & Mary, the University of Virginia, Washington and Lee, and some other schools.

An added stop on that trip was Swarthmore, recommended to my father by guess who?—Branch Rickey—as his daughter had decided to go there. One look at Swarthmore's beautiful campus, friendly atmosphere, and the type of college it was (small [800 students], coeducational, liberal arts, good scholastically), and I was convinced. It was easier to get in then because of the Depression and I was accepted.

I was soon getting the most out of college life. I joined a fraternity (Delta Upsilon) and was president my senior year. I was president of the Inter-Fraternity Council and won letters in baseball and football. Actually, I lacked talent in baseball and size in football, but when there are only 400 men in the college, they have to use everybody. We didn't really play enough games for me to get over being nervous. It was a good day for me when I didn't make an error. We beat Army at West Point my sophomore or junior year and Coach Dunn, who didn't have too many wins to celebrate, went around to each player compliment-ing him on his play. When he came to me he said, "You played a much better game in the field today Lee." What he didn't realize (or perhaps he did) was that they hadn't hit a ball to me. I was actually better in football than baseball. I wasn't nervous in football once the game started (or I got in) and was more aggressive. My 160 pounds weren't much of an asset at center, however.

I worked pretty hard and got decent grades. I was in the honors program my junior year but, confronted with a choice of sacrificing social life, etc., for studies, I went back into course my senior year. The principal reason was that I met and fell in love with a girl in the middle of my junior year. Her name was Jane Hamilton and before my senior year was over we were engaged to be married.

Major companies sent representatives to the campus in those days to interview prospective seniors for jobs, but I didn't attend any of the interviews. I planned to go to work in the administrative side of baseball when I graduated. I had talked with Mr. Rickey when he visited the campus and he had offered me a job as business manager of a minor league team in the Cardinal organization after graduation. I wanted to work for my father, however, for he was now back in baseball as president and general manager of the Brooklyn Dodgers.

His hiring could be traced to the old story of a team in trouble—

down in the standings, a split ownership at loggerheads with one another, financially handicapped, and in the hands of the bank. In this case, the bank was the Brooklyn Trust Company and its representative on the Dodger board was George Barnewall. The McKeever and Ebbets interests finally agreed to let the bank select a man to run the club and Barnewall, acting on the advice of Ford Frick, the National League president, selected Larry MacPhail. Frick knew that he was the best possible man to rescue a distressed franchise.

Home for my mother and father became an apartment on Columbia Drive in Brooklyn Heights. It was a very nice area then and I believe it still is today. The streets were tree-lined and the view across the river of lower Manhattan was spectacular. One weekend in my senior year I told my father that I wanted to go to work for him with the Dodgers after college. It was something we had touched on briefly in the past and I had just assumed that there were no problems with the plan. I was shocked to find that my enthusiasm for such an approach was not shared by the man necessary to put it in place. His thinking was that baseball was too small a business to select for one's profession; that the number of good jobs was too limited; that too many uncontrollable hazards existed to make it a sensible career. He wanted me to go to law school or to the Wharton Business School. All this was good advice I am sure (I have given it to my own sons), but I certainly did not want to go to graduate school for I had plans (not yet divulged to my parents) to get married as soon as possible after my graduation. And I really wanted to work in baseball. After all, I had Branch Rickey's offer as a fall-back. But I certainly wasn't mentioning this to my father.

Finally he said to me, "I will make a deal with you. Try something else for a year and if at the end of that time you still want to go into baseball, I will have a position for you in the Dodger organization." I said that that was agreeable to me but that I had one problem. I explained to him that I had not gone to the college job interviews and that I was at a loss to know how to proceed to find something with an attractive enough future to provide a fair trial under his proposal. He said he would make a couple of calls, that he had something in mind (Could he have anticipated this conversation?). A couple of weeks later he contacted me to say that he had a good job opportunity for me with his old friend Fay Murray who owned the Nashville baseball club. I had met Mr. Murray. He was a very nice man but he was in the livestock business. "Dad," I remonstrated, "Mr. Murray is in the livestock business. I don't know anything about livestock. I'm a city boy. I probably couldn't tell a cow from a steer."

He reassured me. "Business is business," he said. "It doesn't make any difference whether you are dealing with hogs and cattle or nuts and bolts. It will be a desk job working in one of their many offices across the country." (Kennett-Murray Company served as a go-between in the livestock business buying from farmers or ranchers and selling to packing companies.) "You go out to Nashville and talk to Mr. Murray and I am sure you will be interested." So I went to Nashville and Mr. Murray was extremely cordial to me. I stayed at his beautiful home outside the city. I met the people in his office and toured the stockyard.

Perhaps prompted by my father, he told me about all the advantages of a career in business compared to a risky career in baseball. I remember he said, "that I could eventually make many times the income in his business that I could count on in baseball." I clearly remember my very naive answer. "Mr. Murray," I said, "if I could some day make $10,000 a year in baseball, I would be very satisfied. That would be all I would need." ($10,000 seemed like a lot of money at that time and was, but "ever" is a long, long time. We must not have talked too much about inflation in my economics classes at Swarthmore.) Mr. Murray said, "You may feel that way today, but some day your views may change." In any event he offered me a position at the company's Florence, South Carolina office starting September 1st and I accepted. (The starting salary incidentally was $1,800 per annum.)

Jane and I decided to wait to get married until I had reported to Florence and gotten settled in the job. She was living in Rhode Island with her aunt and uncle, her parents having died when she was young. By then, my parents had rented a home in Westchester County and I was staying there. We had the summer free until I had to leave for Florence so she decided to get a job in New York. When Dad heard she was interviewing, he said, "Come work for the Dodgers for the summer, we need a receptionist and relief telephone operator." So my wife to be got into the baseball business before I did. She not only was the receptionist and relief telephone operator, but she did secretarial work for Branch Rickey, Jr., whom Dad had hired as farm director (the MacPhail-Rickey syndrome), and for Buzzie Bavasi (just out of DePauw University—who years later would be general manager of the team). She took a small apartment in Brooklyn and we were able to see each other regularly.

It should have been a great summer but the world started coming apart. Hitler and Mussolini signed their infamous pact. Hitler moved into Austria and Czechoslovakia (Edward Benes, deposed president of Czechoslovakia, had spoken at my graduation); Mussolini into Albania; Japan into China. Neville Chamberlain's "Peace In Our Times" headed for a quick culmination. On September 1st, 1939, Germany was to march into Poland and in response, on September 3rd, France and England were to declare war.

In our private family world, my mother and father were moving apart. My father had become enamored of his secretary with the Dodgers, Jean Wanamaker. Always restless, always looking for the new and glamorous, he had started down a path that eventually separated him from as great a wife as a man could possibly have. My mother was distraught and wanted to get away for a while. After considering various travel alternatives, she simply went to Brooklyn and stayed with Jane, my fiancée. When she disappeared my father became very upset and had detectives searching for her. The last place they would have looked was with Jane in Brooklyn, a half a dozen blocks from the Dodgers office. When my father found out later, he was irate and told Jane "never to darken his doorstep again." That of course ended her employment with the Dodgers. At about the same time, I was off for Florence, South Carolina and my first job.

I drove my Ford Roadster to South Carolina. When I reached Florence, I found the stockyards, partly by following the railroad tracks and partly by smell. I parked my little car and walked back toward the office, livestock pens on either side. When a steer bellowed, I jumped two feet. When I went into the office, I knew right away that this was no office job. The office was very, very small and had just two desks. One was for Jack McCrocklin, the yard manager, and the other for his secretary. Most of the rest of the office was taken up with the workings of a large scale that adjoined the office. Jack McCrocklin was an excellent livestock man and turned out to be a very good friend. The only other employee of the yard was George Betz, Jack's father in law.

The Kennett-Murray yard was engaged in buying livestock, mostly hogs, from farmers at county sales and selling them to meat packers. My job during the first weeks was primarily to feed the stock in twenty some pens—corn for the hogs, mostly hay for the cattle— and to keep their watering troughs filled with water. The last was a tough assignment because when the weather was hot, the hogs liked to lie in the troughs. I had a shovel that just fit the cement trough and I spent much of my time shoveling out the mud the hogs had deposited. The first few times I entered those pens I did so with trepidation and a couple of times I retreated in haste when a big sow came after me.

When stock was brought into our yard, generally by car with trailer, occasionally by truck, our job was to run the animals down the aisle and through a sorting gate operated by Jack and thereafter into the proper pen. When a carload or two of hogs had been purchased, we fed and watered them, sorted them again through the sorting gate, weighed them on our large scale, and loaded them into railroad cars. The last part sometimes took a bit of doing and I never did it without a guilty feeling when I thought of where those hogs were heading. My worst problems came when someone would bring up a truckload of cattle from the swampy range lands farther south. They would have been rounded up western style on horseback, driven into a corral, and then into the truck. Those cows and steers were skinny and mean and had long horns. They weren't too used to people. We banged our livestock canes and shouted at them to get them on to the scale. But occasionally one would turn, lower its head, and paw the ground. If pressed, it would come at you and I quickly learned to scale the fence with alacrity.

We encountered another problem when shipping to the Carolina Packing Company. It sent its own double-deck truck, especially constructed to accommodate hogs. The only trouble was that we did not have a loading shoot for the upper deck. We had to drive the hogs up to the top of our lower deck shoot and then grab them and hoist them up into the upper deck. A 250-pound, squirming hog does not make for easy lifting.

November 18th was to be our wedding date. At one point, we were to be married at Chatham Hall, a girls preparatory school in Virginia where Jane had gone to school. When I heard that the student body would attend the ceremonies, I was less than overjoyed but kept a stiff upper lip. But when Jane's aunt fell and broke her leg I got a reprieve. The site was switched to Tiverton, Rhode Island. Although Jane swore she was not going to invite my father, I ran the proposed date by my family. My father objected—it was the day of the Michigan-Penn football game in Philadelphia and wanted it switched a few days one way or the other. At that point, I did one of the stupidest things of my life—I called my fiancée and made that suggestion to her. Her response was to hang up on me. It so happened that a storm hit Rhode Island at that exact time and her telephone service was disrupted. Both Jane and I spent an unhappy 24-hours until we could get back in telephone contact again and I could reaffirm the November 18 date.

As soon as I arrived in Rhode Island we went together to get the marriage license. The clerk asked Jane: "In what state do you live?" She replied, "Rhode Island." He then asked, "Where were you born?" She answered, "Missouri." His next question was, "Where were your father and mother born?" She said, "Maine and California." Then the clerk turned to me and asked, "In what state do you live?" I replied, "South Carolina." He then asked, "Where were you born?" I said, "Tennessee." And finally he asked me, "Where were your father and mother born?" I answered, "Michigan and New York." At this point, he put down his pen, looked at us and said, "How did you two ever get together?" And we answered in unison, "In Pennsylvania."

I don't think Jane did invite my father but he showed up anyway, exuding charm as he could do when he wished. Jane's aunt and uncle, who had heard her tirades about Larry MacPhail, said to her, "Why dear, we think he is one of the nicest people we have ever met. We don't understand how you could have not wanted to include him."

I took my bride to Florence. I had rented an apartment, which was the second floor of a house owned by a school teacher and her husband. We skipped any honeymoon and drove to Columbia, South Carolina instead and bought a cocker spaniel puppy. And I went back to my hogs and cattle. Jane adapted to it all very well. Her only rule was that I had to take my shoes off before coming into the apartment from work. Heat for the apartment came from a little wood burning stove in the living room. I had to get up very early for work, so it was my job to start the stove. As often as not, it ended up going out and filling the apartment with smoke. It was an experience for us to live in a town like Florence. We liked to window shop on the main street and to eat out. We could literally get dinner for 35¢. The special with everything with it was 55¢. The steak restaurant was $1.00.

Over the weeks that I worked there I began to learn a little about the business and soon I could work the sorting gate and the weighing pen and understood how prices, both buy and sell, were computed. Eventually I would go to county sales around the state with Mr. Betz, bid on the livestock, load our purchases into our truck and drive home. I not only became a competent truck driver but I learned to back trailers expertly up to the unloading shoot. This was tricky business and some farmers never could master it. I could also estimate the weight of a hog within five pounds (abilities I was rarely called upon to utilize in future years).

So passed 1939 and 1940. We rooted for the Dodgers from afar and moaned over the war news. Norway, Denmark, Holland, Belgium, and Luxembourg occupied. And then the breakthrough in France, Dunkirk, the air battle over Britain, and the U-boat war in the Atlantic. I did not bring up the question of a position in baseball. But in the late fall of 1940 my father offered me the job of business manager at Reading, Pennsylvania, a Class-B team in the Interstate League for 1941. Kennett-Murray Company offered me a stockyard of my own to manage if I would stay. I was flattered, but it was not a difficult choice.

2

Prior Seasons—My Heritage

"**P**rior Seasons" requires a flashback to times preceding my own "nine innings." It is about my heritage, my mother and my father, mostly my father. My mother was closer and dearer to me, but my father requires more space. I don't mean to be unfair to him. He was a good parent. He loved his children. He provided me with a college education; taught me to enjoy classical music; got me my first job; helped with the down payment on my first house. He raised his children, by example, not to be prejudiced or obscene. I can't recall him ever being guilty of either, by act or by word. At the same time he was egocentric and, as a result, not always very close to us.

My father was born in Cass City, Michigan on February 3, 1890. His family later lived in Grand Rapids, then in Ludington, Michigan. He attended Staunton Military Academy in Virginia before starting college at Beloit, a small, liberal arts college in Wisconsin. He transferred from there to the University of Michigan and then to George Washington University in Washington, D.C. where he got a degree in law.

My mother, Inez Frances Thompson, was born on September 16, 1889 in Oak Park, Illinois—at that time a fashionable suburb of Chicago. Her father, Frank Thompson, was a vice president of the American Car & Foundry Company, a manufacturer of railroad cars. He had won an award at the International Exposition of 1903 in St. Louis, celebrating the 100th anniversary of the Louisiana Purchase, for his work on the development of refrigerator cars. My mother went to Ferry Hall, a ladies' finishing school in Oak Park. My parents met in Michigan at a summer resort on Hamlin Lake just north of Ludington and were married three years later in Oak Park. My father was only 20 at the time but added a year when petitioning his future father-in-law.

He went to work first for the law firm of Davis & Ranken, later for the firm of Fowler, MacDonald & Rosenberg. While working for the latter, he became close to one of their clients, the Huddleston-Cooper Company. Huddleston-Cooper operated a department store in

Nashville, Tennessee. They became so impressed with the young lawyer in the Chicago law office that when, in 1915, their store needed a reorganization, they hired him to come to Nashville and run the store. He was only twenty-three at the time, a novice in the clothing business, but even then he showed the promotional flair which was his trademark throughout his life.

Europe was at war at the time, but Woodrow Wilson had managed to keep the United States out of it. Two years later, the *Lusitania* was sunk and the United States declared war on Germany. The day Congress declared war, Dad joined the first Tennessee field artillery, a volunteer unit from the "Volunteer State" of Tennessee. Later the unit was integrated into the regular Army as the 114th Field Artillery of the 30th Division. Luke Lea was in command with the rank of Lieutenant Colonel. Lea was a United States Senator; in fact, the youngest senator since Henry Clay. The regiment was sent overseas very quickly. My father became a captain and was in command of Battery B. The unit fought at St. Mihiel and in the Argonne. On the last day before the November 11, 1918 armistice, he suffered a minor shrapnel wound but remained with his Battery when they moved into Luxembourg as part of the peacekeeping force.

That December, Luke Lea came up with a wild, breathtaking idea. Lea was a very dynamic character, in some respects very much like my father, and my father was the first person to whom he went with his way-out, harebrained scheme. The feeling in Allied countries after World War I about Kaiser Wilhelm II was almost as intense as it was against Hitler after World War II. There was much sentiment that he should be made to stand trial for war crimes. While this was being debated in western capitals, however, the kaiser left Germany and went to Holland. (Holland was a neutral country in World War I, and pro-German in sentiment.) They gave him sanctuary and refused to turn him over to the victorious powers.

Lea's plan was to kidnap the kaiser and bring him back to face trial. He had given much thought to the logistics. He knew that the kaiser was staying at the Chateau of a Count VonBentinck in Amerongen, Holland; he had detailed maps of the area; he knew that he could get leave for a small group for the necessary period and he had a way of getting his group into Holland. Lea was a super salesman, and my father was not hard to sell on any exercise that was novel, dramatic, and had a slight chance for success. Plus my father figured that, if they failed, the downside probably wouldn't be too bad—arrest in Holland, sent back to France, maybe even to the United States.

My father recruited the rest of the party—Captain Tom Henderson, Lieutenant Elsworth Brown, three sergeants and a corporal, all from the Tennessee Brigade. Lea got the whole group a leave from January 1st to January 5th and the use of a regimental car, a Winton. They were on their way. The Winton broke down early but Lea was able to get another car, a Cadillac, and once the Winton was repaired, they proceeded forward with both cars. They drove overnight to Liege but had problems at the border and had to backtrack to Brussels, where Lea's friend, Brand Whitlock, was American ambassador to Belgium. Whitlock got them the necessary papers to get in and out of Holland. All of this took time, and when a snowstorm closed the Dutch border on the 4th, time began to be a critical problem.

They crossed the border at Maastrict the morning of January 5th and finally got to Amerongen around 8:00 p.m. They found the castle, and the guard at the gate, completely confused by the sudden appearance of eight Americans in uniform asking to see the officer in charge, admitted them. The three officers were shown into a library and shortly Count VonBentinck, the son of the old count, came in and asked them the purpose of their visit. Lea said he could only reveal the reason for their trip to the kaiser himself. VonBentinck left the room and they could hear him speaking excitedly in Dutch in the next room. They were served port and cigars while they waited. The count returned and told them that the kaiser would not see them unless they explained the nature of their mission. Lea continued to insist upon seeing the kaiser himself.

At this point, the Burgomeister of Amerongen joined them, and as he spoke excellent English, communication was improved. The stalemate continued, however, and it was at last apparent that they would not get to see the kaiser and that the count was stalling for time. It was also obvious that force would not accomplish their objective because the sound of troops could be heard outside. The three American officers decided that it was time to rejoin the rest of their group and beat a hasty retreat. On the way out, my father picked up an ashtray from one of the tables.

When they got into the courtyard they found it filled with Dutch soldiers. They piled into their two cars—my father and Lea in the Cadillac in front—and started slowly forward, not knowing whether or not they would be permitted to pass. As the cars moved forward, the soldiers fell back and they were able to get out of the grounds. Once out, they sped west, were held up waiting for a ferry to take them over the Rhine where the bridge was out; crossed the border; and were finally back with their regiment—about thirty-six hours late and in trouble. The Dutch government had already vigorously protested and the United States Army announced an investigation. The missing ashtray became a factor.* The inspector general recommended that the officers be brought to trial, but the judge advocate reported to General Pershing that the whole episode was simply due to poor judgment, that there should be no court martial, and that the matter should be closed with a reprimand for Colonel Lea. General Pershing followed his recommendation and months later was quoted as saying, "As crazy as it was, I would have given a year's pay to have been with those boys in Holland."

The war over, my father picked up his life in Columbus. There came the glass manufacturing business, the automobile business, that disastrous medical arts building, the Columbus Red Birds, the move to Cincinnati and the Reds, and then the Brooklyn Dodgers. My father's five years with the Dodgers represented the acme of his baseball career. With Columbus, the Cardinals supplied the players. With Cincinnati, though they made a good start and built a solid foundation, the team had not gotten out of the second division before he left. Later, with the Yankees, he joined a top organization already rich in player talent. With the Dodgers, he started close to the bottom from every standpoint—financially troubled, lacking a good off-field organization, with little player talent—and eventually won the National League pennant.

His first year in Brooklyn was 1938. He spent the bank's money to refurbish Ebbets Field and to buy Dolph Camilli, an outstanding first baseman from the Phillies. He also put in lights (the first park to be lighted since he had inaugurated night games in Cincinnati) and brought Red Barber to Brooklyn to broadcast the games, thus breaking an agreement of the three New York teams not to broadcast their games. He made trades and hired Babe Ruth as a coach but the team barely escaped the cellar. In 1939 he made Leo Durocher playing manager and, with the addition of Whitlow Wyatt and Hugh Casey, two veteran pitchers (spotted by chief scout Ted McGrew in the minors), and Dixie Walker, signed after his release by Detroit, the team moved up to third. And in the course of the year, my father and Red Barber arranged with NBC for the first telecast of a professional sports game.

In 1939 he acquired a youngster, Pete Reiser, who had been declared a free agent from the Cardinals by Judge Landis and, in 1940, purchased a young shortstop named Pee Wee Reese from Louisville. In 1940 he also gave players and a lot of cash to the Cardinals for star outfielder Joe Medwick and veteran pitcher Curt Davis. When Medwick was later beaned in a game in Brooklyn by Bob

---

*The ashtray, the head of a wolf with a pipe in its mouth, is on a desk in our New York apartment today.

Bowman of the Cardinals, Dad rushed onto the playing field like a mad bull, challenging Bowman and anyone else in sight. And the team moved up to second. Then in 1941, with the acquisition of three more key veterans by trade and by purchase—pitcher Kirby Higbe, catcher Mickey Owen, and second baseman Billy Herman—the team won the pennant. It was a battle to the wire with the Cardinals, the Dodgers finally clinching the pennant in Boston in late September.

Dodger fans were jubilant and a large crowd filled Grand Central Terminal to greet their returning heroes. Dad had not been in Boston but he sure did not want to miss being on the train when the team arrived, so he cabbed up to 125th Street Station, the last stop before Grand Central, to board the train. Manager Leo Durocher, of course, did not know this and fearing that some of the players would get off at 125th Street to avoid the crowd he talked the conductor into scrubbing the 125th Street stop. So my father was marooned on the station platform as the train sped by and missed the gala festivities. He was characteristically furious and when he caught up to Durocher his first words to the manager who had just won Brooklyn's first pennant in twenty-one years was, "You're fired."

Needless to say, however, Leo was still at the helm when the Dodgers opened the World Series against the Yankees a few days later. They managed to split the first two games which were played in Yankee Stadium and came home to Ebbets Field very much in the running. Then disaster struck. With the third game scoreless in the 7th inning, Freddie Fitzsimmons, their veteran pitcher, was hit in the knee by a line drive and had to be carried from the field. They lost 2–1. The next day it was even worse. The Dodgers led 4–3 with two out in the ninth inning, no one on, and two strikes on Tommy Henrich. Henrich swung and missed the next pitch but somehow Mickey Owen also missed the sharp breaking ball. The ball rolled to the screen and Henrich was safe at first. DiMaggio singled, Keller doubled off the wall, and before it was over New York scored four times and won 7–4. My father went into the Dodgers' clubhouse and walked into the shower to console a disconsolate Owen.

In 1942, after a trip to Havana, the team trained in Daytona Beach, Florida. In the course of spring training the Dodgers' two young stars—Reese and Reiser—got married. They dreaded telling my father because they knew his quick temper and anticipated his reaction. When they found him at his desk in the hotel suite that served as his office and gave him the news they braced for his reaction. He jumped up and ran to the window, "Did you see that?" he said. Perplexed, Reese and Reiser allowed that they had not. "What was it?" one of them ventured. "It was the National League pennant—it just flew out the window."

In spite of, or maybe because of, the new matrimonial state of their two young stars, the Dodgers got off to a good start in 1942 and led by a large margin most of the season. In mid-August they were eight games ahead of the Cardinals, but Dad was concerned. He sensed a feeling of overconfidence. Consequently, he held a meeting of the team and invited the writers to attend and predicted to the players that they were going to lose the pennant. And he was correct, but not really because the Dodgers fell apart. They won 104 games, more than they had won in 1941, but the Cardinals closed with a sensational streak and nosed them out at the end.

There were bigger battles going on—in Europe and the Pacific—and there was no way my father was going to stay out of it if he could help it. In the fall of 1942, he went back into the service as a Lieutenant Colonel—first, on the staff of Major General Brehon Somervell and later as an aide to Judge Robert Patterson, the undersecretary of war. He didn't get into any fighting of course (which he would have liked), but he was on board the flagship of the American Fleet during the invasion of southern France and he did have contact with Eisenhower, Churchill, and others. He was as close to the middle of things as he could get and that is the way he liked it.

3

First Pitch—The Minors

My first assignment with the Dodgers was to go south—to the Carolinas and Georgia—looking for training sites for minor league teams. This was before the days of large, central camps for all organizational minor league players. I picked Wilson, North Carolina for Reading because it had a good ballpark and the hotel looked okay. We found out later that when the trains went through the hotel shook a little and the figure eight front light on the engine came right into our bedroom.

Fresco Thompson was our manager. Fresco had played for the Phillies in those years when almost the whole team hit over .300 and yet the team finished in the second division. It was because Baker Bowl was a real hitters' paradise. In fact, it was so tough on pitchers that one of their best starters (Walter Beck) was named "Boom Boom" as a result of balls rattling off the outfield fences. Fresco was an outstanding person, a good manager, and very funny. A sample of his daily one liners came when we were dining in a Reading restaurant after a night game and a newsboy came in hawking the *Reading Eagle*, the morning paper. When he came to our table with his "Eagle Mister?" Fresco replied without a smile. "No, I'm an Elk."

My wife, Jane, had by now become a great fan. She never missed a home game and we went to almost all the road games—Allentown, Wilmington, Harrisburg, Hagerstown, Lancaster, Sunbury, and Trenton. Plus she took the dog. On one occasion when I called a home game because of rain, she would scarcely talk to me. She kept complaining, "We could have played."

We had a good team. Carl Furillo was a young outfielder, and Al Campanis, just out of New York University, was our second baseman. Thompson and Campanis (along with Buzzie Bavasi) were later to become top executives in the Dodger organization.* Many of the

---

*Poor Al's long career was to end forty-six years later on a sad note—his remarks about the lack of blacks in administrative positions in baseball. Yet

other players got to Triple-A and a few played a little in the major leagues. As the business manager, I did just about everything. I inherited a very capable lady who handled the tickets and made the bank deposits and the concessions were run by Jacobs Brothers. The rest was up to me.

I attended league meetings and worked on the schedule; signed the players to contracts; made the hotel and bus arrangements for our road trips; gave out the meal money; supervised the groundskeeper, clubhouse man, and P.A. announcer; made sure we had uniforms, bats, and balls; paid the bills; called the games when it rained; kept the press posted on developments; and put out a little monthly newspaper about the team. I also got my first experience in speaking in public, relying mostly on some tired baseball stories. During the games, I sat up with our two writers in the press box. It was a good education.

It was all fun, or at least mostly so. One incident that wasn't so much fun involved radio broadcasts by the Philadelphia Athletics over a Reading station. In those days, this was against baseball rules. Today the Federal Communications Commission and the Justice Department would not allow any rules preventing such broadcasts. But it was wrong then and when I could not get any satisfaction from the station or the A's I appealed to Judge Landis (the Dodgers urging me on). The judge held a hearing to consider the matter. Landis was a very dramatic individual and loved creating a big show when circumstances gave him that opportunity. I freely admit I was somewhat intimidated. Whenever I quoted someone as saying something bearing on the case he would tell an assistant to get that person on the telephone and would then verify what I had said. I could not hear the other party so one naturally worried as to whether or not they had properly backed up your statement. I guess they did for the judge eventually ruled in our favor.

The A's ceased to broadcast and also came to Reading to play us an exhibition game to defray any damages that we might have suffered. Connie Mack could not have been more gracious. I have a picture of him sitting at the game with my wife. The Dodgers also came to Reading to play us a game. Leo Durocher was the manager then and Leo and my father came together. I enjoyed it immensely when Reading won the exhibition game.

Fall came too soon and the Dodgers summoned me back to New York to work over the winter in the Brooklyn office, before returning to Reading again to get ready for spring training and the 1942 season. By now my mother and father were separated; Britain was bracing for a possible invasion attempt; the Germans had invaded Russia; the

---

there are few people less prejudiced; and perhaps his remark has sparked a progressive effort by baseball to improve the situation in this area.

Bismarck had been sunk; and Churchill and Roosevelt had signed the Atlantic Charter. Jane and I rented a small, ground floor apartment in Brooklyn Heights on a monthly basis and I helped Branch, Jr. with minor league affairs in the Brooklyn office. I was very fond of Branch Rickey, Jr. He was most helpful to me when I was getting started in the business. Unfortunately, he had diabetes and was never able to properly regulate his eating and living habits and finally succumbed to the disease a few years later.

One day a long-distance phone call came for me. I was amazed when I realized that it was Mr. Rickey calling me from St. Louis. He was very hush-hush and confidential and asked if I could come out to St. Louis to talk to him. He said he would rather that I not tell my father that I was going. I told him I would be glad to come to St. Louis but I wouldn't want to do so without my father knowing. He acquiesced and I made the trip.

I met him in the Cardinal offices and he asked me if I would be interested in going to Toronto as general manager. I was honestly shocked. I didn't know if I knew enough to run a Triple-A team and told him so. He asked a few common sense, elementary questions that my wife could have answered and concluded that I knew enough. Toronto, an independent team with no working agreement and financial problems, had come to him for assistance in finding a general manager. He was prepared to recommend me. He was also prepared to recommend to the other major league teams with teams in the International League that they each sell the Maple Leafs a Triple-A player at reduced prices to help improve the team on the field. He very graciously took me to his home for dinner that evening. (Mr. Rickey was very clever in getting people established in baseball who were thus his protégés. One never knew when they might be able to repay his assistance in some manner.)

Naturally, I accepted the offer of the position at Toronto. I was due to report there January 1st and the salary would be $4,000, which sounded great to me. In the meantime, I was to go to Chicago for the December major league meetings to contact those major league clubs that had teams in the International League about providing a player for Toronto, as Rickey's recommendation of such a course had been quickly agreed upon. I was able to talk to the five major league clubs involved. (St. Louis and Brooklyn were the sixth and seventh.) Everybody was encouraging, but only the New York Giants gave me a player. Bill Terry sold me Burgess Whitehead for the waiver price and Whitehead, if I could get him to report, would be an excellent addition.

Then came December 7th. My sister and I were at my mother's apartment on Park Avenue in Manhattan listening to a radio broadcast of the New York Philharmonic Orchestra when the program was interrupted for that frightful announcement that "The Japanese have attacked our naval base at Pearl Harbor." We were at war. My brother was already in the Navy V7 program. I thought about enlisting. I wasn't sure what would happen to baseball now that our country had been attacked. The news over the next few days was worse. Serious losses at Pearl Harbor; the *Prince of Wales* and *Repulse* sunk off Malaya; the Philippines invaded.

However, we soon learned that President Roosevelt wanted baseball to continue, and with my wife then eight months pregnant, I decided to go to Toronto as scheduled. Just before we boarded the sleeper someone advised me that no one was allowed to leave the country without the permission of his draft board. This was just another of the wild rumors floating around. I spent a fitful night, waking periodically, to find that we had not yet crossed the border, half expecting to be pulled off the train with my pregnant wife in the middle of the night.

We stayed first in a small residential hotel in Toronto. Jane had edema and was a mess. When Peter Campbell, who was president of the club and represented Percy Gardner, the owner, invited us to tea to welcome us to the city, she gamely went along. No notice was taken of her appearance but later, after the baby was born and the edema gone, and Peter saw her again he could not control himself from blurting out, "Why, you are really very pretty. I never realized." The baby had been born in the middle of a blizzard. It wasn't an easy birth and I didn't have an easy time getting to the hospital. I can still remember my feelings—after the relief of knowing that mother and baby were well—as I trudged through the snow getting back from the hospital, that everything was unreal. Here I was, in the snow, a father, in a foreign country, with a new job I was none too secure about, and our country at war. But I was able to find an apartment and soon got my wife and son (Leland S. MacPhail, III) out of the hospital and into our home.

Apartments were scarce in Toronto during the war and this one was so small that when I went to see it and met the landlord, I kept wondering when I was going to see the living room. It turned out that we were sitting in it. I had thought it was the entrance hall or foyer. However, it worked out satisfactorily and later we were able to sublet a small house from people who had gone away for the summer. We had no car as gas was in short supply, but the streetcar service was quite good.

I worked during that winter trying to improve the team. There were a few proven players on the roster: Frank Colman, an outfielder and an Ontario boy with major league experience; Al Rubeling, a good Triple-A infielder; and Carl Fisher, a pitcher. Fisher had been 0–17 the preceding year and I felt we had to move him, if only for PR reasons. I traded him to Seattle for a veteran infielder (Mickey Haslin) who it turned out had a bad knee and couldn't play, and a young pitcher, who it turned out lacked Triple-A ability. (Fisher had an excellent year for Seattle.)

We drafted two outfielders from AA, on the recommendation of the Cardinals: Jim Russell and Nick Gregory. They both worked out well. Russell went on to become a good major league player. I also bought three young pitchers, whom I had seen in the Interstate League the year before: Bill Brandt and Fred Schumann, who had been at Harrisburg, and Paul Mulach, whom we had at Reading. Brandt, and especially Schumann, did very well and Mulach was able to make our team. I picked up Joe Mack to play first base and we had Burgess Whitehead for second. The Athletics had worked with Toronto the year before and they let us have Bill Beckman, an experienced pitcher. So we were making some progress.

I made another trip south looking for a training spot. I thought we could save some money by not going all the way to Florida and picked Camden, South Carolina. Our manager was to be Burleigh Grimes, the old spit-ball pitcher. He had been let go as manager by the Dodgers and my father got me to take him to Toronto. I wasn't enthusiastic at first but he turned out great. We became good friends and I always tried to have Burleigh with me wherever I went in baseball. He was a battler, completely frank and honest, and worked very hard. He was elected to the Hall of Fame in 1969, and our friendship lasted until his death in 1986.

During spring training, I left the team and went to Florida to try to get player help from the major league organizations that had promised it. George Weiss of the Yankees gave us a couple of pitchers on conditional assignment, neither of whom worked out. At one point, it looked as if we had someone from all the clubs that promised help except Branch Rickey's Cardinals and Larry MacPhail's Dodgers. I finally was able to buy a shortstop, Lynn Meyers, from the Cardinals (for whom we had to pay more than I felt we should) and got a pitcher, Ken Drake, from the Dodgers. The Cubs optioned us a catcher, but that position was a problem for us all year long. The deal I had made with Pittsburgh for Brandt and Schumann led to further relations with the Pittsburgh Pirates and after the season started, we made a partial working agreement with them. They then sent us John Wyrostek, a good young center fielder and Joe Sullivan, a veteran pitcher.

It seemed strange to me that baseball was being played while the country was at war, but that was nothing new in Toronto. (Canada had been at war for two-and-a-half years and in an area behind right field of the Toronto ballpark was a place called "Little Norway." It was a settlement camp for repatriated Norwegians, driven out of their country by the Germans.) I got along fine with Peter Campbell, a peppery little man who was our club president. The only fight I ever had with him was about the war, not about baseball. He said to me one day, "What the United States ought to do is to turn its Navy over to the British and let them handle it as they are better qualified to man and operate a fleet." I was really angry and proceeded to tell him all about John Paul Jones, the *Constitution,* the *United States,* the Battle of Lake Erie, the Battle of Lake Champlain, and several other appropriate naval encounters between our countries. It was one of the few times I got in the last word with Peter.

The team played well and attendance was good. I made almost all of the road trips (by train) to Buffalo, Syracuse, Rochester, Montreal, Newark, Jersey City, and Baltimore. We were not allowed to play at home on Sunday, so every Sunday we had to travel to one of the nearer cities to play. This really hurt. This meant we not only played more away games than home games, but gradually the extra travel had its effect. We had one pitcher who, when on the mound and in good condition, was quite effective. Unfortunately, however, that was not the norm. In fact on one occasion he was missing during pregame practice and when the grounds-keepers rolled out the canvas to cover the field for a shower, out of the cylinder came our missing pitcher!

The catching position was our biggest problem, so after we made the working agreement with the Pirates, I went to Pittsburgh to talk to them about player help, particularly to see if they could spare a catcher. I talked first to Bob Rice, the farm director. He said that I would have to talk with Mr. Benswanger, the president and owner. When I talked with Mr. Benswanger, he said that he would go along with any moves that Frank Frisch, the manager, would approve. So, I went down to see Frisch (the great second baseman of his day, known as "The Fordham Flash"). Frisch could not stand to lose and when his team was losing, he became very acerbic.

The day I went down to the Pirate dugout to see him during pregame practice, the Pirates were in the throes of a losing streak. In response to my plea, he announced so loudly that all the players within cannon-shot could hear, "Oh, you want players? Well, you can have them. You can have them all, for all I care. Just bring a truck and back it up to the dugout and load the whole bunch of them in it." I didn't have a truck and didn't want a truckload. I only hoped maybe, at best, to get a catcher; but that wasn't the day for it.

I persevered and finally, one day, Frisch himself called me and said "Look, do you want Spud Davis (the catcher)? Well, we'll let you have him. But I want you to know that when we tell him he's going to

Toronto, he's going to be very angry and without doubt will go home. So, if you want him, you'd better be here when we tell him. We're playing an exhibition game in Albany the day after tomorrow. You come down to Albany and we'll tell him then." I was at the Albany park before the Pirates arrived. When they did, Frisch grabbed me and said "I tell you what, I'm not going to dress for this game so you and I will sit in a box next to the dugout. I will have Davis catch and you can see your new man in action and I'll tell him after the game." That was fine with me.

However, on Davis' first time at bat, the Albany pitcher lost control of a fast ball, inside and up. Davis fell away from the pitch and when his hands came up the ball hit his right hand squarely and broke it badly. Our new catcher was out for the season. I had told Peter Campbell that we were getting Davis but told him not to tell anyone until we were sure he would sign and report. However, Peter was so excited that he leaked the story to a couple of his favorite writers and thus made our loss even more difficult to take. I appealed to the Dodgers and, to their credit, they came to our aid. They had an experienced player-manager managing their Valdosta, Georgia, team named Stu Hofferth. They had Valdosta release him and send him to Toronto and he finished the season for us. There were repercussions however. Buzzie Bavasi was the business manager at Valdosta and Stu Hofferth had been best man at his wedding. He never forgave me for this triple act of larceny taking his manager, his best player, and his best man. Moreover, the releasing of a player and sending him somewhere else to sign was not an accepted way of transferring player contracts and that winter Judge Landis declared Hofferth a free agent.

As the end of the season approached, we were struggling to get into the playoffs. One day, Mr. Rickey called me and said, "Lee, our people at Rochester tell me that all you need to make the playoffs is a little more power. I'll tell you what, we'll try to help you. We have Jimmy Ripple at Rochester. He would be just the man for you, and we have a young first baseman we could send to Rochester to replace him. We'll send Ripple over to you. Just give us a pitcher to help Rochester. Let's see now! Who do you have on your staff? Oh, well, Bill Beckman would be okay. We can trade even up." "Thank you Mr. Rickey," I said.

A week later the Maple Leafs were in Newark and we were rained out. So I hurried over to Brooklyn, where the Dodgers were playing an important game in the pennant race with the World Champion Cardinals. Late in the game, the Dodgers were rallying and there was action in the Cardinal bullpen. I checked the numbers to see who was warming up. No. 43. I looked at the program. Who was No. 43? Bill Beckman. "Thank you Mr. Rickey." Nor did we make the playoffs!

As we played baseball, the war seemed to be going from bad to worse everywhere. In the Pacific, the Japanese took Kuala Lumpur, Singapore, Java, and Rangoon. Bataan fell. On the Russian front, the Germans drove toward Leningrad, Moscow and Stalingrad. In Africa, Rommel launched another offensive. I felt I should enlist. I talked it over with Jane. She was unhappy but understanding. Near the end of the season, I went to the Naval office on Pine Street in Manhattan and applied for acceptance in the Navy V7 program. I took all the tests. When I asked how I had done the officer said if I had done any better they would have figured I was cheating. I took a short medical test. They said that I was accepted but that there would not be an opening until after Christmas. So when the season was over, I resigned my position with Toronto and took my family to New York City.

4

Rain Delay—After Pearl Harbor

After I resigned my position with the Maple Leafs and returned to New York City to go into the service, my wife, baby, and I shared an apartment on East 73rd Street with my mother. To earn enough to pay the rent until I went into the Navy, I got a job at Saks Fifth Avenue as a floor walker. That in itself was an education. I had to okay returns and when things were returned without absolute proof that they had been purchased at Saks, the buyers became angry. I learned how to deal with people and to say "no" politely.

And then, sometime before Christmas, I was contacted by the Navy, which wanted me to come down to Pine Street to finalize my enlistment. Among other things, my pulse had been high on my previous medical examination. When I went down, it was still high. By my third visit, I was alarmed. My doctor-brother-in-law tried to solve the problem with nembutol. The Navy tried to solve the problem by having a Wave slip up on me unawares to take my pulse. Regardless, every time I even started getting near Pine Street, my pulse started racing. At this point, the Navy, and I guess the Army too, closed enlistments and said that entrance to the service thereafter would be through the draft. I was stunned. I didn't want to go back to Toronto. Baseball was further restricting activities, plus I couldn't face returning under such ignominious circumstances. Yet I had to find a job to feed my family.

At this point, a friend who knew my plight, Johnny Jones, came to my rescue. He was the husband of Jane's roommate at Swarthmore and was a teacher at Deerfield Academy, a top Preparatory School in Massachusetts. John said that Deerfield badly needed young teachers, and suggested that I go up and talk with Dr. Boyden, the headmaster. I had always had a feeling that I would like to teach, and I had a true academic interest in American History. If I could link the two, perhaps I could make teaching a permanent career. I went up and talked with Dr. Boyden, who agreed to take me—providing I would come alone for the balance of the semester and live in and take charge of a dormitory.

Not surprisingly, Jane was not enthusiastic, but she was a good soldier and I called to accept the offer. When I did, however, I was told that I couldn't teach American History, but had to teach math. All of the boys were faced with going into the service and all of them needed math to get commissions. While working at Saks I had taken a math course at night at New York University, because I also needed it for a commission. I had always been very poor in math in high school (I never took it in college). Each time I had begun to catch up to the class, it had moved on to something else leaving me floundering along behind. When I needed math for a Navy commission and went to night school at New York University on Washington Square, I started all over. I got an elementary book and reviewed high school geometry and algebra from the beginning. I taught myself more about math than I had ever known before. I actually began to enjoy it and got an A in the course. In a way, it had been a very reassuring experience as it taught me that one's mind could cope with most things, if you gave it a proper chance.

Consequently, as disappointed as I was about the American History, I was not completely discouraged when they said I would have to teach math. Once my teaching career commenced, I became very resourceful. I studied and kept one step ahead of the class and when I had trouble, I simply said, "Now, who can illustrate that problem for the class?" There were always volunteers to come up to the board and work out the problem for all of us, me included. I was not embarrassed about that kind of teaching. In a way, I think that it was more helpful to the students than if I had been on a level far above them and slightly bored with the subject.

The Deerfield experience, aside from living away from wife and child those five months, was great. The village is small, beautiful, and historic, situated on the Deerfield River in northwest Massachusetts. It was first settled in 1677. In 1704, there was an Indian massacre with fifty or more of the settlers killed and most of the rest carried off to Canada. Old Deerfield Street, the main street in the village, is lined with beautiful trees and lovely old colonial houses dating from the early 18th century.

Deerfield Academy was (and is) a fine school. Frank Boyden, the headmaster, was an outstanding person. His first love, after his family, was the school. His next was his horse and carriage, which he drove regularly through the village. His wife was an equally positive human being and taught science. It was a boys' school but accepted anyone, including girls, from the village. When I was there by myself, I spent a good deal of time reading in its library and listening to classical records in a special listening room. I did not have any trouble monitoring the boys in my dormitory. The worst problem I had occurred when the boys on one hall set up all of one boy's furniture (bed, bureau, etc.) in the bathroom. I thought it was a harmless joke and was a little upset when the school started to treat it more seriously.

Part of my job was coaching athletic teams. I helped with the junior varsity and freshman baseball teams. The coach was Lloyd Perrin. He was a great human being and became my very good friend. We worked very well together with the junior baseball teams. (The headmaster was the coach of the varsity baseball team. He was a devotee of the squeeze play and called for it on almost every possible occasion. To his credit, he schooled the players to execute it and even though it was expected, it generally worked.) I knew a little bit more than anyone else about the fundamentals of play and without getting beyond the level of the boys, I believe that I was able to contribute something.

In football, I had the freshman team and I had a great time. I designed a lot of what I thought were very imaginative plays. We used to line up with the strong side of the line to the right and with the back field to the left. At that level, the other team always seemed to have been taught to shift to adjust to the offensive line which left us in good position for a good gain. I got a little carried away with winning and had to be reminded by the powers that be that all the kids had to play whether they could block or tackle or not.

Another hat I wore was that of chaperone for the cast of the *Pirates of Penzance*. This was a joint production by Deerfield and a nearby girls' school. I spent many rehearsal hours there and still know every song from that wonderful Gilbert & Sullivan production. Still another assignment was taking the roll call at collection or vespers, a short, semi-religious gathering for the entire student body. The young masters had to check people in. You simply saw the boys and checked them off your sheet as they came in. They came in so fast you had to know all the boys and to store things in your mind. There could be no calling of the roll. I got so I knew the name of every boy in the school (what a contrast with today when I forget my own telephone number!). A job the whole school took on together was assisting with the fall harvest in the area. Due to the war, farm labor was at a premium or unavailable. Therefore, Dr. Boyden offered the help of the boys to the community. I had charge of a group assigned to harvest potatoes. We would go into the field and down the rows, digging up and basketing the potato crop. There was something basic and satisfying about the work.

As the school year neared its close, I had to think of what to do over the summer vacation period, and I had a few alternatives. Dr.

Boyden wanted me to start graduate work, which was important if I wanted to make a career of teaching. The problem with that alternative was that I could not go for three months with no income. Or I could help out at one of the teachers' summer camps or, having talked to Branch Rickey, Jr., of the Dodgers, I could work for that organization during the summer.

Money and my own desires ruled and I worked that summer for the Dodgers. I was able to return to my family and to the apartment we shared with my mother on East 73rd Street and I commuted to Montague Street in Brooklyn each day by subway. For a part of the summer, to Jane's despair, I did advance work for tryout camp programs that the Dodgers ran. Branch Rickey, Sr. had replaced my father as president of the Dodgers and he was smart enough to realize that an opportunity existed to steal a march on the rest of the baseball world. While the rest of the clubs curtailed activities because of the war, Rickey and the Dodgers operated a nationwide tryout camp program.

I served as an advance man. I would go into an area two or three weeks prior to the camp, arrange for a field, talk to the press, contact the local coaches, and ask them to bring their best kids to the camp. For a month, I went through Ohio, Michigan, Illinois and Wisconsin setting up tryout camps. Others worked in other areas. Though the benefits might not have been immediate, they were realized in time. I also served as road secretary for the major league team when their regular traveling secretary was ill. Another small bit of experience at another level of our game.

When school recommenced in the fall, they provided us an apartment in the village. Jane and Lee were now with me and it was a pretty hard life to beat. Life was so idealistic that I began to think I ought to make teaching my life's work. It would have made my wife happy and if I had had a supplemental income (which I didn't) to allow for travel and a few little extras in day to day living, it would have been great. Baseball was still in my system, however, and more important, although the Allies were now beginning to win, the country was still at war. What brought me up short was a notice from Selective Service that, family or not, I might be subject to the draft soon. Enlistments for officers had opened up again and I was determined to try again. I got my file reactivated and reported for the requisite physical. This time, it wasn't at Pine Street in Manhattan. With the change in venue, miraculously, my pulse was normal and I was accepted in the United States Navy.

I was sworn in on May 25, 1944 and ordered to report to the Boston Navy Yard for temporary duty until November 1st, the start of the next course at Harvard Business School for supply officers. We were lucky to be able to find an apartment on the second floor of a house again. It was in Newton, a Boston suburb, and very close to the house in which Jane had been brought up. During the course at Harvard, however, I had to stay in the dormitory. Other than being away from my family during the week, I enjoyed the time there.

It was an experience to be going to school in the Cambridge surroundings, though the atmosphere was not quite what it normally is. I studied hard, partly because being able to go home on weekends depended on maintaining a satisfactory average. Your rank in class also determined what kind of assignment you got when the course was over. So the incentive to work was there. I also enjoyed drilling, which I had never done before. As officers, we all had to be able to take a group through basic drills. I particularly enjoyed marching around Harvard Stadium and singing while we marched, songs such as "A Yellow Ribbon" and "Grand Old Flag."

I ranked quite high when the course was over and got my first choice in type of assignment, a new destroyer not yet commissioned. It was the type of ship I wanted to serve on and the fact that it was still being built meant more time in the Boston area with my family. While waiting, however, I did have to spend some time in Bayonne, New Jersey at Ships' Stores and Commissary School and in Bath, Maine, where the ship was being completed. During this period, Franklin Roosevelt had died and Truman became President, and on May 7th, 1945, Germany surrendered. Japan was still a formidable foe, however, and progress in the Pacific was slow and costly in American lives. My ship, the USS *Turner* (DD-834), was now ready for sea and had been equipped as a radar picket ship. That meant that the torpedo tubes had been removed and added radar equipment and mast installed. These ships were posted outside the fleet to provide early warnings of Japanese air attacks. The only drawback was that the Japanese strategy was to knock off the picket ships and many of them had been lost.

Our first destination was Guantanamo Bay, Cuba for "shakedown." The Atlantic was rough going down there and for many of the crew, including me, it was our first time at sea. Needless to say, many people were seasick. I was okay until I had to stand watch in the decoding shack. This was about the size of a telephone booth, on the deck near the bridge, entirely enclosed, right under a forty millimeter gun. I would still have been all right except that the man on duty before me had been sick and left the bucket he had used there. I eventually learned that the best way to avoid sea sickness was to continue to eat and get some fresh air. When the ship was really rolling, I used to find a safe place on deck when I could and munch on soda crackers. It was tough to try to eat meals when the chairs in the wardroom—though tied down—wanted to tip over and dump you on the deck, and glasses and plates had to be secured on the table by "fiddle boards." Yet I always tried to eat something. I felt a little strange on board at first because almost all of the other young officers knew each other, having taken pretraining together. As a result, on my first few shore leaves I went with the chief petty officers. This brought a lecture from our exec. This wasn't done in the Navy. Officers did not socialize with the men, even chiefs.

We had finished shakedown and were in Pensacola practicing with Jeep aircraft carriers preparatory to going to the Pacific when the bomb was dropped on Hiroshima. That was an act that today brings emotion, grief, regret, and nervous concern for the hazards now confronting the world. At that time, at least for me, there were feelings of awe and horror but there was also a realization of the great number of American lives that had been saved by not having to invade the last strongholds on Japan itself. One of those lives saved could easily have been my own and I think of that and of my children who might not have been born had the war not ended when it did. Once Japan surrendered, the pressure on our ship and division to get to the Pacific quickly abated. We returned north to Casco Bay, Maine, Washington, and Norfolk before starting for the Panama Canal.

During the Guantanamo-Pensacola period, our second son, Allen, was born in the Naval Hospital in Chelsea, Massachusetts (as I remember, the charge was $8.00 and we got a $3.00 refund). Then when Jane was able to travel with a child and a baby, she went to Columbus to stay with my mother. My mother, once her marriage had deteriorated, had returned to Columbus and her friends there. I got to Columbus for a quick visit to see my family and new son while our ship was in Washington. In Norfolk, my brother's ship, the USS *Philadelphia*, was also in port. They had seen rough duty in the Mediterranean—off the African coast, Sicily, Italy, and in the invasion of southern France. Their sister ship, the USS *Brooklyn*, was sunk at their side and the *Philadelphia* had been reported lost so many times it became known as the "Galloping Ghost of the Sicilian Coast." The *Philadelphia* was changing captains and they had a party at the Norfolk Officer's Club. I went with my brother and in the spirit of the evening, in response to the taunt that "destroyer sailors can't drink," I bottomed up quite a few lethal bombs and suddenly was quite drunk. With difficulty, my brother got me on and off the bus and back to my ship. Of course, our captain and others knew of my plight and bright and early the next morning I was sent off to the Navy Yard with orders for many scarce and hard to find items (including a new ship's bell). It was a difficult day.

In the fall, we headed for the Panama Canal with a stop in Lake Charles, Louisiana for Navy Day. While in Lake Charles, I ordered a general provisioning for the big voyage ahead. On an occasion like this, the entire crew was turned out to load and store the supplies. We were getting the stores from the Navy Base at Port Arthur, Texas and they were being trucked over. Normally, when we had ordered things on the east coast, they could only fill about half our orders and I ordered expecting that. At Port Arthur, they had everything. The stuff kept coming and coming and we were finally out of room to store it. I had to send some things back and stored some bags of potatoes on deck. I had been told in one of our courses that this was permissible but it sure didn't make a hit with our captain who wanted his ship neat and trim.

It was interesting going through the canal and we enjoyed some leave at San Diego and then in Hawaii, my first time there. I was a little disappointed in Waikiki Beach. I thought it compared unfavorably to Ludington, but the island, of course, was beautiful. At sea, en route to Hawaii and then to Japan, I was enthralled. In the Caribbean, I loved to see the fluorescence and the flying fish. I also saw a whale and a couple of men caught a huge hammerhead shark. In the Pacific, it was porpoises. Sometimes great schools of them dotted the horizon as far as you could see. I used to like to lie on the very bow of the ship and watch them play in the waves cut by the ship, another practice that the captain didn't quite approve of. I am sure he must have muttered a few oaths about his Naval Reserve supply officer.

My duties as supply officer included stocking the ship with everything needed except fuel and ammunition. It also included feeding and paying the crew. I kept a large amount of money in my office safe and was always very nervous when I made out my periodic reports for the General Accounting Office. It wasn't always easy because, when we got to Japan, we were paying in yen and often had to pay the men on other ships that had no supply officer. I had a good petty officer (Henry Childs from Evansville, Indiana), however, and we managed to balance out each time. Whenever I had to get money to replenish my funds, I was required to wear a side arm. Even though we had had practice using it, I never felt comfortable wearing it. It made me nervous.

Feeding the crew was not a big problem and strangely there were very few complaints about the food. One problem I did have was that the stewards mates were in my division and were my responsibility. They were young black boys and were often put on report for being out of uniform or something. I thought at times that they were unfairly picked on and defended them as best I could at "Captain's Masts." Another problem was the galley. Whenever there was an inspection, they invariably found fault with the cleanliness of the galley. It could look bright and clean but I think it was a Navy rule that the inspecting officer find something to criticize in the galley.

My watch and battle stations included, at various times, the decoding shack (a buzzing in my ears today is, I believe, the result of sitting under that forty millimeter gun), combat information center, and a twenty millimeter gun station. For relaxation, I occasionally played bridge in the Ward Room, usually with the captain and the commodore, who was flag officer for our division and came onboard in Hawaii. I had to win a little at bridge to pay my Ward Room food bill as most of my salary went directly home to Jane. All in all it wasn't bad duty, but I have to admit to feeling a little melancholy on Christmas Day in Tokyo Bay.

Fortunately, our ship never had to fire a shot in anger while I was aboard her. The only military danger was from old floating mines still remaining in Japanese waters. We did have to go through a few wild storms and then the waves would go completely over us and we could not see our sister destroyers on the other side of the giant troughs. We went over a tidal wave once, but at sea it was a gradual rise and fall and really nothing. Once we reached Tokyo Bay, I had to go ashore to order supplies and went in to Tokyo. I can still visualize the sight— miles of rubble with only brick chimneys standing—the rest of the area having been burnt down by incendiary bombs. Yet the people seemed surprisingly friendly and this only three months after peace was signed.

The assignment given our destroyer division was to visit the various ports of Japan and take a census of the shipping. What ships, how many tons, and so forth. So we saw quite a bit of Honshu Island. (One view I particularly remember was going up Suruga Bay with Mount Fujiyama behind us.) In one place they had a little dinner for some of the officers from our ship. Our captain and exec were both there and they were very handsome. Yet for some reason the Geisha girls all seemed to be paying attention to me. One wanted me to teach her to sing "When the Moon Comes Over the Mountain." I couldn't figure it out and then it occurred to me later that because I was short and had a round face and slanty eyes maybe I looked more like what they were used to than the Adonises in my group. Or maybe I just looked less dangerous.

With two children, I soon had enough points for discharge and like everybody else, I was ready to go home. But I could not be discharged until I was relieved. I had to wait until there was a supply officer available to replace me. Finally that day came. Ensign Robert Sporcik came on board and very happily I turned my accounts and the $41,123.16 in my safe over to him and left the *Turner*. When the moment came it was a little sad. I had many good friends on the ship, although most of them had already gone home. I was detached from the *Turner* on April 11, 1946. On April 19th, I boarded the USS *Rockbridge* (APA-228) for the trip back to the United States. The Golden Gate Bridge as we steamed under was a beautiful, beautiful sight to see.

5

Early Innings—The Kansas City Blues

When my father returned to civilian life from the Army he decided to try to put a group together and see if he could buy a major league team. He tried first to get the New York Giants but was unsuccessful. Then Colonel Jacob Ruppert died and the ownership of the New York Yankees went to his estate. Trustees for the estate indicated they were interested in selling and my father entered into negotiations with them. He had a backer by then whose financial position was beyond question and he had been issued a letter from a New York bank stating that the bank would stand behind any agreements entered into by Larry MacPhail. A verbal agreement was eventually reached for the sale of the Yankees and affiliated minor league clubs for $3,000,000. Though this was a lot of money in those days, it was an incredible deal for it included Yankee Stadium, the Newark team with its stadium, and the Kansas City team with its stadium.

My father was feeling very good about it and was prepared to sign the formal papers the next day. Then he got a call from Judge Landis. Landis had found out about the deal and also found out who was putting up the money. He told my father that his backer was not acceptable and would not be approved because he was involved in horse racing. The Judge was adamant and Dad was crushed. Was he going to lose this outstanding opportunity? His reaction was typical of the man. He simply went forward with the deal the next day and signed the papers, the Trustees having no idea that his financing had just evaporated. At least this gave him a little time to try and put a new group together. That afternoon he stopped at the "21" Club on 52nd Street in Manhattan, one of his favorite haunts. While he was standing at the bar, contemplating his problem, in walked an old friend, still in his Marine uniform, Dan Topping. Dan came from a very wealthy Long Island family that had made a fortune in tin. He had owned the Brooklyn Dodgers professional football team that played at Ebbets Field and he and Dad had gotten to know each other then and were friends. Dan quickly agreed to be part of the syndicate to buy the Yankees and, in addition, he knew someone who would take the balance. The someone was Del Webb, a large real estate developer who lived in California. The deal was quickly put together. Webb and Topping each put up half the money; each of the trio would own one third of the team; and Dad would run it and receive an appropriate salary. (Over a period of time, it was a great deal for Topping and Webb. They sold the land under Yankee Stadium and took a ninety-nine year lease on it. They eventually sold both the Newark and Kansas City teams and their stadiums. And finally, years later, they sold the Yankees to CBS for $14,400,000.) While I was still in the service, my father contacted me to tell me that he would like me to run the Kansas City Blues as soon as I got out of the Navy. So in addition to the thrill of getting home and seeing my family, I had a good job waiting for me in baseball.

The 1946 season was well under way by the time I got to Kansas City in June. My father had brought Frank Lane into the Yankee organization and he was running the Blues. He was also serving as farm director midwest. The Yankee organization was so large that they had divided it into three geographical areas. George Weiss was vice president and farm director and in overall charge of the entire minor league operation. Frank was glad to welcome me aboard so he could concentrate on the scouting and the lower classification clubs and leave the Blues to me. I was again blessed by having a very able person, Gertrude McClure, to handle the tickets. She had been there for years and was a great lady. Frank was a real character. He was volatile and had a hot temper. We shared an office and I got an education just listening to his half of phone conversations. I heard many scouts and minor league managers get told off in major league fashion.

Like Toronto in 1942, Kansas City in 1946 was still suffering from wartime housing problems. I found an apartment for my little family but it was almost as small as the one in Toronto. Still it worked out fine. It was in a development called "President Gardens" and was a few miles south of the city, about a half hour from the ballpark. We were lucky in that the people across the hall were about our age, from the New York area, and had children the ages of our two. Zoe and Bill Eansor became our close friends and remained so for many years, until we lost Zoe to cancer. Her father owned the Mohawk Carpet Company and Bill was their regional sales manager. They loved baseball and became our regular companions for games, dinners out, and family picnics.

The 1946 team wasn't going anywhere. It was composed primarily of older, experienced players. Many young prospects in the

Yankee organization were still in or just getting out of the service. The best thing that happened on the field that year was that Carl DeRose pitched a perfect game. The only other one I ever saw was not to come until 1956 when Don Larsen did it in the World Series. Bill Meyer was our manager. He had been in the Yankee organization for years, was highly regarded by Weiss, and respected by the players. If Bill had a problem it was that he drank too much. In those days, we made all the trips to the cities in the American Association (Columbus, Toledo, Indianapolis, Louisville, Milwaukee, Minneapolis, and St. Paul) by train. Bill used to board the train for each segment of the road trip with a brown bag containing a bottle, which he took into his drawing room. The players all knew what was in the bag. At various times, some of us would share it with him until time to retire. It would either be Goldie Holt, the coach, Ernie Mehl, a writer, or me. I made most of the trips.

Later on in the season, Bill Meyer had a heart problem and was out of action. We thought it was only going to be a short period. I talked to Weiss and we decided to put Goldie Holt, the coach, in charge of the team. Dad called later and said he thought we should get a replacement for Meyer until he could return to the field, but I went along with Goldie. We lost a few games and one night in the middle of a night game there was a long distance call for me. It was from New York and it was my father. Without any introduction or pleasantries, he said "Who is managing your team?" "Goldie Holt," I replied. And he said "If he is still managing on Friday, you're fired," and hung up. With my job at stake, I called Burleigh Grimes and he arrived before Friday and took over for Bill. That was one of the few run-ins I had with my father while working for him. Actually, I didn't have that much day-to-day contact with him as I had worked with Branch, Jr. with the Dodgers and then with George Weiss with the Yankees. The only other flare-up occurred the next year, 1947. Dad had made a big speech over the winter in Kansas City in which he promised that the Yankees would not recall any players from the Blues. Now they wanted to recall Jerry Coleman but were embarrassed to do so. So they wanted me to say that the exchange of players (and the Blues were to get a good proven infielder back plus a pitcher) was made to help the Blues. I refused to do it and the whole idea was dropped.

Frank Lane was elected president of the American Association after the 1946 season and moved to Columbus where the League office was located. Frank convinced Weiss that I could handle both jobs. When George offered me some help I put in a request for my brother Bill. Bill had been discharged from the service before me and in 1945 and 1946 had served as the Yankee road secretary. Dad and

George okayed Bill's coming to Kansas City and George also let me hire Herm Krattenmaker, my Swarthmore College roommate and a very bright and able guy, to help with the two jobs.

Spring training, 1947, was in Lake Wales, Florida, a beautiful little town in the lake and orange grove district in Central Florida. The Newark Bears, our sister team, trained in Sebring just south of us. The Yankees themselves were at St. Petersburg. I didn't want to be away from my family that long so I decided to bring them down. I thought I was lucky to be able to rent a cottage on a large estate at Mountain Lakes, an idyllic spot just outside Lake Wales. What a great place for Jane and the kids—or it should have been. Al, the two year old, fell in the yard and a weed went into his eye. We took him to the local hospital, then to an eye specialist in Orlando. The latter told us he was probably going to lose his eye. Jane and I were both devastated. Fortunately, the Lake Wales doctor treated the eye with penicillin. Penicillin was a new drug then, only recently available to the public. Del Webb then sent his private plane for us and flew us up to New York Hospital where he got the treatment needed to save the eye. Today the eye is 20–20.

We had a really outstanding Triple-A team in 1947. It was one of the best athletic groups that I have ever been associated with. The regular lineup consisted of Steve Souchock, first base, Joe Muffoletto, second base, Odie Strain, shortstop, Jerry Coleman, third base, Eddie Stewart, left field, Cliff Mapes, center field, Hank Bauer, right field, Gus Niarhos and Charlie Silvera, catchers, and Bill Wight, Fred Bradley, Cal McLish, and other pitchers. Bud Metheny, Frank Secory, and Harry Craft were also on the team. Bill Meyer had recovered and was the manager. We won the pennant, drew well, and enjoyed a great season. The Yankees also won, so it was quite a year for the organization.

But what really made the Blues outstanding for me was the caliber of the men on the team. They were not only good players but top-flight people with a great interest in the game. The majority of them played in the majors and then stayed in baseball after their playing careers were over. Steve Souchock managed and scouted in the Yankee organization; Jerry Coleman became a major league executive, manager, and now is a major league broadcaster; Eddie Stewart managed in the minors; Harry Craft and Hank Bauer were major league managers; Bill Wight and Cal McLish were (and are) major league coaches and top scouts. Charlie Silvera managed in the minors and coached in the majors. Bud Metheny became a college coach and Frank Secory a National League umpire. It was a year to remember, and having Bill and Herm there to share it with me made it even more enjoyable. Del Webb used to come to Kansas City quite often and we got to be friendly. Late in the year, he told me that he had been talking to Dan and my father and that they wanted me to move into the New York office next year. So when Jane and I went back to New York to the World Series we started looking around for a house.

The World Series in 1947 was a wild affair. The Yankees had their scouts and minor league executives, myself included, on hand. Whenever the Dodgers and the Yankees met you could expect drama. The Series opened in the stadium and Frank Shea and Allie Reynolds put the Yankees two games up. At home in Ebbets Field, with Hugh Casey in relief, the Dodgers won by 9–8 in Game 3. Game 4 proved to be one of the most historic games in Series' history. Floyd Bevens was pitching a no-hitter for New York going into the ninth, but had only a one-run lead. With one out in the ninth, Furillo walked. Al Gionfriddo ran for him, and with two outs, stole second. Pete Reiser, who was not able to play because of an injured ankle, then came up to pinch-hit. Bucky Harris, the Yankee manager, fearing the long ball from Reiser, a left-handed hitter against his right-handed pitcher, ordered Bevens to intentionally put the winning run on base. I was sitting right next to the dugout and can still see Bucky pointing to first base. Cookie Lavagetto then pinch-hit and hit a double off the right field wall to score both runners and tie the Series. Shea came back to win Game 5 on Joe DiMaggio's home run and the Series returned to New York. In Game 6, Gionfriddo made his famous catch off Joe DiMaggio to save the game and tie the Series once again. Then in Game 7, Tommy Henrich's bat brought the Yankees from behind and Joe Page came in to nail down the victory and the World Championship.

It was a tremendous thrill for my father because the Series involved his two teams, the Yankees and Dodgers, with players on each that he had been responsible for, plus his manager, Bucky Harris. And he really celebrated. It started in the clubhouse at the stadium. We drove into Manhattan with him and unfortunately he was at the wheel. We went up a down ramp on the expressway but somehow made it to the city without an accident. Jane and I went to my sister's apartment where with my mother, sister, and my sister's husband we had our own private little celebration before I went over to the Hotel Biltmore and the "Victory Party."

As soon as I walked into the ballroom, I knew that something had happened. But people were reluctant to tell me the sorry details—that my father had argued with and then hit both Weiss and Topping. Everyone was still there and I was soon thrust in the middle of it. Dad had told Weiss he was fired and I remember telling George to ignore it, that he didn't mean it. However, the damage was already done.

The press were all there and there were screaming headlines the next day: "The Battle of the Biltmore." Topping and Webb agreed to buy my father's one-third share and he was out. As it turned out, it was the end of his baseball career. I wondered what would happen to me. I am sure that under the circumstances Topping, Webb, and Weiss would all have welcomed my resignation. But I had a wife and two kids and needed the job and just waited to see if the ax would fall. George eventually talked to me and said I could stay but they would want me to return to Kansas City, rather than coming to New York. So I went back to Kansas City.

During the winter, Bill Meyer was hired by the Pittsburgh Pirates and got a richly deserved opportunity to manage in the major leagues. Joe Devine and Bill Essick, the Yankee scouts on the Pacific Coast, recommended Dick Bartell, a former New York Giants shortstop, for the Kansas City managing job. Weiss had great confidence in Devine and we took Bartell. He was the type people would sometimes describe as "The Bantam Rooster Type"—short, outspoken, a battler. On paper, we had what looked like a very fine team. Ralph Houk was our catcher. We had a top rookie hopeful at first base, Dick Kryhoski, who had outstanding left-hand power. Paul Krichell, the dean of the Yankee scouts, had signed Dick and could see him starring in Yankee Stadium. We expected big things of Hank Bauer in the outfield. The pitching looked okay and we eventually got Al Rosen, a super player in our league, on option from the Cleveland Indians to play third base. The Indians had agreed to option him to us as part of a deal in which they got a player from New York. Harry Craft gave us some added experience and served as coach.

The team should have done well but didn't. It was Bartell's second managing job but he still didn't seem to know how to handle his players. He was biting and sarcastic. If he did not get the response he wanted, he fined people. Sometime in mid-season he fined a pitcher, Don Johnson, $100 for something unreasonable. The other players were angered and all contributed to pay the fine—and they gave it to Dick in pennies. He was furious! It all came to a head on the road when the players, including the natural leaders, Houk, Bauer, and Rosen, all said they would not play for Bartell any longer. Harry Craft stepped in and cooled things down and after a couple of phone calls with me, the revolt subsided.

After the season, George Weiss told me that they would now like me to come to New York. They offered Bill MacPhail a job running the Amsterdam, New York team which understandably wasn't to his liking. Bill then went to work for Frank Lane, who was then general manager of the White Sox, and went to Memphis and later Colorado

Springs, before returning to Kansas City as publicity director, when Kansas City became a major league team in 1955. We were sorry to leave Kansas City. It is really mid-America with fine people. We had made some good friends, including Ernie Mehl and Joe McGuff of the *Kansas City Star,* who covered the Blues, and Larry Rhea, our broadcaster. I had also enjoyed working closely with the scouts and our minor league teams in that area. We had a roster of teams larger than the entire organizations of major league teams today.

Kansas City, of course, was our Triple-A team, Beaumont, Texas in the Texas League was our AA affiliate, Denver in the Western League was Class-A. In those days, classifications continued through B, C, D. Quincy, Illinois in the III League was our Class-B team; Grand Forks, North Dakota and Joplin, Missouri were Class-C; while Fond du Lac, Wisconsin, Independence, Kansas and McAlester, Oklahoma were Class-D. I visited them all pretty regularly and, in addition to spending time with the managers, got to know the team owners well—often several per team. I also spent a lot of time with the scouts. We used to conduct many tryout camps and had a training camp in Branson, Missouri in the Ozarks where we sent the better players from the tryout camps for a more extensive look. All of our area scouts came into Branson with their better prospects. Many good players made their way through Branson—Mickey Mantle, Bill Virdon, Whitey Herzog, Jerry Lumpe, Norm Siebern, Bobby Winkles, and many more.

Tom Greenwade brought in Mickey Mantle, and because he was only seventeen years old his father came with him. Mickey played shortstop at the time. He was very green and made lots of errors but anyone could see his great, natural talent. He had outstanding speed, a fine arm, and was a switch hitter. He showed power both ways, but the tremendous power he had as a major league player developed as he grew bigger and stronger. He signed a Class-D contract for a very small bonus. The only question was which team he would report to—McAlester or Independence. The latter was closer to his home in Commerce, Oklahoma and that's where his father wanted him. So that's where we sent him.

This was really the part of baseball that I enjoyed most. I have always felt that, salary aside, the best job in baseball is that of the farm director. Things have changed though; the title itself has pretty much disappeared from job descriptions and the job has generally been divided between scouting on one hand and the handling of the minor league teams and player personnel on the other. Similarly, there are really few general managers in baseball today, with the job usually divided between business operations and the baseball operation itself. The business operations generally include stadium operations, tickets, marketing, concessions, broadcasting, and finance. Baseball operations usually encompass publicity, the schedule, travel, and the overall responsibility for player development, as well as, of course, the makeup and signing of the major league team.

Now, however, I would be operating out of the New York office—new circumstances, a new environment, and in daily personal contact with George Weiss. Running my own little realm, halfway across the country from the main office, was a thing of the past.

6

Long Home Stand—New York

So in the fall of 1948 we picked up where we had left off in the fall
of 1947 and started house hunting in the New York area. We
bought a house in the Edgemont section of Scarsdale, right across the
street from the elementary school. It was a happy home for us for ten
years. I could walk to the railroad station and walk from Grand
Central Station in New York City to the Yankee offices at 57th and 5th
Avenue. Gene Martin had been running the Yankee farm system in
the east and we worked together as "co-farm directors." Gene had a
long background on the field and in the office and we got along fine.
We reported, of course, to Weiss, and I got to know him a little better.
He was a hard man to know—reserved and all business. His wife
Hazel was just the opposite, outgoing and lots of fun.

Early that year George called me in and started talking in an
oblique manner, unusual for him. He was obviously a little flustered
and I could not figure out what he was trying to get at. Finally, he
asked me if I was sure I could always be loyal to the organization. I
offered that I had no thought of going to another club, but that wasn't
what he was concerned about. Apparently they—Dan, Del, or
George—worried that I might be inclined to tell things to my father
who would, in turn, relay them to the press. In any event, it was rather
an unsatisfactory and unresolved conversation. I certainly didn't pass
along any negative things to my father, but then neither did I have
any control over what he might say—and the fact that I was working
for the Yankees wouldn't restrain him in the least.

Weiss really watched expenses and was particularly tough about
the scouts' travel accounts. I had to okay them and then send them to
him for approval. It was somewhat like the inspection of the galley in
the Navy. It was almost as if there was a rule that something had to be
found to complain about—if only to encourage close scrutiny on my
part in the future. I used to hold a big batch of expense accounts back
and wait until I knew things were very pressing for George. Then I

would take them in and say, "George, could you please sign these? I am a little late with them." That way I got by with just a few sighs and a shaking of the head.

Weiss was very tough with the players, both with respect to their salaries and to their work habits, and he didn't have a good relationship with them. I eventually became a sort of go-between in this area. Like all the rest of us, he liked to win and, although he didn't show it, got nervous at games. He had a habit of leaving our club box before the last half of the ninth to go downstairs to his office—he said to avoid the crowd—but I sometimes thought that he did not like sitting through those last three outs. (Years later, in a way, I found myself emulating his example.) He was also superstitious and thought departing was lucky. My daily contact was almost solely with George. I didn't see too much of Topping or Webb, although they were always friendly. Del would usually see the team play on the west coast but, of course, was in New York for the World Series. (He used to give me problems then by coming into my office and appropriating a block of World Series tickets out of the allotment I handled for our players, scouts, and minor league clubs.) Dan was at home games regularly, often with his wife of the moment—all of whom were young and attractive. (I remembered my father relating how, when Dan had broken up with Sonja Henie, the skater, she would not let him in their house to get his clothes, but how she finally relented and let Dad—whom she liked—come in and retrieve a few things for him before she gave his entire wardrobe to the Salvation Army.)

Gene Martin and I were responsible for the scouting and our minor league clubs nationwide. The division into areas ceased. We were not directly concerned with the major league team. George had an assistant to work with him there. After Newark was sold, we had a working agreement with Richmond in the International League; Herm Krattenmaker, my old roommate, ended up there as general manager. And after Kansas City entered the majors, we worked with Denver in the American Association. Birmingham (later New Orleans) was our AA team. We owned the Class-A team at Binghamton and had B, C & D teams scattered from coast to coast.

We had some fine scouts, which are the key to everything. If your staff does not sign boys with ability, all the work on player development will produce meager results and winning players advancing to the majors will be rare. Because of our fine scouts we had a steady stream of good young players coming into our system. In addition to players mentioned in earlier chapters, there was Gil McDougald, Andy Carey, and Billy Martin (via Oakland) from the Coast; plus Tony

Kubek, Bobby Richardson, Lew Burdette, Bill Skowron, Woody Held, Norm Siebern, Jerry Lumpe, Russ Snyder, and others.*

A few we had got away. Lew Burdette was struggling a little; I had to talk him out of quitting once in a hotel in Charleston, West Virginia. Then when he was ill in spring training, George put him in a deal with Milwaukee for Johnny Sain, another loss I blame myself for. Don Bessent, a right-handed pitcher, was moving along very well up through our farm system when he hurt his back. A top doctor told me he would be lucky if he walked again. I left him exposed to the draft and the Dodgers drafted him. Unfortunately, both of these men came back to haunt the Yankees in the World Series. In 1956, Bessent won the second game in relief for Brooklyn and pitched well in another game. And in 1957, Burdette beat the Yankees three times to gain the World Championship for Milwaukee.

And then there were disappointments. Dick Kryhoski never really made it, nor did Frank Leja or Tommy Carroll or Bob Weisler. All were young men who we felt had more than the requisite physical ability, but who, for various reasons, fell by the wayside. But enough of them made it to give the Yankees the greatest record from 1949 through 1964 that any organization ever had or, most likely, will ever have again. In sixteen years the Yankees won the American League Championship fourteen times and the World Championship nine times. In the period 1949 to 1958 (covered by this chapter), they were in the Series every year but one and won five consecutive World Championships.

In addition to the young white players we signed, we finally started trying to acquire good, young black players. The Kansas City Monarchs of the Negro League rented our stadium in Kansas City and they had promised us first chance at any of their players. In 1950 I worked out a deal with Tom Baird, owner of the Monarchs, to purchase the contracts of Elston Howard and Frank Barnes. Barnes had an excellent arm but had other problems and we eventually let him go to St. Louis. But Howard was outstanding; an outstanding player and an outstanding man. Baird also told me about a young

---

*On one occasion, George asked me to look up our reports on a young, high school catcher in the western Pennsylvania area, see if I thought he was a top prospect, and then come into his office. We had three or four reports and it appeared the boy was a marginal professional prospect. You would sign him, but not go overboard. I went into George's office to report what I had learned and found Bear Bryant, the Alabama football coach, with him. When I gave him my report, Bryant was so happy I thought he was going to embrace me. The player was Joe Namath and my information had satisfied Bear that he would be able to get Joe to come to Alabama on a football scholarship.

shortstop he had and I sent Tom Greenwade to see him. At the time, he had a bad ankle and Tom wanted to see more. When we did not act immediately, Baird felt free to assign him elsewhere (he also didn't like the price I was able to extract from Weiss in the Howard-Barnes deal), and sold this boy's contract to the Cubs. The player was Ernie Banks. Can you imagine how formidable the Yankee lineup would have been with Ernie Banks inserted in it?

Tom Greenwade later acquired Vic Power for us and was involved in another deal that should have brought us Luis Marquez. However, Bill Veeck heard we were trying to purchase Marquez and flew down to Puerto Rico to offer more money and to try to derail the deal in any way he could. As much as anything, he was simply trying to bedevil Weiss. Nothing would have pleased Bill Veeck more than to steal a player from Weiss and the Yankees. We had a signed agreement but Veeck managed to foul things up, both with regard to Marquez and with regard to Artie Wilson, another player we were trying to acquire. There was a big fuss and the matter finally went to Commissioner Happy Chandler for a decision. Chandler awarded Marquez to Cleveland and Wilson to the Yankees. The ruling came out completely opposite to the way the Yankees felt it should. This decision soured George Weiss on Chandler. Del Webb was already against him and the Yankees then took the lead in putting together enough votes to eventually unseat Chandler as commissioner.

When Elston Howard first reported for spring training with Kansas City at Lake Wales, Florida, he couldn't stay with the team at the Walesbilt Hotel. I was able to arrange good accommodations for him at the home of the high school principal. It left me with a not-so-good feeling, but we were baseball people, not crusaders, and I guess I was more concerned with how he fared on the field rather than off it. Elston had done some catching but had played the outfield more. At one of our Instructional Schools, Bill Dickey convinced us to concentrate with Ellie behind the plate and it was a good move. The Yankees had lagged behind in acquiring black players for the organziation and now many other teams had blacks on their major league teams. Certain segments of the media were beginning to put pressure on us for this. By 1954 Vic Power was making his presence felt. Vic was an outstanding fielder at first base—I am not sure I have ever seen anyone any better—and a good right-handed hitter with power. He was an aggressive player with an aggressive attitude, and the latter had caused a few problems in the clubhouse. Weiss and Topping wanted to be certain that the first black player to play for the Yankees would be a role model. We thought we had the ideal man in Howard, although Elston, who in 1950 was at Muskegon, wasn't as close to the majors as Vic. In any event, Weiss resisted the pressures to bring up Power—eventually trading him to Kansas City—and in 1955, Elston became the first black to play for the Yankees. He was a fine young man and handled himself very well.

Almost as important as the scouts were those who managed the minor league teams. They not only had to teach and instruct but had to oversee the off-field habits and behavior of many young men who, in the lower classifications, might well be away from home for an extended period for the first time in their lives. Moreover, in high school, these boys had been the outstanding stars. Now they were thrown into tough competition in an environment where they were just another member of the group. Often their morale would get down and here again it was the manager who had to be aware of the situation and pick them up.*

We had an excellent group of experienced managers, most with a background of major league play. In those days players who had completed their major league careers were more apt to be interested in staying in the game and would accept managing jobs at even the lower levels. Today, the players make so much money that when they retire most are not interested in working in baseball and those that are will not consider managing below the Triple-A level. Among the fine managers working for the Yankees during the fifties were Mayo Smith, George Selkirk, Harry Craft, Ralph Houk, Eddie Lopat, Phil Page, Bill Skiff, Vern Hoscheit, Freddy Fitzsimmons, George Stirnweiss, and Rogers Hornsby. Gene Martin left in the early fifties but I had Johnny Johnson and George Pfister to help me in the office or in the field. They were able and completely dedicated. Several years later, both ended up working in top positions in the Commissioner's office. John eventually became president of the National Association and successfully guided the affairs of the country's minor league teams for many years.

While working with the scouts and the minor league teams, our life, of course, still revolved around the Yankees and their day-to-day problems and successes. I saw almost every home game when I was in New York and a few games on the road. Casey Stengel had taken over for Bucky Harris after the '48 season (another Larry MacPhail man gone). Casey was a very unusual individual. He was one of a kind. He already had had a long career as a major league player and manager

---

*It wasn't only the very young players who got discouraged. In 1975, when he was demoted from the Yankees to Syracuse, Ron Guidry made up his mind to give it up and go home. He was actually on the road heading for Louisiana. Fortunately his wife Bonnie convinced him to turn the car around and head instead to Syracuse.

and Pacific Coast League manager and now, in his first year as a Yankee manager, was fifty-nine years old. On the surface, he sometimes acted like a clown. He spoke in "Stengelese," his own lexicon, which ignored grammar and might or might not have subject or verb. Things or people were seldom referred to by name—instead by a description that might or might not be recognizable to the listener. Sometimes when he did not want to comment on something he made his remarks incomprehensible on purpose. When he was first hired and exposed to the press and others, some thought the Yankees had lost their minds to hire him. Weiss and Webb knew him well from contacts with him in the Pacific Coast League and again Joe Devine's influence probably played a part. They knew he had a fine baseball mind and after you had been around him a while and got used to his manner of speaking you could follow him—at least some of the time.

There was a great deal of talent on the Yankee roster and Casey wisely realized he should find a way of getting most of the squad into games. He was probably the first manager to use the platoon system extensively. Some of the players didn't like it but when it produced results they grudgingly accepted it and year by year their respect for their manager grew. In 1949, Casey's first year, the team was beset with injuries. Red Patterson, the publicity director, even numbered them in his press releases. The number of injuries reached into the seventies, but the team held on and won the pennant by one game by beating Boston both games of the final series of the year at Yankee Stadium. And in the World Series that year they beat the Dodgers four games to one. The opening game was a classic with Allie Reynolds and Don Newcombe locked in scoreless combat until the bottom of the ninth, when "Old Reliable," Tommy Henrich, lined a shot into the right field stands at Yankee Stadium. Eddie Lopat, Vic Raschi, and Joe Page (in relief) won the other games.

In 1950 Vic Raschi duplicated his twenty-one win season of the previous year and the Yankees edged Detroit and Boston for the Championship. Phil Rizzuto was the League's MVP. The World Series was a sweep against Philadelphia. Most of the games were close, a tenth-inning DiMaggio home run winning one of them. Another victory came on the bat of current American League president, Bobby Brown. And the fourth game was won by a twenty-one-year old rookie, Whitey Ford. In 1951 it was Cleveland that challenged, but the Indians' ninety-three wins proved five short. This time, Ed Lopat, as well as Raschi, won twenty-one games and the League's MVP was a young man named Yogi Berra. Gil McDougald was the Rookie of the Year. It was DiMaggio's last season and Mickey Mantle's first.

In July we had our third child, the first of our post-war family. We named him Bruce Thompson (after my mother). I went through the usual worrying and pacing that fathers experience. When I got my wife and child home I relaxed. A day later the Yankees were playing the Chicago White Sox in an afternoon game at the stadium. At the time, the White Sox were battling New York for the lead. It was a key game and was tied in the ninth. In the bottom of the ninth, Joe Collins hit a home run into the right-field seats. We celebrated in the press room. I was celebrating two events and I celebrated a little too much and a little too long. When I finally got home I was met by an irate wife, left alone to tend child and baby. I could not blame her.

In 1952 it was again Cleveland that provided the toughest opposition, but again their ninety-three wins was a little short. This time the margin was two games. This season the Yankee ace was Allie Reynolds with twenty wins, and the World Series foe was, once again, the Dodgers. The teams split the first two games at Ebbets Field but the Dodgers then won two of three at the stadium. They were one game away from victory and returning to Ebbets Field. Raschi faced Loes in the sixth game and Mickey Mantle hit a home run to break a late inning tie for a 3–2 win that evened the Series. Allie Reynolds opposed Black in the final game and led in the bottom of the seventh. The Dodgers then loaded the bases with one out and had Duke Snider and Jackie Robinson coming up. Casey brought in Bob Kuzava. Snider popped up, two out. Robinson popped up—but for a moment no one seemed to have it. Then Billy Martin dashed in to make his historic ankle-high catch on the run in the middle of the infield and the Yankees held on to win. I missed the first two games of the Series because the Kansas City Blues were playing the Rochester Red Wings in the Little World Series and I stayed with George Selkirk and his charges through their Series. Though Rochester won, we had a fine team at Kansas City (Vic Power, Bill Skowron, etc.) and it made us proud to have both the Yankees and Blues in post-season play.

About this time we developed a new approach to player development that proved very successful for us. I think Joe Devine and I conceived the idea jointly. The concept was to bring all of our best young prospects together in the fall for a two- or three-week session with the best instructors in the organization. The Yankee coaches were part of the staff. Jim Turner worked with the pitchers, Bill Dickey with the catchers, Frank Crosetti with the infielders. Our top minor league managers were also there and Harry Craft worked with the outfielders. Casey Stengel was in overall charge on the field. He also had his own routine of teaching base running, taking the whole group from base to base and letting them know what they should be thinking about in all situations. Johnny Neun, an excellent detail man, was the camp coordinator. It worked very well. It gave better instruction to the players than we could give them in the lower minors. It was an incentive and reward for the players to be chosen to attend and was a maturing experience for them.

It also gave our major league people an early look at the prospects in the organization. It was here that Casey's eyes popped out when he saw Mickey Mantle perform. It was also here that the decision was made to move Mickey from shortstop to the outfield, before he killed someone in the stands behind first base with his very strong but erratic arm. After operating the school for several years, we thought it would benefit from more game competition. Consequently we got other clubs to start the same type program and to engage in a series of games with us. This was the start of the Fall Instructional League program that all the clubs take part in today in Florida and Arizona.

The results of the 1953 season were similar to those of 1952. The Yankees finished seven games ahead of Cleveland and then met the Dodgers again in the Series. This time the first two games were played in the stadium and New York took a two-game lead behind Sain and Lopat. The Dodgers came right back however, winning the first two in their own borough. Carl Erskine struck out fourteen (a record at that time) to edge Raschi 3–2 and the Dodgers beat Ford to tie it. However the Yankees battered Johnny Podres (11–7) and took a 3–2 game lead back to the stadium. They appeared to have the Series won the next day when they led 4–1 in the ninth with Reynolds on the mound. Carl Furillo kept the Dodgers alive by hitting a three-run homer to tie, only to have Billy Martin drive in Hank Bauer with the winning score in the bottom of the ninth. The Yankees had thus won five consecutive World Series, a tremendous accomplishment. During these years they were very consistent, winning between ninety-five and ninety-nine games each year. In fact, the Yankees won so consistently that it often seemed to those of us in the organization that the rest of the world was pulling against us.

After the 1953 season Red Patterson, whom my father had hired from the *Herald Tribune* to work for the Yankees as director of publicity, left to join the Dodgers. Red and George Weiss had never hit it off too well. Their personalities simply did not jive. One small example: pennants of each of the American League teams were regularly displayed above the roof of the Yankee Stadium upper deck and it was customary to fly these flags, starting from the outfield, in the order of the team's standing in the league. In a game toward the latter half of the season in which the Yankees were not in first place, and were trailing their opponent of the day in the standings, they staged a rally to take a good lead. If the game ended that way the Yankees would pass their opponents. Red, jubilant over the big Yankee inning, directed a member of the Yankee maintenance staff to switch the flags in the middle of the game. The fans noticed and cheered, but Weiss was furious. He thought it was uncalled for showmanship—and he was also superstitious. There were other more serious differences and Red resigned.

To replace him the Yankees hired Bob Fishel from a Cleveland advertising agency. Bob had worked with both the Indians and the Browns and was well qualified. He stepped right in and became an immediate favorite with the press and his coworkers, as well as with George and the owners of the team. Bob and I worked together over the years and became very close friends. He was completely devoted to his work and to the game. (I thought so much of him that years later I tried to hire him for the commissioner's office, but was glad that he hadn't accepted when I returned to the Yankees. Later I tried again, this time successfully, to get him to join me when I became president of the American League.)

In 1954 our new rookie sensation, Bob Grim, won twenty games and was Rookie of the Year. Yogi Berra had another banner season and was again named MVP. The team won 103 games, seven more than their average of the preceding championship seasons, yet they finished second. The Cleveland Indians, behind the superb pitching of Bob Lemon, Early Wynn, Mike Garcia, and Bob Feller were unbeatable, finishing with 111 wins—a number of regular season wins that has been surpassed only once in baseball history (116 by the Chicago Cubs in 1906). But without the Yankees as their representative, the American League lost the World Championship. This was the year of Willie Mays' great catch and throw and Dusty Rhodes' pinch hitting. Leo Durocher, my father's old manager and sparring partner, and the Giants, won four games to none.

After the 1954 season, the Philadelphia Athletics were purchased by Arnold Johnson and moved to Kansas City. Johnson was a friend of Dan Topping and was in the concession business. It worked out well for the Yankees as they sold Johnson the Kansas City territorial rights and the stadium. It also worked out well for Johnson, who got a major league team and eventually ended up getting the concession rights for Yankee Stadium. It didn't end there. Weiss became the new team's unofficial advisor on baseball matters and recommended Parke Carroll (who had been general manager of the Yankees' Newark Bears) to be G.M. Relations between the Yankees and Athletics naturally were close. When we couldn't sign an amateur player because of roster restraints, we recommended him to the A's. (Clete Boyer is the best example.) And there were frequent deals between the teams. Parke hired Bill MacPhail as director of publicity and apparently talked to George about my joining them as a vice president for player personnel. (I learned later they were not the first team that had asked about me.) George then worked it out with Dan and Del that I would become vice president and director of player personnel for the Yankees and I got an increase in salary.

Bill DeWitt had gone and from that point on I served as assistant to Weiss and became more and more involved in major league player matters. Under George's tight guidelines, I did most of the work signing the players. Also, as neither Casey nor George liked to talk to players being sent out, I inherited that duty. Actually I did it in unison with Casey. He didn't mind doing it that way and I found out it worked very well to have both the field manager and the office represented in moving a player. (Later as general manager of both Baltimore and New York I followed the same procedure without fail.)

When Kansas City became major league, we shifted our American Association Triple-A team to Denver. We needed a manager for Denver and the choice was mine. I had always felt that Ralph Houk would make a good manager. He was smart, interested in the game, was a good competitor, and a leader of men. He had experience in all levels from Class-D to the majors. I had talked to him a little about managing and knew he was interested. When I mentioned Houk to George, he was all for it. So Ralph became manager of the Bears. We had a very young team there—good talent but not much experience— and they got off to a very bad start. I knew George was concerned and some people were saying we had moved these kids along too quickly— that we needed some more experienced players. Houk wouldn't panic and stuck with them and before long they were winning.

Ralph was at Denver for three seasons and did an outstanding job there. The club was owned by Bob Howsam and his family. Bob's father-in-law was a United States Senator from Colorado and Bob had previously operated the Denver club in the Western League before Denver moved up to the American Association. Bob was from old German stock and a very careful operator. In many ways, he was a little like George Weiss. He watched costs very carefully and was very concerned about the reputation and image of the team. He and Ralph did not get along without an effort on both of their parts. An early difference of opinion came when Bob shut off beer to the clubhouse. A later, more serious, difference came after a fight on the field between the Bears and Omaha at Omaha. Denver had rallied and won the game and Ralph felt pretty good about it. Bob, though, was very upset about the reports he received of the incident and sent Ralph a scathing telegram. Ralph was mad and ready to quit. I got his long-distance call and was finally able to calm him down and in proper mind to continue.

One other incident with Ralph came late in 1955 when Denver

was fighting for the pennant. Billy Hunter (who later became a major league manager) was playing shortstop and providing the necessary experience for another young team. Unfortunately Billy broke his leg in a play at the plate and was obviously out for the season. Ralph reached me in Winston-Salem, where we had a team in the Carolina League, and he was frantic. (As well he might be—losing your star shortstop in the home stretch of a pennant race was not an event to be accepted with equilibrium.) But I reassured him. "Ralph," I said, "we have a shortstop to send you from our Quincy club. I'll call them immediately and he'll be there tomorrow. Believe me, he'll do the job for you." Well, the young shortstop from Quincy did get there in time to play the next night but he made three errors and cost Denver the game. But from that point on he did indeed do the job, filling the shortstop position admirably. That young man's name was Tony Kubek.*

In my new role, in addition to continuing with player development, I spent a good deal of time with the major league team. In spring training I went to St. Petersburg instead of to Lake Wales and as a result spent a lot of time with Casey. I was sort of his personal chauffeur and companion and ate (and drank) with him often. Everyone thought that Casey was a great drinker. I learned that, although he always had a glass in his hand, on most occasions he didn't really drink that much. His managing reputation was established with the World Series he had won despite all the injuries, that first year (1949) with the Yankees. As the successes continued, his reputation continued to skyrocket. He was very canny and his reputation was deserved.

He was also, on occasion, lucky. I remember one such occasion during a game in New York: the Yankees were leading in the ninth but the opposition filled the bases with none out. Casey turned to his bull pen, where two men were throwing. One was Virgil Trucks, a veteran pitcher, not having a good year and nearing retirement. He had just been acquired by the Yankees and hadn't pitched for ten days. The other was Johnny Kucks, a young sinker ball pitcher who had been doing an excellent job, since being called up, in tough late-inning situations. Casey picked up the phone to the bull pen and said, "Send in Kucks." Darrell Johnson, the bull pen coach, misunderstood. He thought Casey had said, "Send in Trucks." So in came Trucks. Everyone was aghast and Casey almost fainted, but by the rules

---

*Tony was a very interesting young man. Son of a former professional player, as a youngster and even in his Yankee days he was very quiet. Today he is a top major network broadcaster and is never at a loss for words!

Trucks had to pitch to at least one man. He did, and the batter popped up the first pitch. The next hitter hit the first pitch back to the pitcher and the Yankees completed a game-ending double play. The crowd was thrilled, the press ecstatic. Casey was indeed a "master strategist."

In 1955 the Yankees bounced back and won the American League Championship again. "Bounced back" is hardly the right description, considering their 103 wins in 1954. But in 1955, they finished three games ahead of Cleveland rather than four behind them. The team leaders were Mantle, who led the league in home runs, and Yogi, who repeated as MVP. In October, though, the Dodgers, after failing seven times to win the World Series, finally came out on top; and they did it after losing the first two games in Yankee Stadium. It was the first time a team had won the World Series after being down two games to none. The Dodgers swept the three games in Brooklyn behind Podres, Labine, and Craig; lost Game Six to Whitey Ford; and then finally won when Johnny Podres pitched a shutout in Game Seven to edge Tommy Byrne, 2–0. The play of the Series came in that game, when in the sixth inning, with two men on, Sandy Amoros came up with Yogi Berra's slicing drive to left.

The Yankees reversed the script in 1956, however, beating the Dodgers in seven games after the Dodgers had won the first two games in Brooklyn. The highlight of this series was Don Larsen's perfect game in Game Five, which was the third straight Yankee win and gave them a 3–2 lead in the Series. It was the first no-hitter, let alone perfect game, in World Series history. Game Six was a nail biter, with Clem Labine winning 1–0 in ten innings. Then in Game Seven Johnny Kucks' win brought the World Championship back to New York. Tommy Sturdivant had won the fourth game, and with Kucks winning the seventh, it was a thrill for me to see two of our young pitchers come through. The 1956 season belonged to Mickey Mantle, as he won the triple crown (hitting 52 homers) and was the MVP.

One night during the 1957 season a group of Yankee players went to the Copacabana, a New York nightclub. It was primarily the group who played the hardest off the field as well as on and included Mantle, Ford, Bauer, Berra, and Martin. Johnny Kucks was with them, and some of the wives. When a noisy customer started heckling Sammy Davis Jr., the entertainer, Bauer told him off and a fight ensued. Of course, the press found out about it and it was national headline news. Plus, the man filed a suit against Bauer. Topping and Weiss were upset. They were concerned about the fast-paced life that some of their players were living and, rightly or wrongly, decided that Billy Martin was the leader and had to go. This was not a decision that Casey could accept easily. Billy had always been his boy. He had had him at Oakland before they both came to New York and Billy was Casey's kind of player—a tough competitor. Weiss and Topping were adamant however, and Casey finally had to give in. The deal was made and Billy's contract was assigned to Kansas City. It was announced after a game between the teams in Kansas City. Casey didn't have the heart to tell Billy, and as I was with the team, I got the assignment. I didn't enjoy it too much either.*

In the course of the 1957 season I made my first major league deal. We were looking for a back-up relief pitcher. I learned from my friend Buzzie Bavasi that the Dodgers were willing to sell Sal Maglie, who was nearing the end of his outstanding career. Sal was just what we were looking for—an experienced, gutsy competitor. Moreover, he would be new to our league and American League hitters would not be used to his style of pitching. Unfortunately Weiss was sick but he okayed the deal and Topping gave me a green light to spend any reasonable amount necessary. Buzzie and I met in one of his favorite Manhattan seafood restaurants to close the deal. When the sale was announced, Buzzie made sure that both the restaurant and I received publicity, neither of which made Weiss very happy. Buzzie, Chub Feeney, and I became good friends over these years. About the same age, we had comparable jobs with the three New York teams, and we all lived in Scarsdale within a few miles of one another.

In 1957 the Yankees won ninety games to beat the White Sox, a new runner-up. Boston was third. Mantle was again the MVP, and Tony Kubek was Rookie of the Year. Once again the World Series went down to the seventh game. This time the opponent was the Milwaukee Braves; and this time the seventh game was at Yankee Stadium. I felt sure that we would win this one. Lou Burdette had already won two games in the Series. It was against all odds for him to win the third and Don Larsen was pitching for New York. But it was Burdette, helped by Eddie Mathews' bat, that prevailed.

When contracts went out for the 1958 season, to my dismay, Weiss had insisted that Mantle's contract reflect that, record-wise, he had not

---

*Later, even with Martin gone, Weiss still worried that some of the players were leading too merry a life on the road. From time to time he would have detectives check to see what might be going on. On one occasion, following a day game, the assigned detective waited in the lobby to pick up the trail of anyone going out for an evening on the town. When two players slipped out together around nine p.m., after having had dinner, the detective slunk along behind. Unfortunately for him however, he hadn't focused on the right people and was following Bobby Richardson and Tony Kubek, two young men with most exemplary habits, and the trail led to the downtown YMCA, where Bobby and Tony engaged in a tough ping pong encounter.

matched his triple crown performance of 1956. (He only batted .365 in 1957.) Mantle refused to sign for a cut in pay, and the controversy dragged on. Our offer was increased, as I remember, to reflect a small raise. I remember urging Mickey to sign (I didn't want him missing once spring training started), telling him that someday I would make it up to him. Mickey was eventually signed before spring training began and came back with another good season, again leading the league in home runs.

Bob Turley was the other star, winning twenty-one games, the Cy Young Award, and playing a hero's role in the World Series. Again, the October foe was Milwaukee. Again the Series went seven games. Again, as in 1956, the Yankees lost the first two games and, in this Series, they were down three games to one. I remember how hard I was pulling for us to at least win Game Five and send the Series back to Milwaukee. It was Turley who did it, shutting the Braves out and beating Burdette. Feelings were aroused in Milwaukee when the teams returned, as someone in the Yankee party had reportedly referred to Milwaukee as a "bush town." All over the city there were figures of Yankees hanging in effigy. The Yankees stayed alive by winning Game Six. Ryne Duren got the win in relief, but it was Turley who came in to save it. Then in Game Seven, when Larsen ran into trouble, Casey called on Turley one more time. He responded by holding the Braves the final 6⅔ innings to nail down the win. It was only the second time in history that a team had been down three games to one and triumphed. Hank Bauer was the hitting star for the Yankees with ten hits, four home runs, and eight RBIs. I think that this Series might be the greatest thrill I ever experienced in baseball. I can still see some of the plays in my mind's eye—particularly a catch by Elston Howard and Bill Skowron's long home run to left, which pretty much clinched that seventh game.

Late in the 1958 season when Baltimore was playing at the stadium, Paul Richards asked if I would stop in his office in the visiting clubhouse before the game to talk with him. Paul was both manager and general manager of the Orioles, who had been in the American League since moving from St. Louis in 1954. Paul came right to the point: he asked me if I would consider coming to Baltimore to work with the Orioles. I was taken completely by surprise. I had given no thought to working anywhere else, and I did not know exactly how to respond, other than to tell him that I was completely happy with the Yankees. I didn't think a great deal about it. Then after the season I received a call from a gentleman named Joe Iglehart, who introduced himself as one of the owners of the Orioles. He asked if I would have lunch with him at the Racquet Club on Park Avenue in Manhattan. We had lunch, and he pursued the subject that Paul had opened with me. His big sales point was the superior lifestyle in Baltimore compared to New York. (Actually, I was perfectly happy with our home in Westchester and with our lifestyle.)

The situation with the Orioles was that Paul was not business-operation–minded. All of his energies were devoted to the field and they wanted someone to come in as general manager to supervise the organization off the field and to watch the exchequer. What they wanted in part was someone to say no to Richards when he chose to ignore the budget. I later found out that Joe was on the Board of CBS and had heard good things about Bill, my brother, who had moved to CBS from the A's to serve as sports director. When Joe had brought Bill's name up in Baltimore, Richards had said, "If you're going to hire a MacPhail, the one with the baseball experience and the one you should be interested in, is Lee." I wasn't too much interested at that juncture, but the Orioles kept pushing, asking Weiss and Topping for permission to make me an offer. Eventually it came to a head. Jane didn't want to leave New York. I really didn't want to either, though I knew that if the job as general manager was open to me, I probably should take it. Weiss didn't want me to leave. Then Dan Topping called me in and said, "Lee, look, George is probably going to be here for a long, long time. This is an opportunity for you to get out on your own and show that you can run a team yourself. I think that you would be making a serious mistake to turn down an opportunity like this."

I took the advice as an act of friendship and called Joe and arranged to go down to Baltimore and meet with their Board of Directors, but I said that before I went any further I wanted to make absolutely sure that this was okay with Richards—he was the one giving up the position of general manager. I had heard rumors that there was disharmony in the Oriole organization, and if Paul and I were going to work together as a team I wanted to be sure that he was one hundred percent in favor of the move. So I met Paul in Memphis, Tennessee (halfway between New York City and Waxahachie, Texas, Paul's home). We had a good meeting. I was satisfied and shortly thereafter agreed to join the Orioles as general manager, at a salary of $35,000 and five percent of the net profits. And so my time with the Yankees came to an end. I had been with them thirteen years, ten in New York. In those ten years they had won the pennant nine times. (That's a lot of victory parties, all of which began with Casey's dancing with his wife, Edna, to the strains of "Casey would waltz with the strawberry blonde and the band played on.") No baseball person could have asked for a more pleasant sojourn.

7

Good Road Trip—Baltimore

I signed the contract with the Orioles on November fifth and was soon at work in my Memorial Stadium office. My move from the Yankees to Baltimore started a game of musical chairs in baseball. To replace me, the Yankees got Roy Hamey to give up his job as general manager of the Philadelphia Phillies and return to New York. The Phillies then hired John Quinn, who had been the general manager of the Milwaukee Braves. Then Milwaukee needed someone and lured John McHale away from the Detroit Tigers to replace Quinn. Finally, the Tigers brought the game to a close by elevating my good friend Jim Campbell from their own organization to serve as their new general manager.

In Baltimore I served on the Board of Directors and worked closely with Jim Keelty, who was president, and with Joe Iglehart and Zan Krieger, major owners. There was a third major owner, Jerry Hoffberger, president of the local National Brewing Company, but for some reason Jerry was not involved in the operation of the club and did not serve on the Board of Directors. This may have been because of the rivalry between the National Brewing Company and another local brewery, the Gunther Brewing Company, as Gunther's was owned by the Krieger family. There were no problems. Keelty was president but did not spend much time with the baseball team. Zan liked to be closely involved and would stop regularly in my office to discuss whatever was going on. Joe was with the W.E. Hutton Company, stockbrokers, and his office was in New York City. In addition, he was treasurer of CBS and on its Board, so this also kept him in New York. He was, however, a great Oriole fan and never missed a home game if he was in Baltimore.

We had a good staff in the office. Jack Dunn was my assistant. His family had owned the Triple-A Orioles and had given up their territorial rights in order to help bring major league baseball to the Baltimore area.* Jack was about my age and had been working in

---

*His grandfather, Jack Dunn, signed Babe Ruth to his first professional contract.

baseball since he graduated from Princeton. Jim McLaughlin was farm director. He had worked for the Browns in St. Louis. Harry Dalton was Jim's assistant in the scouting and player development area. Harry had gotten his indoctrination in baseball while in the army. He had been at an army camp near Colorado Springs and had offered his services gratis to the local team. The general manager of that local team happened to be my brother, Bill MacPhail, and Bill had put Harry straight to work.

Herb Armstrong was older and a legend around Baltimore, where he had taught and coached. He was in charge of stadium operations—the ground crew, ushers, etc. (the stadium belonged to the city of Baltimore, so it was responsible for major maintenance). John Lancaster was the public relations director. He was an Amherst graduate and had recruited Bob Brown, also from Amherst, to be his assistant. (Harry Dalton was the third member of our Amherst triumvirate.) Elmer Burkhart a former Oriole Triple-A pitcher, was the ticket manager; plus the team had a capable young accountant, Joe Hamper, who looked after things on the financial side. Later I hired a young man named Jerry Sachs, who asked only for an opportunity to work. It was a case similar to my brother hiring Harry Dalton at Colorado Springs. Jerry became an important part of our organization and after I left became a key executive for the Washington Bullets and Sports Complex. And there were the ladies. Every professional baseball team, at all levels, relies heavily on the dedicated secretaries who work extra hours and look after all the important details. I was very much pleased with the staff and got to appreciate them more the longer I was there.

One thing I learned very quickly was that, at this point in time, Baltimore was a Baltimore Colts town. The Orioles had not done much since their arrival in 1954, and the Colts, with John Unitas at quarterback, Lenny Moore in the backfield, Gino Marchetti at defensive end, and Raymond Berry as a receiver, were an exciting and very competitive football team. The Colts, at times during my stay in Baltimore, were almost like a religion to the sports fans of the city. One would not have believed at that time that things could go downhill for them as they did, and that some years later Baltimore would not even have a professional football team.

Jane and I found a house in Baltimore in the Guilford section, near Johns Hopkins University. It was a very nice residential area. When I turned into our one-block Kemble Road it seemed almost like a secluded harbor in an otherwise stormy sea. I had been lucky on one of my first public appearances in Baltimore, at a McCormick Company dinner, to sit next to Dr. Forbush, the headmaster at Friends School, a private Quaker Preparatory School. I told him about my concern in moving my boys from Scarsdale and he offered to take them all at Friends School. That was a very fortunate occurrence for my family. Although we are Episcopalians, my years at Swarthmore had generated a great respect for Quaker traditions and education. The fact that our house was only five minutes from Memorial Stadium was another plus.

In my new position I was suddenly called upon to do a lot of public speaking, and at first I was very nervous about it. I used stories to add some humor to my remarks. I found that if I could get my listeners to laugh, it relaxed me, and I got along better. One night I told a story that was slightly off-color. It got many laughs but after the dinner a man came up to me and told me that he had his son with him at the dinner and that he did not think my story was appropriate for a sports gathering when young people might be there. It was a good lesson and was the last off-color story that I ever used in speaking.

One of the first things I did in Baltimore was to finalize the arrangements already in progress to have the Orioles train in Miami. They had been training in Scottsdale, Arizona—a great spot but out of the way for Baltimore. The different time zone in Arizona was an impediment from a publicity point of view and there were also many more Maryland-area people in Florida than in Arizona in the spring. I also liked the Florida weather for training and liked the fact that we would be closer to more of the other teams. Along with the A's in Palm Beach, we were the first team to train on the southeast coast of Florida. Once we were there, it helped to attract first the Yankees to Fort Lauderdale, and later other teams to the area. Miami became, along with Vancouver, our Triple-A affiliate.

Spring training was the first opportunity I had to evaluate the players on the Oriole roster and to spend some time with Paul Richards. The team stayed at the McAlester Hotel in downtown Miami, and we had a small suite on the top floor. It had a patio looking out over downtown Miami. Jane came down to join me. That was important to us, even though at times we felt that we might have left the children without ideal supervision. It was a period for us to be together, to enjoy the games, to dine out with other baseball people, and to "luxuriate" in our little hideaway suite. During this period I tried to get close to Paul and though everything was quite friendly, I could not seem to break through his shell. It was the manner of the man. Ours was not the same as the relationships I had with the field people in the Yankee organization: Ralph Houk, Jim Turner, Bill Dickey, Ed Lopat, Harry Craft, Mayo Smith, George Selkirk, etc. With them I was able to talk at great length, to discuss players' strengths and weaknesses, and to analyze the plusses and minuses of our organization. I simply was unable to do this with Paul. I was able to do it, however, with Eddie Robinson, a coach and special assistant, who was a great help to me in my first years with the Orioles. The spring training facilities worked out extremely well. Clubs had played occasional spring games there for several years, so we knew that the stadium, clubhouses, lights, and fields were good. The city installed a batting cage in the right-field area and an extra infield in the left-field area and made office space available to us under the stands. Everybody, except perhaps Paul, was happy with the switch.

The 1959 Oriole team was pretty much a veteran ball club with fill-ins in several spots. In fact, when we first met the Yankees, with all of their young players who had meant so much to me, dressed in their traditional white pinstriped uniforms, I wondered if it wasn't the "good guys" playing the "bad guys" and that I was on the side of the bad guys. However, it didn't take me long to get over those feelings. And there was some talent in our lineup. Gus Triandos caught, Bob Boyd was at first, Billy Gardner was at second, Chico Carrasquel at short, Billy Klaus started the season at third, and Bob Nieman, Gene Woodling, Al Pilarcik, and Willie Tasby were in the outfield. Woodling and Triandos had been part of the famous Yankee-Oriole deal of a few years earlier, when Baltimore traded Bob Turley and Don Larsen to New York in a deal that included seventeen players. Woodling had a good season for us in 1959 and was named the most valuable Oriole. Pitching was the best part of the club, with Hoyt Wilhelm, Billy O'Dell, and Skinny Brown leading the staff.

Wilhelm won his first nine decisions and got the team off to a good start. One of those wins, his eighth, came at Comiskey Park in Chicago, in a game that looked as if it might be curtailed by a major league "first." A swarm of insects took over the pitching mound in the first inning and defied the waving of towels, sprays, and whatever. Finally at Bill Veeck's suggestion, they brought in some fireworks, already set up behind the outfield fence for a post-game fireworks show. When they set off a few bombs on the mound the insects disappeared and the game was able to continue.

In the first week of June our team was actually tied for first place for one day with the White Sox. But the next day Rocky Colavito of the Indians hit four consecutive home runs in Memorial Stadium to drop us back a spot. After the All-Star Game, we started going with young players. Brooks Robinson, a brilliant third base prospect, was recalled from Vancouver. A trio of young pitchers (Milt Pappas, Jerry Walker, and Jack Fisher) began starting regularly and they responded sensationally. Pappas and Walker each pitched shutouts in a doubleheader win over Washington and a few weeks later, Walker and Fisher did the same against Chicago. Paul Richards was great with young pitchers. In fact, he was an excellent manager all around, both from the standpoint of teaching and because he got the most out of his players' talent. The White Sox won the pennant but they got all they could handle from the Orioles. The two teams split the twenty-two-game series after a number of incredible battles: one went eighteen innings, two went seventeen innings, one, sixteen and two, ten. The Orioles won seventy-four games, lost eighty, and finished sixth.

That fall Paul and I determined to go with the "kids." The Orioles—thanks to a capable scouting staff and an open budget for signing bonuses—had excellent talent in their system. The only problem in this area was a major schism within the organization. On one side were Richards and his coaches and some of the scouts. On the other were Jim McGlothlin, the farm director, and the rest of the scouting force. It got so bad that I was afraid that the handling of players and the reports on players would depend to some degree on whether the player was a Richards-acquired player or a McGlothlin-acquired player. It was an intolerable situation which I knew had to be eliminated. I did everything that I could to repair the rupture and, in the final analysis, I reluctantly told Jim, who certainly was not entirely at fault, that he was going to have to change or we would have to let him go. I reasoned that the ex-general manager and manager had to be considered before the farm director. When Jim was unbending, I eventually had to dismiss him. That may have been the only occasion in my entire career when I had to dismiss someone from an off-field position. I was able to get the Washington club to agree to take Jim, for he was a capable man but, although he could have commuted there from his home, he refused the offer. In another development preceding the 1960 season, I was made president as well as general manager. I never completely understood all that was involved in the situation. Primarily, it was the fact that Jim Keelty did not have the time to devote to the club. There also may have been some politics at play on the Board of Directors level. In any event, from my personal point of view it at least showed that they were satisfied with my performance to date and that, if there were factions within the Board, I was considered neutral between them.

With our decision to go with youth in the 1960 season, we decided to trade one of our experienced pitchers in an attempt to bolster our outfield and to add a little speed and offense. We therefore dealt Billy O'Dell to San Francisco for Jackie Brandt. Billy Loes, a real character, went with O'Dell and we got a couple of players with Jackie, who was also a character in his own right. I negotiated the deal with my friend Chub Feeney, and it proved a good one for both teams. My view on trading was that the objective was not to try to outsmart someone, or even to gain an advantage, but rather to give up something you could spare for something you needed more. This trade was a good example of that. If you were long in one department and short in another—with respect to position, offense or defense, right-handed or left-handed strength—you could usually rectify this only by trading. We also got a break in filling our hole at first base when I was able to purchase Jim Gentile from the Dodgers. Paul was not enthusiastic about that deal, but as we were not giving up any players, I went ahead anyway. We felt pretty good about our club as we went south for spring training. We knew that our team was very young, but we definitely felt that we were headed in the right direction.

We were scheduled to play a three-game exhibition series with the Cincinnati Reds in Havana that spring but the Cuban Revolution had occurred, Castro had taken over, and conditions were very unsettled. There had been a couple of incidents during the Winter League season, with gunfire breaking out at the ballpark. Our players were concerned about having to go, and reports were that the Reds' players felt the same. Gabe Paul was then general manager of the Reds. I met with Gabe and Powell Crosley (my father's old employer) in a hotel in Miami to discuss the situation. It was clear that neither team wanted to go, but Gabe was very concerned about cancelling the game because the Reds had a working agreement with the Havana club. The owner of the Havana team, Bob Maduro, was a friend of Gabe's and he was afraid that it might hurt Bob's position in Cuba if the Reds refused to play. I therefore said that I would be willing to take the initiative and declare the game would be cancelled because the Orioles would not go, and that the series would be played in Miami instead. That was the way it was handled. There was a great outcry in Cuba against the Orioles and against me personally. I have kept the Havana papers that carried a front-page headline reading "Lee MacPhail, Public Enemy Number 1 of Cuban Baseball."* Commissioner Ford Frick and the State Department said that they had played no role in the decision (and they hadn't). Gabe said that the Reds wanted to play the games in Havana and had done everything they could do to encourage us to do so but, as the home team, the decision was up to the Orioles.

The Oriole team in 1960 included seven rookies and most of the players on the roster were in their twenties. The only real veterans were Wilhelm and Brown, Walt Dropo (a back-up first baseman), and Woodling. In addition to Gentile and Brandt, other additions to the team included two young pitchers from the farm system, Chuck

---

*Our two youngest boys were on spring vacation and in Miami with us at the time. As Miami had a large Cuban population they weren't too sure how safe we were and for a couple of days, when out in the car with us, they would occupy the floor of the back seat.

Estrada and Steve Barber, a new rookie double-play combination of Marv Breeding and Ron Hansen, plus Clint Courtney, a back-up catcher. Despite its youth, the team was in the race all the way. Paul Richards came up with the "big mitt" to assist in catching Wilhelm, (we had had 49 passed balls in 1959, a record) and it definitely helped when Hoyt was on the mound. At the start of June the Orioles served notice that they could be troublesome by sweeping a three-game series from the Yankees in Baltimore. Moreover, the breaks began to fall our way. In August we were trying to cling to a late-inning 3–1 lead against the White Sox when Ted Kluszewski, the big Sox first baseman, hit a home run with two men on to give Chicago the lead—or so it seemed. Actually, Umpire Ed Hurley had called time just before the pitch and the home run was nullified. Understandably, the White Sox were beside themselves, but the decision held, and the Orioles got by the two remaining innings to win. Then when the Yankees returned to Memorial Stadium in early September the Orioles swept them again, passing them and taking a two-game lead. Three youngsters, part of what became known as our "kiddie corps" (Pappas, Fisher, and Estrada) were the starters for the Birds. One hundred and fourteen thousand people saw the series. That was a new plateau for support for baseball in Baltimore.

In mid-September, the Orioles had to make a final visit to New York. So far they had not won a game there in 1960. Going into Yankee Stadium, they trailed the Yankees for the league lead by one percentage point. Obviously, the pennant was on the line. We chartered a bus and took our entire office staff to New York for the series. It was a reward for them for all of the hard work they had put in throughout the hectic season. Well, unfortunately, they didn't get to see an Oriole win. The Yankees won Friday and Saturday and then swept a doubleheader on Sunday. Of course, everyone felt bad. I didn't actually feel as bad as one might expect. I realized that the team was extremely young and really wasn't ready to win it all. I was satisfied that we had made tremendous progress and were on the brink of winning a championship. Gentile, Hansen, and Robinson— three new young regulars—all had had fine years. Our young pitching looked awesome. (Little did I realize that final success would continue to elude me throughout all of my remaining days as a general manager.) In 1960, we finished second, winning eighty-nine games and edging the White Sox for the runner-up position. The slogan around Baltimore that winter was, "It can be done in '61." Preseason ticket sales reached new levels. Everyone was confident that at last we had a good chance to win the pennant.

In the fall of 1960 we operated an Instructional League team in Scottsdale, patterned after the program we had initiated while I was in

New York. I had quickly placed the Orioles in such a league after I joined them, and we had a good crop of young players in Arizona that fall. Then, suddenly, the American League expanded, placing a team in Los Angeles and one in Washington, D.C. to replace Calvin Griffith's organization that had moved to the Twin Cities of Minneapolis and St. Paul. There was to be an expansion draft and the existing teams would be permitted to protect only a limited number of players. This was tough for us because we had some fine young prospects all through the organization. We had had good years scouting and signing during my first two years there, adding players such as Dean Chance, Arne Thorsland, Boog Powell, Bob Saverine, and others, to the many prospects we already had. We could not protect them all. We had to balance the major league needs for 1961, when we hoped to challenge for the pennant, with younger prospects for the future. In making up our protected list we finally got down to one open space, and we had two nineteen-year-old pitchers just signed that year out of high school whom we were very high on, Dean Chance and Arne Thorsland. Harry Dalton wanted to protect them both, but that would have meant giving up Al Pilarcik, who we expected would be playing a great deal for us in 1961, and I ruled that out. (As it turned out, I was wrong.) We agonized over the choice between Chance and Thorsland. Paul had worked with them both and was particularly high on Thorsland. We protected him and left Chance exposed. The Angels took him and in a short period of time he became an outstanding pitcher for them, and on one occasion pitched a no-hitter against us. Thorsland hurt his arm the following spring and had to give up baseball. Those are the kinds of breaks that can drive a general manager wild.

We had one other player whom we could not protect and did not want to lose, Chuck Hinton. He was from the D.C. area and could both catch and play the outfield. Based on his minor league record, he probably wouldn't have been taken because he had not been outstanding in 1960 and was not well known to the other clubs. Unfortunately, however, he was playing on our Instructional League team and playing very well. These teams were well scouted by Los Angeles and Washington, the two expansion clubs. It was a break that they would not have had except for the timing of the vote to expand. We were sure that we would lose Hinton. Paul, therefore, devised a one-act play designed to fool the scouts of the expansion teams. He had Hinton play the outfield in pre-game practice and had the fungo hitter hit a fly ball against the outfield fence. Hinton, who wanted to stay with the Orioles, had the lead role in Richards' drama. He went back after the fly, crashed into the fence, and fell to the ground. He lay there until Richards and the Oriole trainer and coaches ran out to him and had him carried off the field on a stretcher. The story was then allowed to leak out that his shoulder was badly injured and that he probably would have to have surgery. (I wasn't in Arizona and plead not guilty to being one of the producers of this play.) In any event, it must not have been a convincing performance because when the drafts were made, Hinton was quickly selected.

By now Frank Lane was serving as the A's general manager, and I made a trade with Frank that I thought was one of my better ones. Jerry Walker's pitching had leveled off, and I was able to trade him (with others) for Dick Hall, Russ Snyder, and Whitey Herzog. I knew Snyder and Herzog from Yankee organization days and Dick Hall was a Swarthmore college graduate, so you might say that I was prejudiced. I felt that Russ and Whitey would be serviceable players for us and give us some depth, and I had high hopes for Hall.

From the time I arrived on the Baltimore scene, I was anxious to do something to improve the stadium itself. The fans were too far from the playing field, there were too many posts, and too many good seats without seatbacks. We also needed something like a Stadium Club for the convenience of season ticket holders. We discussed these problems at length in our Board meetings and in staff meetings. The city did not have money to spend on the stadium but we worked out a deal whereby we put up the money but could deduct it from the city's concession share over a period of time. This arrangement allowed us to bring the box seats right down to the field (previously, there had been an eight-foot wall); to eliminate many posts from the loge box areas; to construct a restaurant for season ticket holders within the stadium (we called it "The Hit and Run Room"); and to put in seat chairbacks. The latter was a problem because it reduced seating capacity for football, but the city agreed to add a section to the upper deck in both right and left field to make up for any loss of seats.

It turned out, unfortunately, that IT (winning the pennant) could *not* be done in 1961. The final Oriole won-lost record was better than in 1960, but the Yankees, led by Whitey Ford with twenty-five victories on the mound and by Roger Maris with the bat, were just too tough. It was Maris' year. Sports fans all over the country watched as he made a run at and then broke Babe Ruth's season home run record of sixty. Home run number sixty, which tied the Babe, came off our Jack Fisher at Yankee Stadium. (The only solace for the Orioles in Maris' record breaking year was that it drew good crowds to Memorial Stadium for the late season Yankee series. And when one game ended in a tie and had to be completely replayed, we got an extra gate.) Maris also led the league in RBIs and was the MVP. For the Orioles, Jim Gentile had a sensational year, hitting .302 with forty-six home runs and 141 RBIs. He also had five grand slams, tying a league record. Two of them came on back-to-back plate appearances in Minnesota. Dave Philley had a record twenty-four pinch hits but, overall, we simply could not match the Yankees' team performance.

The players were also distracted by rumors that Paul Richards was about to leave the Orioles to become general manager of the new expansion National League franchise in Houston. It was a chance for Paul to work in his native Texas, and it was a good move for him financially. One could not blame him for wanting to make the move, but the publicity about the possibilities of his going ran on and on and in my opinion had a negative effect on the team. I think it also distracted Paul, and the Orioles may not have received the intense concentration that he usually gave to them. It finally got to the point where I asked him if he would either sign a new Oriole contract or resign. On August thirtieth, when the team was playing in Los Angeles, Paul announced his resignation. He managed his last game that night. Jack Fisher pitched and won, but walked fourteen men. Paul had never been a favorite with some of the umpires, and he felt that some of the balls called on Fisher were not balls but represented an effort to get him to come out and argue. Then the umpire would be able to get his last shot at him. True or not, Paul stayed in the dugout as his seven-year term with the Orioles came to an end. He had his plusses and minuses, but he was an excellent manager on the field, great with pitchers, a good judge of talent, and did a fine job for the Orioles. Luman Harris, his coach, finished up the season as manager, but after the season Luman and the rest of the coaches, including Eddie Robinson, joined Paul in Houston. It was now my job to find a new manager, and perhaps coaching staff, for the 1962 season.

With the Yankees, we always had people managing our top farm teams who were prospective major league managers. If something had happened to Casey Stengel, there would have been Ralph Houk, Eddie Lopat, Harry Craft, or Mayo Smith available—people we knew and who knew the organization's players and methods. That was not true in Baltimore in the fall of 1961. I was going to have to go outside the organization to find a replacement. My father kept after me to hire Leo Durocher, but I hoped to find someone fairly young who had not bounced about from managing job to managing job. I talked with many people (and vowed to myself that I would not be caught again in a situation in which my selection of a manager had to be based on other people's judgment) and finally settled on Billy Hitchcock.

It would have been impossible to find a finer human being than Billy Hitchcock. I guess that is why friends such as John McHale and Jim Campbell recommended him to me. Moreover, he had had good experience managing in Triple-A and coaching in the majors. I don't really know why Billy did not make a better manager. For one thing, Richards was a tough man to follow. He was very quick in his decisions and gave the impression of always being one move ahead of the action on the field. Billy was more tentative and it sometimes struck observers that he was unsure of himself. I think that this was apparent to the players and also to the press. Also some of his moves, even though they may have been statistically correct, backfired on him. Few people stop to remember that a manager must generally play the percentages. If he pursues a course that will succeed six or seven times out of ten, he has made the correct move. But alas, three or four times out of ten it will work the other way and everyone will immediately conclude that he made a bad decision. Billy also had problems with the press. He should have been good for the working writers as he was there and would talk. Again, he was following in Paul's footsteps, and Paul had been more debonair about it—charming when he wanted to be, unavailable when he did not want to talk.

Whatever the reasons, the team did not play up to its capabilities that year. One problem was fitting our outstanding young slugger, Boog Powell, into the same lineup with Jim Gentile. Both were really first basemen and there was no designated hitter rule in those days. The team's final won-lost record was eight games under .500. Attendance fell below the 800,000 mark, the lowest number the team had drawn since coming to Baltimore. It was a real turnaround, and in the wrong direction. But some interesting events also unfolded during that season. We were looking for a pitcher, and the Yankees had released Robin Roberts, and I thought that he might be able to help us. Ralph Houk had succeeded Casey Stengel as Yankee manager and when I checked with Ralph he indicated that Robin might be worth a try. We invited him down for a workout. Darrell Johnson caught him and reported that he was throwing very well. We eventually signed Roberts and he did a fine job for us. It was a pleasure to have a player of his stature on the club.

Another memorable event occurred in August and, for Oriole fans, at least partially compensated for a lackluster season. The Yankees, in first place, came to Baltimore for five games in three days and the Orioles came to life and swept the series. Brooks Robinson had an outstanding series and Robin Roberts bested Whitey Ford to win the final game, 2–1. Tony Kubek homered for the Yankees' run in that game, but Brooks and Gentile homered for the Orioles.

Late in the season a tragedy befell us. The city had put in escalators to the upper deck. They were really for football but we were glad to have them as a convenience for our fans as well. Shortly after they were installed, there was a Kids' Day with hundreds of youngsters bussed to the stadium for the game, something that all baseball teams do regularly. The group was to sit in the upper deck where they were well supervised. To get to their seats, they used one of the new escalators. On the ascent some of the kids began roughhousing. Someone fell and they began to pile up at the top, with no space for those coming up. The guard was knocked down and unable to reach the emergency switch immediately. A few children were hurt, but not too badly, but one little girl had been killed. It was a terrible tragedy, and I have never felt much worse about anything.

I did my best to shore up the weaknesses in our lineup to prepare for the 1963 baseball season. Ronnie Hansen, after his Rookie-of-the-Year season in 1960, had been playing with back problems and was no longer able to cover the ground at shortstop. Our other most acute problem was catching. We had not been set there since Gus Triandos' days. I was able to make two trades in an effort to correct these problems. In both cases, of course, we had to give up something to get something. One trade was with my old friend Chub Feeney at San Francisco. We had good reports on John Orsino, a young Giants catcher. We gave up pitchers Jack Fisher and Billy Hoeft in order to get Orsino, Stu Miller (a relief pitcher), and Mike McCormick. We wanted Miller because we were contemplating trading Hoyt Wilhelm, whom Billy had moved from a starting role to relief. Hoyt had trouble holding men on and fielding his position. Teams could run on his knuckleball, and there was always the danger of the passed ball. These problems had made him relatively ineffective in relief for us in 1962. Billy and I thought he must be reaching the end of his career. That shows you how smart we were. Hoyt pitched ten more years and saved many, many games. We were lucky, however, in that Stu Miller far surpassed our highest hopes for him.

   Our second trade was with Chicago for Luis Aparicio. Louie was the best shortstop in baseball. An excellent fielder, he was also a good offensive player, able to get on base, and an excellent base stealer. I could not believe that Chicago was willing to trade him. My negotiations were with Al Lopez and Ed Short and they wanted plenty. Wilhelm and Hansen we expected to have to give up, but they also wanted two top young prospects, Dave Nicholson and Pete Ward. Nicholson might have been great. He had tremendous power. He was easily pitched to, however, struck out a lot, and had not shown real progress the last year or so. We were willing to take a chance and let him go. One could not worry about a traded player doing well and making you look bad. We had to worry about filling the holes in our own club and improving our own team. We could not be building for the future forever. After 1960 the fans wanted a legitimate pennant contender. The last player the White Sox extracted from us was Pete Ward, and in many ways he was the hardest for me to agree to give up. He had a good bat and was a real battler. We also got Al Smith, a proven veteran outfielder, who unfortunately was pretty close to the end of his career. And so we believed we were reinforced and hoped we were ready for 1963. We were encouraged in spring training when our new catcher. John Orsino, hit three home runs his first three times up in his first game against the Reds in Tampa, and almost hit another on his fourth. I thought: "What have we here?"

The club got off to a good start and was in first place going into June, but then went into an incredible slump, losing twenty-two out of thirty games. We could never get back into the pennant race. But the new players performed well. Orsino was a bear-down player and hit a respectable .272 with some power, tying Al Smith for the club lead. Stu Miller was sensational, appearing in seventy-one games and finishing fifty-nine, both league records. He had twenty-five saves. Luis Aparicio was a revelation at shortstop and led the league with forty-two stolen bases. In addition, Steve Barber won twenty and Boog Powell had twenty-two home runs and eighty-two RBIs. But it was not enough. The team finished fourth of ten, and the attendance continued to decline. Hitchcock somehow lacked the magic touch and in addition, he had just not caught on with the Baltimore public. I reluctantly decided that we would have to make a change. I hated it but knew that it was the right move. I had hired Hank Bauer as a coach, with Billy's approval, before the 1963 season and, after looking over the rest of the field, I hired Hank as manager. He had had a season and a half managing for Finley at Kansas City so it would not be all new to him. Moreover, I knew that he had good baseball instincts and was a battler. We held a November press conference to let the writers fire questions at him. What Hank didn't know, because he had left Baltimore at the end of the season (and what I should have warned him about), was that some of the writers were blaming our disappointing showing in 1963 on a lack of conditioning and a disregard for any curfews. One of the first questions asked Hank was whether he had any rules about drinking. "Yes, I do," said Hank. "The players are not allowed to drink in the hotel bar, that's where I drink." That sort of shook everybody up, but the rest of the conference proceeded more satisfactorily.

Nineteen sixty-four was an exciting year on the field. Things also were occurring that affected my family. My oldest boy (Leland S. MacPhail III) was in college and he and his high school sweetheart, Carol Witt, decided to be married that June. In July we had a surprise 75th birthday party for my mother in Columbus. Bill, Marian, Jane, and I were all able to be there, and we had most of mother's longtime friends at a celebration at the Columbus Country Club. We were so glad we did this because she enjoyed it thoroughly, and a year later she had a heart attack and we lost her. That was my first experience with losing someone whom I loved and was close to. I was able to see my father fairly frequently during this time, either at his horse farm in Bel Air, twenty-five miles north of the city, or at Oriole games (at which time he gave lots of unsought-after advice on how to run the team).

We had a good team in 1964; the infield of Powell or Norm Siebern, Jerry Adair, Aparicio, and Robinson was as good as you could ask for. Our pitching was strong, with young starters such as Pappas, Barber, Dave McNally, and Estrada and two newcomers to the ranks, Wally Bunker and Frank Bertaina. To balance all of that youth were Robin Roberts, Mike McCormick, and the veteran Harvey Haddix, plus an outstanding bullpen of Stu Miller, Dick Hall, and Wes Stock. We had needed a left-hander in the bullpen and I had picked up Harvey Haddix, a great performer over the course of a long career, and a clone of our coach Harry (the Cat) Brecheen. We also had a good group of coaches. In addition to the "Cat," Sherm Lollar, Gene Woodling and Billy Hunter were Hank's assistants.

The outfield and catching departments were not as strong as the infield and pitching. In the outfield, Brandt and Synder were back. And because of a new baseball rule that allowed clubs to draft any first-year players not protected on a major league roster, we were able to "steal" Paul Blair from the Mets. Sam Bowens moved up from Rochester with good credentials. We also acquired Joe Gaines from Cincinnati and Earl Robinson from the Dodgers organization. In Robinson, we were hoping for another late-blooming surprise, as with Gentile. Gentile, however, we had to let go as we just could not fit Jim and Boog into the lineup at the same time, although we continued to use Boog in the outfield for some time. Jim's play had fallen off markedly, partially I feared because of his off-field habits. We traded him after the 1963 season for Norm Siebern, a former Yankee. Another trade made after the 1963 season was with Washington, for an outfielder on whom we had had good reports as an amateur. As a matter of fact, under circumstances that were similar to the Yankee recommendation of Cletis Boyer to Kansas City, I had recommended this player then to the expansion Washington club, which at the time was run by my friend George Selkirk. Although this young outfielder was clearly not yet ready to play in the major leagues in 1964, I gave them Buster Narum, a pretty good young starting pitcher, for him. The young outfielder's name was Lou Piniella, and Lou spent 1964 playing for Earl Weaver at Elmira in the Eastern League, our Class-A team. Behind the plate, we were counting on Orsino, who was backed up by Dick Brown. Unfortunately, Orsino was injured midway through the season. We were lucky to be able to pick up Charlie Lau as a replacement but this, as well as the loss of Boog Powell for a month, hurt us badly.

The team got off very well and around June 1st had a 30–15 record and led the league by one-half game. On June 23rd, in a home game against New York, the Orioles staged a rally that excited the city and got the fans thinking pennant. The Yankees led 7–2, with two outs in the bottom of the eighth. The Birds then exploded for seven runs to take the lead, and the large crowd went wild. Charlie Lau had two hits in the inning. Maris homered for the Yanks in the top of the ninth but Stu Miller then struck out Tom Tresh to give Baltimore a 9–8 win. The Orioles then went on to put together a seven-game winning streak and build a four-and-one-half game lead. The Yankees, White Sox, and Orioles battled through July and the first half of August, taking turns with the lead. In late August the White Sox swept a four-game series from the Yankees to move ahead. But the Orioles then went into Chicago, and led by Brooks Robinson, won three of four to reclaim first place. The race continued nip and tuck through the first half of September with Baltimore holding on to first place. (It was probably during this period that I developed the habit or superstition, when watching a road game on TV or listening on radio, of taking a walk around the block rather than enduring the agony of those last three outs when we were leading going into the bottom of the ninth. When I turned the corner on my way back home, I could see our upstairs window. If all was well, Jane put the window shade all the way up. If tragedy befell us, she pulled it down. Happily, because we had good relief pitchers, it wasn't pulled down too often. My "routine" seemed to work, so I continued this practice as long as I was with a team.)

On September 17th, however, the Yankees started an eleven-game winning streak which, in effect, won the championship for New York. They finished one game ahead of Chicago and two ahead of Baltimore. It was a great race, and it produced a song that was a hit in Baltimore that summer, called "Pennant Fever." Brooks led the league with 118 RBIs and won the MVP Award; Wally Bunker had a 19–5 record. Hank Bauer was selected as Manager of the Year. The team had won ninety-seven games and performed magnificently. We drew well over the million mark. There was a great deal to be happy about, but I surely wish that we could have won the pennant.

Over my years in Baltimore, I had grown closer and closer to Joe Iglehart. Zan Krieger was my friend but, because of circumstances, I saw more of Joe. His wife was not living and he became almost like part of our family. He spent a lot of time with Jane and me in Florida during spring training, and any of our boys who might be down there. We had dinner together more nights than not. He was dedicated to the Orioles and was always "upbeat." His stock expression when asked how he was, was "fine as silk." He did complain, however, that he had never won the lucky number award even though he had purchased a program at every regular season game for years. The lucky number was announced each night over the loudspeaker at the top of the seventh inning and was good for Oriole tickets and various gifts of merchandise. We decided to give Joe a little thrill and arranged with the program vendor, who was located at the gate where Joe always entered and bought his program, to give Joe a specific program, the lucky number of which we had carefully recorded. Then at the top of the seventh inning, while all of us watched gleefully from the press box, we had the PA announcer go through his regular spiel and announce Joe's number as the lucky number. We watched him start up with surprise and then show it to all the people seated in his box. We then had the PA announcer announce "Your attention please, ladies and gentlemen, we regret to announce that there has been an error in the lucky score-card number announced to you. The correct number is . . ."—and he changed the last digit by one.

Sometime before the start of the 1965 season, Joe talked to me about joining with him and others to buy the Orioles. Joe and Zan's stock together constituted a controlling majority, and they had a buy-sell agreement with each other. If either wished to end the agreement he could set a price for his stock and the other individual would have first option to buy it. If he didn't take it then the original partner could buy the stock of the other at the same price. Zan Krieger began to feel that he had too much money tied up in the team and was not getting sufficient return from his money. Zan also owned the local hockey team and had other pressing investments. Perhaps he and Joe might also have had some differences, but if they were major ones I did not know about it. In any event, Zan had apparently said something to Joe which started Joe working on plans to purchase Zan's stock.

Joe wanted me to be part of the ownership group he was putting together. I was interested, although I didn't have any money. (Joe said "no problem" and took me to the bank.) A day or two later I was having lunch with Zan. He had an expression, "What's new, Lee?" that he used when he wanted to be updated. I said that I was surprised to learn that he was going to sell his stock to Joe. He was clearly surprised and said that that was not his intention. I told him that if that was so, there had been a misunderstanding, and that he should call Joe at once to straighten it out. He was quite upset and did call Joe right after lunch—and there was a misunderstanding. And this misunderstanding led to a strong difference of opinion between them which eventually resulted, in June of 1965, in Zan's buying Joe's stock. Zan called me in Detroit, where I was with the team, to give me the (sad for me) news. Furthermore, as Zan wanted to sell rather than buy more, he sold Joe's stock and perhaps some of his own to Jerry Hoffberger, thus giving Jerry complete control. Jerry became Chairman of the Board and Zan became chairman of the Executive Committee. Actually there wasn't any Executive Committee, and though Zan apparently understood that decisions would be made by him and Jerry together, it did not work out that way.

This really changed things for me. It was not that I had any problem with Jerry. He had always been very friendly, even when I appeared before the State Legislature in Annapolis to speak against night racing at his racetrack in the Baltimore area because I thought that it would hurt the Orioles. But Jerry had not selected me to run the team and I have always felt that someone who owns a team should have an unencumbered right to select his own top people. All of this made me a little uneasy, as did some of my first meetings with Jerry. He made it plain that he thought the team should be drawing more people than it was. Actually in those years, with a team in Washington shutting the Orioles off from the Washington Metropolitan area and Virginia, the Orioles really did not have much drawing area. Going north we ran into the Phillies at Wilmington; to the west were mountains; and to the east Chesapeake Bay and an expensive toll bridge. Outside of a little triangular territory to the northwest that included York, Lancaster, Harrisburg, Gettysburg, Hagerstown, and Frederick, Baltimore baseball pretty much had to rely on Metropolitan Baltimore for its major support (which is why an expansion team in Washington could present difficult problems for baseball). Jerry also wanted me to be more of a showman and to have a higher profile. He suggested a sport coat in Oriole colors and a bright red convertible. This just wasn't me, and was a role I didn't want to try to play. However, as the 1965 season got under way, I had other things to concern me.

One problem occurred off the field and came to a head before Hoffberger took control. CBS wanted to buy the Yankees and the league was split as to whether it should be permitted to do so. Some of the clubs feared that CBS ownership in the league would adversely affect our network broadcasting arrangements. We had debated the question at Oriole board meetings, and the board was undecided. Joe Iglehart, who was on the CBS board, made himself ineligible to participate in the decision making. The board then appointed a three-man committee, Zan Krieger, Jack Dunn, and myself, to attend the coming league meeting, hear all the arguments, and determine the Oriole vote. Jerry Hoffberger had let it be known that he was opposed to admitting CBS well before the league meeting was held. All of the other clubs had also clarified their positions on the issue. The White Sox led an anti-block. It became very apparent that the deciding vote would be cast by the Orioles. All the other noses could be counted. We attended the league meeting and heard Dan Topping's fervent request for approval. Dr. Frank Stanton represented CBS and answered questions. Then during a recess, I asked if Dr. Stanton could sit down with Zan, Jack, and me and talk a little more. From my point of view I found him forthright and convincing. Although it was my desire to be able to vote for CBS for Topping's sake, and because my brother was now sports director for CBS, I honestly would not have done so had I not thought that it would be a good owner. When the meeting was ready to resume I looked at Jack and Zan. Jack said, "I will vote whichever way you vote, Lee," and Zan said that he would too. So Baltimore voted yes and CBS bought the Yankees. Little did I know that the move would someday have an impact upon my own future.

We did not make many changes in our team for the 1965 season. We had some new young players knocking on the door. We had Curt Blefary, whom we had drafted from the Yankees in the same way that we got Paul Blair from the Mets. We had moved Curt to the outfield. Davey Johnson had been signed but was playing in the minors and Jerry Adair was still the second baseman. Jim Palmer had been added to the pitching staff. Lenny Green, Earl Robinson, and Joe Gaines were gone. We were counting on Powell, Brandt, Blair, Bowens, Blefary, and Snyder in the outfield. The pitching was pretty much the same, except that arm problems hampered Chuck Estrada, and Wes Stock and Mike McCormick were gone. Again, the team played well, winning ninety-four games. Still it wasn't enough. This time the Twins bested the Yankees and the Orioles finished third. Curt Blefary came along in great fashion and was the Rookie of the Year. Once more Stu Miller was the Most Valuable Oriole. But once more, we were disappointed.

Somewhere toward the end of the season I was contacted by John Fetzer, the owner of the Tigers. Ford Frick had retired and Fetzer and John Galbreath, the owner of the Pirates, had been appointed a committee of two to pick a new commissioner. They wanted to recommend Spike Eckert, an Air Force General, for the job but were concerned about his lack of baseball experience and wanted me to assist him. I really wasn't that interested, but again, I was concerned as to whether or not I was really Jerry Hoffberger's type to run the team. I knew it would be difficult PR-wise for him to let me go and yet I didn't feel that I really wanted to stay on that basis. Jerry had talked with me further about the marketing problems and toward the end of the season suggested that it would be in everybody's best interest if I had someone to help me in that area. I told him that that was certainly okay with me if he felt that it was needed. Then on October 15th, Frank Cashen, a National Brewery executive, was made executive vice president of the Orioles. This was fine, but I must admit that I was upset that I wasn't advised of the announcement date ahead of time or invited to attend the press conference. I began to look more seriously at the position of executive administrator to the commissioner and to listen more intently to John Fetzer. Jane and I were visiting my sister over Thanksgiving in her home in Pawling, New York when John reached me again. He represented my proposed role as something that was important for the game. I told him that I would do it but that I owed it to Jerry to talk with him first. Jerry urged me to stay and emphasized that I was still president of the club and in charge, and Frank Cashen, whom I liked, also came to see me and urged me to stay, saying that he knew we could work well together. I appreciated their words but somehow it seemed to me that it was time to move along.

Baltimore had been great for my family and for me. We had enjoyed some wonderful associations, not only with the team itself but with the press and broadcasters. People like Bob Maisel, Lou Hatter, John Steadman, Bill Tanton, Ernie Harwell, Herb Carneal, Bob Murphy, Frank Messer, and Chuck Thompson simply cannot be surpassed. Yet I've always felt that it was good for one to change his life every eight or ten years and to enter a new working environment to avoid getting into a rut. Jerry asked me to stay at least through the major league meetings, as this was an important time with respect to trades. I agreed and said that I would continue to pursue my efforts to add one more good bat to the Oriole lineup. He also asked about a replacement for me. He was considering Frank Lane, whom I had hired for the Orioles, but I thought that the organization should really go for someone younger and I urged him to give the job to Harry Dalton.

So I went to the major league meetings representing the Orioles, even though I was there on a somewhat unusual basis. I was convinced that what the team needed was one more good hitter with power— preferably a right-handed hitter. Jim Russo, who did most of our scouting at the major league level, told me that there was a chance the Reds would deal Frank Robinson. Frank had had some problems there and at one point, for some reason, had wielded a gun in the dugout. Bill DeWitt was running the Reds and Bill and I were good friends from our Yankee days. He was candid with me. They would deal Frank but needed an established starter and a top reliever. At the meetings, I made a trade with Fred Haney of the Angels for Dick Simpson, giving up Norm Siebern. (Again, with Norm, it was the same problem of not having a spot for him at first base because of Boog Powell. We had played Boog in the outfield in order to play first Gentile and then Siebern at first, but it had simply not been satisfactory.) After we got Simpson, I found out that the Reds were very much interested in him. Now all we needed was the relief pitcher as we had starters we could put in the deal. Darold Knowles was a good young pitcher but couldn't seem to fit in on our staff. Some of our people thought that he didn't throw hard enough (actually he became a better pitcher than we anticipated). So we put Knowles with Jackie Brandt and got Jack Baldschun from Philadelphia, one of the proven relief pitchers in the National League. DeWitt was now ready to trade Robinson for Milt Pappas, one of our best starters, Simpson, and Baldschun—and now it was my turn to be concerned. Was there any real problem with respect to Frank Robinson?

Again I was fortunate to have a good friend in the right place. Jim Turner, the former Yankee pitching coach, was with the Reds. Despite the fact that he was working for the Reds, I knew that Jim would tell me the truth. I called him and laid it on the line. Was there a problem and was Frank a good person on the club? Jim was the "Southern Colonel" type, so I felt that he would not lean over backward for Frank, although perhaps this was unfair. In any event, he could not have given me a more positive report. I then told DeWitt that as far as I was concerned we had a deal but that, as he knew, I was leaving and I would have to clear it with Harry Dalton, the general manager-to-be. I then sat with Jerry and Harry and told them that this was the deal that could be made and it was their decision. Jerry very properly left it to Harry. Harry stewed a little, asked for an extra player and eventually got a marginal pitcher thrown in, and closed the deal. Once the deal was closed we were all exuberant. Harry Dalton's remark was "Oh boy, cannons at the corners!" And with Frank Robinson in left, Curt Blefary in right, Boog Powell at first, and Brooks Robinson at third, the Orioles did indeed have "cannons at the corners." I was unhappy that I wasn't going to be around to watch.

The author, second from left, with his sister Marian, mother Inez, seated, and brother Bill in Columbus, Ohio in 1925.

Commissioner Landis with Larry MacPhail at the opening of Columbus Redbird Stadium, June 3, 1932.

The author with his Reading manager Fresco Thompson, 1941.

The author's first wife, Jane Hamilton MacPhail.

As sworn into the U.S. Navy in May 1944.

The author and Jane had four sons (from left): Lee III, Bruce, Allen, and Andy. Andy is now general manager of the Twins.

Outside Memorial Stadium in Baltimore after having been hired to run the Orioles in 1959. (Associated Press photo.)

Observing a spring training game in Miami with Yankee General Manager George Weiss, 1960.

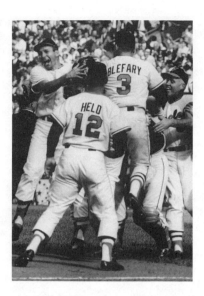

Brooks Robinson leaps for joy to celebrate the Orioles' 1966 world championship.

With Commissioner Eckert (left) and Orioles' world championship manager Hank Bauer (right), 1966.

With Syd Thrift (left), later to become General Manager of the Pirates, and Oakland owner Charles O. Finley.

In the Yankee Stadium press box, the author is seated between George Weiss and his father, Larry MacPhail. Longtime Yankee team physician, Dr. Sidney Gaynor, is in the rear.

This was the team CBS put in place to run the Yankees in 1967 (from left): president, Mike Burke, manager, Ralph Houk, and the author as general manager.

Mickey Mantle Day, 1969, as Joe DiMaggio presents a plaque to Mickey. In the background between them is Yankee announcer Frank Messer.

Old Timers' Day, Yankee Stadium, 1970, was the day Casey
Stengel returned after a decade's absence to have his uniform
number 37 retired.

A presentation for Yankee owner George Steinbrenner.

In the Yankee stadium press box with friend Joe Iglehart and the Yankees' Gabe Paul, who succeeded the author when he went to the American League.

Signing Bobby Murcer to a $100,000 contract in 1972, when such figures were still considered worthy of a press conference.

Wedding day of the author and Gwen Dayton, October 26, 1974.

From left, Joe and Mildred Cronin, Gwen MacPhail.

Presenting a Manager of the Year award to Billy Martin for his work with the 1974 Texas Rangers.

At Tiger Stadium with former Detroit owner John Fetzer.

With Yogi Berra.

A gathering of the MacPhail family at Cooperstown's Hall of Fame, in 1978.

Louisville Slugger representative Pee Wee Reese and the author present a Silver Bat award to George Brett (without pine tar) for winning the 1980 batting championship.

With A.L. President Joe Cronin (left) and Orioles' skipper Earl Weaver.

Longtime National League President Chub Feeney, Commissioner Bowie Kuhn, the author, and Warren Giles, Feeney's predecessor.

The author with his longtime friend and associate Bob Fishel (left), his brother Bill, and his wife Gwen at the 1983 World Series.

8

A Backup Role—View from the Top

Following many years as National League president, Ford Frick had served baseball well as commissioner. His decision to retire after the 1965 season caused a problem for the clubs with respect to the choice of his successor. He was only the third commissioner in baseball history so no precedents as to how to go about selecting a new commissioner had been established. The clubs met in Dearborn, Michigan in July. They discussed the matter and considered a list of possible candidates suggested by clubs in advance of the meeting. They finally picked a two-man committee—John Fetzer, owner of the Tigers, from the American League, and John Galbreath, owner of the Pirates, from the National League. They then took a straw vote poll of the suggested candidates for the guidance of the committee. I was surprised to find that my name was on the list and flattered to be on any list with some of the people who were on it.* Everybody had a different idea of what kind of man and what kind of experience would be best for the role of a commissioner. The game was changing, and perhaps the kind of individual needed when Landis, Chandler, or Frick was elected would not be the kind of man needed in 1966.

The two Johns decided to go for a strong business leader and back him up with a baseball man. Their choice for commissioner was William "Spike" Eckert, an Air Force General. I was to be the man to back him up. The announcement was made in late November, but I was able to continue with the Orioles through the December meetings, and then close my work for them with the trade that I felt really improved the club. I was sorry to leave the Orioles but was satisfied with what we had been able to accomplish while I was there. The club had been in debt to the bank and in the second division when I came. We paid off that debt, and the club made money each year that I was there. After the first year, we finished in the first division every year

---

*Potter Stewart, Curtis LeMay, LeRoy Collins, Philip Hart, Arthur Lane, William Rogers, Byron White, Richard Nixon, Eugene Zuckert.

but one and had some fine young prospects moving up in the farm system.* Now I was taking on a new type of assignment.

My first meeting with Spike Eckert was at a dinner at a restaurant on the Baltimore-Washington Parkway, midway between the two cities. There were only three of us there, Eckert, a man from Galbreath's promotional firm who was spending some time with Spike in the Washington area before he took over, and myself. Spike was most pleasant and seemed genuinely pleased that I had been selected to assist him. I liked him, but was amazed at how soft-spoken, low key, and almost retiring he was. Not at all what I expected an Air Force General to be like or, for that matter, the kind of person I would have expected the two Johns to select as commissioner of baseball.

Our first job once our term began was to find new office space for the commissioner in New York as we were losing our offices in the RCA Building. The Mets had moved from their downtown offices to Shea Stadium and wanted to get out of their lease for their space on Fifth Avenue, so we took over their offices there. Our next job was to try to "beef up" our organization. Fortunately Charlie Segar was staying. He had been Frick's right-hand man for many years, and was experienced in all that went on. What we needed was someone to handle the public relations and press duties. Frank Slocum had been taking care of these matters for Frick on a part-time basis but was not remaining, so this was pressing. I recommended Bob Fishel to Spike but Bob did not want to leave the Yankees. I then recommended Joe Reichler, a top AP writer. Joe joined us and did an excellent job for baseball for many years. The commissioner inherited Mary Anargeros, Frick's secretary, a great lady, so he was well set there. (Mary served Frick, Eckert, and Bowie Kuhn before retiring.) Ann Groom, my secretary in Baltimore, came up to help me. And so the reign of Spike Eckert began.

Things went well for me personally. We found a really lovely colonial house in Hartsdale, not far from where we had lived in Scarsdale. I was back together with all my old Westchester friends. Johnny Jones, our Deerfield friend, was now headmaster at the Riverdale School in the Bronx, an excellent preparatory school, and we decided to send our boys there. Jane stayed in Baltimore with Andy, our youngest, until the end of the school semester in February, but Johnny recommended that we have Bruce, who was in high school, come up right away and live in the dormitory in order to get oriented as quickly as possible. Bruce has never completely forgiven us for this.

---

*From the foundation established, both on the field and off, the Orioles went on to become the winningest team in the major leagues over the next two decades.

He said we moved him "in the middle of the semester, in the middle of the week, in the middle of the day." Later when I wanted to take him somewhere and suggested that he leave some of his things with his friends, his reply was "what friends?" But of course, things eventually worked out well, and both boys loved Riverdale.

Jane bought a Norwegian elkhound puppy with the Scandanavian name of "Tosket" (Foolish One) to which we all became devoted. She had a lovely coat and the breeder had told Jane that they only shed once a year. He was right but that once lasted twelve months. Tosket grew big enough to fill the role of a watchdog, but she had a very friendly temperament. That was fortunate as she had to put up with our black, half Siamese cat that accompanied us from Baltimore. His name was "Oriole," the only cat named after a bird.

I liked Eckert very much. He was a soft-spoken, considerate man. That is not to say that he didn't have a temper. He was all business and wanted very much to do a good job. His general knowledge of baseball was extremely limited and this worried him very much. He was terrified that he might make some terrible goof—not know who Paul Waner was, or who Joe McCarthy had managed for, or whatever. When the day's work was done, he would stay in the office or go to his room in the New York Athletic Club and read baseball books by the hour in an effort to prepare himself. That winter I went with him to visit as many of the owners as we could arrange to see. I took him to lunch with some of the New York press and these one-on-one meetings went fine. But the general press treated him very badly from the first announcement. Because he wasn't a baseball name, it dubbed him "the Unknown Soldier." Someone came up with a story that somehow baseball hadn't hired the general it intended to pick—that it had wanted General Eugene Zuckert and instead got Eckert. And the meetings we had with the press on our travels or at meetings did not go well. I was always with him and was generally described as "the man who was there to show him where second base was." At one press conference, things were going stiffly when one writer, trying to be friendly and loosen things up, said, "Commissioner, do you ever read the comics?" Spike answered that he sometimes did. "Well, what is your favorite comic strip, commissioner?" "I am not sure, I would really hate to have to pick one." A natural answer—but the press portrayed him as a man who couldn't even pick his favorite comic strip.

Speeches were also a problem and he was called on to speak at many sports dinners. In the service I imagine that any speeches he gave were on serious military subjects and that the speech would be written out and he would read it. To my surprise, he tried this at the Chicago Baseball Writers Dinner, his first major speech. In those days, at the Chicago Writers Dinner, they put liquor bottles on the tables and some guests were noisy and obstreperous before the speeches were half over. They were even a little further along when Spike got up to make the final address of the evening and started from his twenty-page manuscript. You can imagine the reaction—which was less than civilized—but Spike bowed his neck and read right through it. After that disaster Joe and I talked with him about making his speeches shorter, lighter, more off-the-cuff—and definitely not read. He tried, but to assist himself, he put his notes on cards, which he consulted as he spoke. Disaster struck again when on one occasion the cards got out of order and the speech came out in improper sequence. The clubs didn't help either. Instead of trying to assist him, some baseball people called to rant and rave about inconsequential problems. He was perpetually worried about what the next long-distance call might bring. As a consequence he had me sit in his office with him for ready consultation on telephone calls, and I literally spent most of each working day in those first months sitting in his office, listening to his long-distance calls.

The first real baseball problem we encountered came during spring training. The Atlanta Braves had signed pitcher Tom Seaver of the University of Southern California to a contract. Unfortunately, however, they had signed him prior to the close of USC's college schedule. This was definitely a violation of baseball's college rule. I had no alternative but to tell my friend, John McHale, who was now in Atlanta with the Braves, that the contract had to be voided and that Seaver was a free agent. Tom and his father tried to get his eligibility at USC restored, but without success. We were then faced with a dilemma as to how this should be handled. We had two concerns. Frankly, we did not want to set up a bidding-war leading to a contract far more lucrative than his Braves' contract. On the other hand, we felt responsible to the player. It wasn't his fault that a baseball signing rule had been broken. The ideal for us would be to have him sign with another club for the same terms. So it was my idea to advise the clubs of the Braves' terms and to invite any club that would match them to advise us by a certain deadline. This would make them eligible for a drawing. My worry was, what would we do if no club was willing to match the terms? What would happen to Tom Seaver, who could not go back and pitch a senior year for his college? Tom and his father okayed our approach and we waited for the clubs' reactions. I thought that I had an ace in the hole, as Rod Dedeaux, Tom's coach at USC, worked for the Dodgers. Surely the Dodgers would be willing to match the Braves' offer! But we did not hear from the Dodgers. It later turned out that Buzzie Bavasi was very much involved in salary negotiations with Sandy Koufax and Don Drysdale. These two ace pitchers were threatening to pool their talents, negotiate together, and not sign until both were satisfied. With that kind of crisis on his mind, Buzzie forgot to send a wire putting the Dodgers in the draw. However, the Phillies came in and a little later, a second club. It looked as if we would have to draw between the two. Then at the last moment, Bing Devine was able to convince George Weiss to enter the sweepstakes, and the Mets were in. We were in a hotel in Fort Lauderdale. The three club names were placed in the hat and Commissioner Eckert drew the Mets' name. What a great break for the Mets. It made their new franchise.

The Braves caused the Seaver problem; the Braves also caused an earlier controversy—the legitimacy of their move from Milwaukee to Atlanta. One of the first bits of advice I had given the commissioner was never to say something "was a league affair." Ford Frick had often taken that position. It irritated the press and damaged his image. So I advised the commissioner not to consider that anything was outside of his jurisdiction. (Later when I became a league president I did not necessarily subscribe to that thinking.) Then on the occasion of the Braves' move to Atlanta—which the National League had prevented the previous year because a lease obligation remained but apparently now favored—Eckert stayed carefully outside of the controversy. I personally thought that the proposed move was wrong. The Braves were leaving a city where population was limited but which had supported baseball well. But apparently Warren Giles and Walter O'Malley had told Eckert that he must stay out of the decision making and Spike, being new, was not about to go to war with these two and accepted their ultimatum.

After the opening of the season a situation developed—not alarming at the outset—which would eventually have great consequences for baseball. The players had a loose organization centered around a player-representative from each club, elected by the players themselves, to help look after their common affairs. They had a judge in Milwaukee, Bob Cannon, who served them on a part-time basis. As a general rule the players selected to be player representatives were the older, more experienced players. This made sense, except that it also meant that there was more of a turnover of representatives than was desirable. The players wanted more permanence and stability in their organization. They wanted to hire Bob Cannon on a permanent basis and possibly establish a full-time office in a two-team city. Bob Cannon was a sensible, reasonable, fair-minded man. He was willing to leave the Bench and to take on the assignment. Bob Friend, a veteran Pirate pitcher, had been representing the players on the Pension Committee and had therefore worked closely with John Galbreath, who was also the owner of the team for which he played. He therefore, quite naturally, approached Galbreath, told him the problems, and asked him if the clubs would possibly assist the players in making the desired changes. Galbreath was sympathetic and brought the matter to the commissioner and the Executive Council.

The Executive Council in those days was composed of six owners, three from each league, and consisted of Walter O'Malley of the Dodgers, Gabe Paul of the Indians, and alternates Bob Carpenter (Phillies), Don Grant (Mets), Bob Reynolds (Angels), and Tom Yawkey (Red Sox). The players' request made sense to them, and they were given strong assurances that there was no intention of forming a militant union, such as had been considered several years earlier when the players hired Norman Lewis as their attorney. The council was assured that no real change was intended, other than to give more consistency and effectiveness to their organization. The clubs knew and respected Bob Cannon. He was no revolutionary. And so they approved of the change and offered to help with the necessary financing. In my new role, I sat in on these Executive Council deliberations. There was no concern expressed nor opposition raised by anybody, nor did I have any misgivings. The players as a group accepted the lifetime Reserve System arrangement which existed in baseball; were not overpaid; and were entitled to any peripheral assistance that could be given them.

Once the plan moved forward, complications arose. Bob Cannon, after accepting, raised the problem of his judicial pension and wanted the players to match it. A disagreement arose between Cannon and the players, and he temporarily withdrew from the picture. Then the players began looking for an alternate to Cannon. One of the players suggested Chub Feeney, but Chub wasn't interested. Robin Roberts of the Phillies then went to Professor George William Taylor of the Wharton School of Business (who had written New York's Taylor Law) for advice, and Taylor recommended Marvin Miller. Roberts says today that he went to Eckert and told him that if Miller wasn't satisfactory to the clubs he would not present his name. If that is so (and if Robin says it is, it must be), I never heard this. I don't know whether or not Eckert relayed this to the owner members of the Executive Council or not. In any event, the players moved ahead. Now Cannon got back into the picture, and the players held a meeting of all the player representatives in spring training to elect their director. They invited Eckert to attend, and he asked to bring me with him. That created a problem in the minds of some of the players as I had, until very recently, been a club operator. They were not sure that my presence was appropriate, but they acquiesced. Eckert and I were simply witnesses to what went on. Miller and Cannon both came into the meeting at separate times. I don't remember that anyone else was even considered. There was still some resentment toward Cannon over the prior misunderstanding, and he was also asking to keep the offices in Milwaukee where he lived.

The vote was taken and Marvin Miller was elected, subject to ratification by the players of a majority of the teams following meetings in spring training. Once elected, cries of warning started coming from club people who had been apprised of Marvin's record and reputation with the Steelworkers. It was obvious that we were remiss in not researching Miller's background more carefully and possibly in not trying to divert the players from Miller before his election was ratified. There was some opposition and the players of some of the teams did not vote their approval, but the necessary majority did, and a new era was born.

Marvin Miller is a very intelligent, hardworking man with very strong labor instincts and feelings. He was bright enough to feel his way at the start, until he knew that he had the unquestioned backing of his group. He went to work on obvious things, such as the minimum salary (which was a ridiculous $7,000 per annum), and the amount of the clubs' contribution to the Pension Plan. He also worked to establish a system of independent arbitration of player grievances rather than leaving such to the decisions of league presidents and a commissioner elected by the clubs. The clubs eventually assented to this, providing that any decisions of discipline involving the game on the field would still be decided by the league presidents and that anything involving "the integrity of the game" would still be decided by the commissioner. Marvin was very clever; and he was dealing with people, including Commissioner Eckert and his aide (me), who were naive and uninformed about labor matters. We did put together a small group of advisers from the clubs who had experience in this area; and Dick Meyer, a vice president of the Cardinals who was used to dealing with unions at Budweiser, became our leader and was most helpful.

Looking back with the knowledge of hindsight, one can clearly see other errors made by the club representatives. For example: The clubs agreed that no rules (other than playing rules) that affected the benefits of a player could be changed without negotiations (and agreement) with the Players' Association. There was to be a year before this went into effect. The clubs should have taken advantage of this year of grace to make any important rule changes necessary to protect them from the future onslaught of labor negotiations. Such action was not considered, and no significant rule changes were made. Second, the clubs should have made absolutely certain—in black and white—that the arbitration procedure had no jurisdiction over their Reserve

System. They thought that this was very clear—and, in truth, the arbitration procedure was not supposed to impinge upon this—but eventually there was an arbitrator, Peter Seitz in 1976, who reached out to make a landmark decision in this area and his jurisdiction was upheld by a Federal Court.

Thus was lost baseball's basic Reserve System. I am not saying that the Reserve System as it existed was right and proper. Under it an eighteen-year-old boy who signed a minor league contract could be controlled by the organization with which he signed throughout his entire career. He went wherever his contract was assigned or was placed on an Inactive List which prevented him from playing with anyone else. He had to sign whatever contract was tendered him. His only alternative was to hold out and not play. The only protection that the rules gave a player was the draft, which provided that after four years' professional service, if he had not been placed on a major league roster, he could be drafted by some other major league team. Once on a major league roster, a player could be optioned back to the minors three times. Thus an organization could keep even well-qualified players in the minors for seven years, if it did not have a position open for them on its team. The other protection was the major league minimum salary, but this of itself was unreasonably low. The system was clearly weighted in favor of the clubs and was unfair to the player. Yet there had previously been very little resentment or discontent on the part of the players. In fact, when Congressman Emanuel Celler held hearings clearly aimed at demolishing the system, the best witnesses for the clubs, testifying before Congress, were the players—from veterans such as Ted Williams to rookies such as Mickey Mantle. (Mantle's testimony, which followed shortly after a classic performance by Stengel in Stengelese, was, "I agree with everything Casey said.") And in practice, the clubs were seldom guilty of unfair treatment. The general feeling was that a happy club was more apt to be a good club, plus public sentiment was often on the side of the player in contract disputes and clubs were inclined to be responsive to public opinion.

Nevertheless, the system was clearly unfair. A few people (and I numbered myself among them) suggested moderate changes, but ownership was always opposed. I remember one owner stating at a meeting that anyone who proposed any changes in the Reserve System should be fired. Nevertheless I feel that those of us who tried to consider both sides with some degree of fairness are culpable for not fighting harder to make changes, although our efforts would not necessarily have prevented the events that caused the pendulum to swing too far back the other way in the players' favor. A few years later the clubs did propose and establish a system of salary arbitration, under which an independent arbitrator determined salary disputes between club and player. This was intended to serve as a substitute for free agency. Ironically, free agency eventually emerged anyway and the clubs were whiplashed between the two—free agency and salary arbitration—a Catch 22 situation for the clubs.

During my years in baseball I was always interested in trying to help bring about new procedures that I felt would help the game and all of the clubs as a group. I had a particularly good opportunity to do this in my role as executive administrator under the commissioner. Moreover I had been involved in matters of this nature while I was with the Yankees and Orioles and would continue to be involved in them throughout my baseball life. Some of the things that I feel I helped bring about were the College Rule, the free agent draft, the Fall Instructional Leagues, the Summer Rookie Leagues, divisional play, the designated hitter, the general manager's meetings (Joe Brown of the Pirates and I were the co-chairmen of the first such meeting, which was held in Ligonier, Pennsylvania), central scouting, and procedures for the expansion drafts. My good friend, Chub Feeney, collaborated with me in many of these ventures—but not for the DH!

The league presidents are in charge of the League Championship Series (which did not exist in 1966) but the commissioner is in charge of the All-Star game and the World Series. So Spike and I met with the umpires and managers before the All-Star game in 1966 and went through the other pregame preparations. The game was played in St. Louis, in its brand new downtown stadium, and as we were still in the era before TV started influencing game times, it was played in the afternoon. St. Louis can be hot in July and this July day was hot even for St. Louis. I sat with Eckert in a front box and Spike had asked Casey Stengel to sit with us. Someone asked Casey what he thought of the new stadium. His reply was, "Well, I know one thing. It holds the heat very well." Actually this game, plus one in Minnesota on another scorching July day, is what influenced baseball to go to night games for the All-Star game.

Sometime during the summer I got a call from Dan Topping. Although he had sold the Yankees to CBS he had retained ten percent of the stock and remained as president of the team. The Yankees had been doing very poorly. Age had caught up to their stars and the team needed rebuilding. Dan asked me if I would be interested in coming back to the Yankees and I made it clear that I would at least be interested in talking about it. I had promised Fetzer and Galbreath only one year, and I had told them when they hired me that I would like, at some point, to get back to a team. Joe Iglehart—since he was out of the Orioles organization and CBS owned the Yankees—was on

the Yankee Board and he also talked with me. I told them all, however, that any serious discussions would have to wait until the end of
the season.

I was, of course, following the pennant race in the American
League with great interest and pulling for the Orioles. (They had an
unbelievable June, winning twenty-six games while losing only seven.)
Frank Robinson was everything and more than we had hoped for and
eventually won the triple crown and was the League's MVP. The
young pitchers were outstanding, and Hank Bauer won his second
award as Manager of the Year. I was as proud of them as if I were still
there. Next this very young team came up against the Dodgers in the
World Series. Moe Drabowsky was the hero in the first game in relief,
striking out eleven in 6⅔ innings and Jim Palmer and Wally Bunker
(both twenty-one) and Dave McNally (not much older) shut out Los
Angeles in the next three. The Dodgers scored only two runs in the
entire Series. Drawbowsky's performance highlights the breaks that
often befall teams in baseball. At the winter meetings in December of
1965, in addition to a power hitting outfielder (Robinson), we had
been shopping for a relief pitcher. We were interested in two players
on minor league rosters, both of whom were available in the draft. We
had decided to go for the second player over Drabowsky, but our first
choice was drafted right before our turn to choose. We were a little
dubious about taking Drabowsky, but we had lost the other pitcher
and it was now our turn. I thought, "What the hell," and took Moe.
Sometimes it is better to be lucky than smart!

At one point in the Series I ran into George Weiss, who com-
mented, "That is a very fine team you put together, Lee." It made me
feel very good, as I looked up to George as just about tops among
knowledgeable baseball people. His opinion probably meant more to
me than that of anyone else in the game. He had asked the year
before if, at the end of the season, I would come back to New York
and join him with the Mets. There was, of course, no way that I could
even consider that at that time. I was signed to a contract with the
Orioles and in the middle of a close pennant race but, more than that,
I never would have left Joe Iglehart and Zan Krieger. But, again, it
meant a great deal to me that George would want me. I have been
fortunate to have been associated with three mentors in my baseball
life—my father, Branch Rickey, and George Weiss. They all had an
influence on my career. All three were to end up in Baseball's Hall of
Fame.

The end of the 1966 season found the Yankees at the very bottom
of the American League standings. CBS had purchased Topping's
other ten percent of stock and had made Mike Burke president of the
team. The season was barely over before Mike contacted me and we

started talking. I had told Spike Eckert of my desire to get back with a team and he was most understanding. Moreover, John McHale had left the Braves and was available to replace me. I knew that I wasn't leaving Spike in the lurch. My talks with Mike progressed rapidly. My relationship with Ralph Houk and Joe Iglehart's friendship with William Paley of CBS, of course, paved the way. I would be executive vice president and general manager with complete responsibility and authority for player matters. After a year, I would also become president. The salary was fine, but the Yankee Employee Profit Sharing Plan (which my father had put in, and under which they put fifteen percent of your salary into a trust fund for you) was not, at that point in time, too big a factor, because the team was not making a profit. While working for CBS my brother had done very well with his stock-purchase plan, so I asked for and was given some rights in this area. (Unfortunately, the stock never got up to my option price—so I wasn't that smart a negotiator.) In any event, the public announcement was made and I was once more back with the Yankees.

And the year ended on a happy note when I was selected by my peers as *The Sporting News'* "Executive of the Year," both for my work with the commissioner and for the fruits of my work for the Orioles. It was a good feeling to win the award my father had won while with the Dodgers, the year I graduated from college.

9

Rally from Behind—Yankee G.M.

The Yankees held a press conference at the stadium to announce my return as general manager. I was very candid with the press. I told them that, in my opinion, we had a tough uphill climb ahead and that it could possibly take us five years before we would again be serious contenders for the American League pennant. I know that my lack of optimism about the immediate future concerned Mike, and he had a point. After all, he had to sell tickets, and I wasn't being much of a promoter. On the other hand I felt that the fans were entitled to know the situation and that it was better to have them expecting little and reasonably happy over modest progress and a few moves up in the standings than having them disappointed and disillusioned. Some people probably said that I was also protecting myself and perhaps they were right, but I did know that it wasn't going to be either easy or quick.

The Yankee stars who had won five straight American League pennants from 1960 through 1964 had either retired or were in the last years of their careers. A few had been traded. The team had fallen from first to sixth place in 1965 and from sixth to tenth (last) in 1966. Maris and Mantle had been hampered by injuries. Yogi Berra had gone from player to manager, and had been released as manager after the 1964 World Series and replaced by Johnny Keane. Elston Howard was in his late thirties. Bill Skowron had been traded to the Dodgers in 1963. Bobby Richardson retired after the 1966 season. Tony Kubek never really recovered from the neck injury suffered in the 1960 World Series against Pittsburgh. Andy Carey and Gil McDougald had retired. Of the pitchers who started World Series games in the 1960–64 period (Ditmar, Turley, Ford, Terry, Daley, Stafford, Coates, Downing, Bouton, and Stottlemyre), only Ford, Downing and Stottlemyre remained. Moreover, Downing had arm problems and Whitey Ford was thirty-eight years old. Only Joe Pepitone at first, Clete Boyer at third, Tommy Tresh in the outfield, Elston Howard catching, and Mantle and Maris were proven major leaguers, and age and injuries handicapped the last three. Even more serious was the fact that the scouting staff had also gotten old. The great talent seekers, such as Paul Krichell, Joe Devine, and Bill Essick were gone, and other standbys were slowing down. The needed replacements were not on Yankee minor league clubs and the new free agent draft ensured that no club could expect to sign many more than their fair share of good high school and college prospects.

At least I was very happy about our manager. Ralph Houk and I had been friends since our Kansas City Blues days. We became particularly close in the 1950s when Ralph managed the Denver Bears and I was Yankee farm director. We went to spring training together in Lake Wales, Florida, and our wives were with us and also good friends. Ralph had been a U.S. Ranger in World War II and had been parachuted behind the German lines in Holland in 1945 (that was the Allied push that provided the story for the movie, *A Bridge Too Far*). He came out of the service a major, and throughout his baseball career had the image of a tough combat officer and the nickname "Major." Near the end of the war, a close service friend in his outfit was killed. When the war was over and Ralph returned to Kansas, where both he and his deceased friend had lived, he went to visit his friend's widow. The lady eventually became Ralph's wife, Betty.

On the baseball field, as a player, Ralph was a tough competitor. As a manager, he retained that competitiveness and was also an excellent handler of men. He always protected his players, never showed them up, and was always liked by them; but he demanded their respect and dedication to their jobs. When Paul Richards left Baltimore, I would have hired Ralph to replace him in a minute, but of course by then he had replaced Casey as manager of the Yankees. So it was very gratifying to me to be reunited with Ralph. I think that he felt the same and I know that he was glad to be back on the field and relieved of front office duties.

Ralph was concerned about the spirit and morale of the club. We talked at length about the problems confronting us and finally determined that, as tough as it was, the only thing to do was to "clean house" and "go young." We would open up positions and give youngsters a chance to make it if they could, and at the same time we would be creating a new, and less complacent, attitude. The only veterans we would definitely keep would be Whitey Ford and Mickey Mantle, plus perhaps Pepitone and Tresh to help keep us respectable. To take some of the wear off Mickey's legs, we decided to talk to him about trying first base. The other veterans we would trade or, if necessary, release. Looking back, maybe we carried our youth program too far, too fast, but it seemed to us the best way to go. Mike Burke let us make the decisions and only asked that we keep him advised of what we were doing. We had a few young players on the roster or in the organization around whom we hoped to build: Bobby Murcer (who was in the service), Steve Whitaker, Roy White, Frank Fernandez, Jerry Kenney, John Ellis, Rusty Torres, Stan Bahnsen, Fritz Peterson, and a few others farther away. So we started off right away trading Clete Boyer to the Atlanta Braves for Bill Robinson, an outstanding young outfield prospect, and letting Roger Maris go to the Cardinals (the only club willing to take a chance with him). Our 1967 opening day lineup in Washington was as follows: Tresh lf, Robinson rf, Mantle 1b, Pepitone cf, Howard c, Smith 3b, Clarke 2b, Kennedy ss, Stottlemyre p.

Mike Burke was a very interesting man. He had a background that could not be matched: star football player at the University of Pennsylvania (offered a pro contract); in the OSS in World War II (with service behind the lines in France); consulting work in Hollywood during the making of *Cloak and Dagger,* based upon his own war experience (with Gary Cooper as Mike Burke); working as general manager for Ringling Brothers, Barnum and Bailey Circus; and vice president for CBS in charge of diversification and the acquisition of new businesses—in which role he recommended that CBS underwrite the play *My Fair Lady.* It was also in that position that he recommended to CBS that it purchase the Yankees (although the initial idea may have come from William Paley, who was a baseball fan and a personal friend of Dan Topping).

Mike dressed with an elegant continental flair, but he was careful to combine this with a shirt with slightly frayed collar and cuffs. Mike also had a very winning personality. He and I got along fine. He concentrated on the stadium, the public image, the broadcast, and the finances. We were both on the Yankee Board, which also included William Paley, Frank Stanton, and Joe Iglehart. I found the Board meetings fascinating, which were generally held in Bill Paley's office. He was really interested in baseball, whereas Frank Stanton was not— but I never met anyone I thought more intelligent, or quicker to comprehend things, than Frank Stanton.

Mike and CBS retained almost all the old Yankee off-field organization and it was a good one, composed of some very fine people. Jimmy Gleason and Mike Rendine handled the tickets. (Today, Jimmy is ticket manager for the New York Giants.) Bill Guilfoile was Bob Fishel's assistant for public relations and when Bill joined the Pittsburgh Pirates (and later went to work for the Hall of Fame), Marty Appel (now a vice president with WPIX TV), took his place. Pete Sheehy, a Yankee legend, was in charge of the clubhouse and Jimmy Esposito in charge of the field. Jimmy had been groundskeeper at Ebbets Field. And Jackie Farrell was director of the speakers bureau.

Jackie was just a wisp of a man—barely five feet tall, he could not have weighed 100 pounds. On one special promotion night, a player was given a huge St. Bernard dog. Since he had no place to keep it he gave it to Jackie, and after the game, Jackie put the dog in the back seat of his car to drive it home. The dog was very friendly and put his paws on the back of the front seat and his head right over Jackie's. Jackie's head barely cleared the dashboard and when they drove up to the toll booth of the George Washington Bridge, all a flabbergasted toll taker could see approaching him was a car with a St. Bernard at the wheel.

Jackie enjoyed telling a story about his father, who earned his living managing fighters. One day one of his friends came to him and asked him if he would manage his son's career. Jackie's father asked what weight or class the boy was, but the friend replied that he was not a fighter but a singer. Jackie's father was regretful but adamant; he had enough trouble with the boxers and was not going to manage singers. And Mr. Sinatra had to look elsewhere to find someone to manage Frankie's career.

Despite a good start on opening day in Washington, 1967 was a struggle. We should have known that it was going to be so, when Bill Rohr of the Red Sox almost pitched a no-hitter against us on opening day in Yankee Stadium. (Elston Howard singled in the bottom of the ninth.) About all that can be said for the season is that we did get out of last place, finishing ninth. Bill Robinson and Steve Whitaker had tough seasons. Bill hurt his arm in winter baseball at just about the exact time we made the deal for him—a fact that neither we nor (I hope) the Atlanta club knew. He had had a great arm and it was one of the tools that most attracted us to him. Bobby Murcer was still in the service. We had optioned Roy White to the Dodgers' Triple-A club in a deal to obtain John Kennedy. We hoped Kennedy could fill our big gap at shortstop, but he couldn't. Charlie Smith, whom we had obtained from the Cardinals in the Maris deal, was mediocre at third base. We had let Elston Howard go to try Frank Fernandez behind the plate, but the result was uncertain. Pepitone (only thirteen HR) and Tresh (.219) had bad seasons. Horace Clarke did a workman-like job at second base, but had trouble making the double play. The pitching (Mel Stottlemyre, Al Downing, Fritz Peterson, with Jack Aker and Steve Hamilton in relief) was good. The staff ERA for the season was an excellent 3.24, but Whitey Ford developed bone chips in his elbow and had to retire in mid-season. This was a very unhappy blow. Whitey had epitomized the spirit of the Yankees. The happiest development of the year was that Mickey Mantle moved from the outfield to first base and played 144 games there. (I told Mickey that the move would add years to his playing career and was the favor I had promised him when he signed his contract in 1958—but I don't think he was convinced.) But the 144 games meant that he had passed Gehrig in total number of games played by a Yankee, and in addition he passed the 500 mark in total home runs.

That June, the second of our four sons, Allen, who had been born while I was at sea in the Navy, graduated from Dickinson College. Jane and I went to the ceremonies, which were held outside on the lawn, under beautiful elm trees, on the Carlyle, Pennsylvania campus. Behind the platform was an early colonial stone building which dated back to the 1700s when the college, the fifth oldest in the United States, was founded. It was a perfect day, a perfect setting. The faculty and graduates, in caps and gowns, were formed and ready to start the academic procession, when the music suddenly stopped and an announcement came over the public address system, "Will Lee MacPhail please report to the college office for an emergency phone call?" Jane was naturally upset and worried about the two younger ones at home. I located the office and the phone. The voice on the other end belonged to Gabe Paul, general manager of the Cleveland Indians. "Lee, would you have any interest in Gary Bell?" Gary Bell was a pitcher Gabe had been trying to unload for a month. I had told him at least three times before that we had no interest in Bell. I could have shot Gabe but, in any event, it didn't prevent Al from graduating.

In 1968 we did show some improvement. Although the offense was anemic, the pitching, again, was excellent (2.79 staff ERA). The addition of Lindy McDaniel after the All-Star break was a big plus. At one point he retired thirty-two straight hitters in relief. Mel Stottlemyre won twenty-one games and pitcher Stan Bahnsen was the Rookie of the Year. Mantle played 144 games again; Roy White had a good year; and Bill Robinson a good second half—but Pepitone and Whitaker disappointed and Downing's arm problems persisted.

The highlight of the year was probably a doubleheader in August against Detroit, in which outfielder Rocky Colavito came in as a relief pitcher and did an excellent job in a 6–5 Yankee win. Then in the nightcap Colavito played right field and hit a home run as the Yankees won the doubleheader. The team hit only .214, last in the league, but we played over .500, winning eighty-three and losing seventy-nine and finished in fifth place (of ten). We were encouraged. We had shown progress. We were at least respectable and hopefully we would soon be contending. We were trying very hard to rejuvenate our scouting staff. We had a team based in Clearwater in the Instructional League and we were doing everything we knew how to do to sign and develop prospects.

After the 1968 season the American League finally voted to permit

Charlie Finley to move the A's from Kansas City to Oakland. It came as something of a shock to me. Finley needed a three-quarter vote to gain approval and we had had a solid block (which included Boston, Detroit, and New York) to oppose the move. Somehow, the night after the first day of a two-day meeting, Yawkey and Fetzer changed their minds and Mike Burke went along with them. I never did get a satisfactory explanation of their thinking. I know part of it was their belief that we were not doing Kansas City a favor by keeping Charlie there as he was feuding with everyone, including the very influential *Kansas City Star*. They may also have worried that Charlie would sue but I think they were more likely to have decided that Kansas City would be better off with an expansion team. The league voted to supply one in 1970. Once the approval for the move was known however, pressure (led by Senator Symington of Missouri) quickly built to supply Kansas City with a team immediately. Though many people had left, Joe Cronin reconvened the league in a night session. At this night session, with a bare quorum present, the league agreed to give Kansas City a team for 1969. And, although there was no adequate ballpark and no properly financed ownership, it was later agreed that Seattle was to be the companion expansion team with Kansas City. This was a blueprint for future trouble, but it did have some good aspects. By 1969 we would have twelve teams, which provided a couple of advantages over operating with a ten-team league. First, it was much easier to construct a sensible schedule for a twelve-team league than for ten. Second, playing with all twelve teams in one league did not make sense. The situation called for divisional play and the American League was unanimously in favor of it. The National League, which at times moves with the speed of the tortoise and the adaptation to change of the dinosaur, was strongly opposed to divisional play. When we said we were going forward with it in any event, they made a compromise agreement with us. They joined us in divisional play and we abandoned consideration of reducing the schedule to fewer than 162 games.

The other big issue of the winter of 1968–1969 involved Eckert and the commissionership. Some of the clubs felt that the choice of Spike Eckert had been an unfortunate one. He had had a three-year trial and it was not turning out completely satisfactorily. I was not in accord with that thinking. I felt that, given time and help, he would work out well. He had certainly not done anything really wrong to justify his being fired. The antis said he had certainly not done anything, period. I knew some of the people who were gathering votes against him (Mike Burke was one), but they did not discuss this with me as they knew how I felt about Spike. Then at the annual meeting at the Palace Hotel in San Francisco, I ran into Spike and he asked me if I had heard anything about a move to replace him. I replied that I had not, thus demonstrating how poorly attuned I was to the politics of baseball, for within the next twenty-four hours, Eckert was let go as commissioner and the clubs once more set about trying to find and reach agreement on someone to occupy the top position in the game.

A meeting was quickly convened at the O'Hare Inn in Des Plaines, Illinois. This was one of the only major league meetings I did not attend between the mid-1950s and my retirement in 1985. The clubs were encouraging one representative per club meetings and Mike seemed to want to go alone. This was okay with me. The voting quickly settled in along league lines, with the American League supporting Mike Burke and the National League backing its new president, Chub Feeney. There was a little support for Joe Cronin and Bob Cannon. Any candidate needed three quarters of the votes in each league. They went through several ballots with little change in clubs' positions. By the eleventh ballot, when he saw he could not be elected, Mike Burke withdrew his name. The National League continued to back Feeney. My name appeared on the tenth ballot, but on the twelfth and thirteenth ballots the American League cast eleven votes for John McHale. There was a question as to John's availability and by the fifteenth ballot, the American League was backing me and the National League, Chub. Sometime around three or four a.m., I got a call in New York asking me my feelings about being considered for the position. The designated callers were Mike Burke and Bowie Kuhn, who at that time was National League counsel. I told them (once I woke up) that I honestly did not want the job and thought that the position, in the present circumstances, probably needed someone with talents different from mine but that I would not refuse if the clubs really wanted me to serve. I don't know after which ballot the call was made, or whether my response had any bearing on the course of the meeting. In any event, on the eighteenth ballot I received eleven votes and Chub eleven, and after nineteen ballots (MacPhail ten, Feeney eight, Cronin three, abstain three) the delegates gave up and the meeting was adjourned.

Sometime after that, CBS brought up the question of my taking over the presidency of the Yankees, as had been promised when I accepted the job. I was getting along fine with Mike and was not being interfered with. Nor was I adverse to being able to concentrate entirely on trying to rebuild the team on the field. I also knew Mike had not given up hopes of becoming commissioner and a change in his status at this time would not have been helpful to him in that regard. To Joe Iglehart's disappointment, I told CBS I was content to forego the presidency and to continue things as they were.

The leagues met again that winter in Miami Beach and discussed possible ways to eliminate the league verses league impasse that was preventing the election of a commissioner. A joint league committee was set up to seek a solution. It was agreed that each league's committee would first meet separately. I was on the American League committee along with John Fetzer, Mike Burke, Gabe Paul, and one or two others. At this meeting of the American League committee members, Gabe and I suggested Bowie as an interim commissioner, at least for a year, to give everyone time to work things out. We made this suggestion to the joint committee and as the suggestion came from the American League and as Bowie was the National League attorney, the two leagues were finally able to break the deadlock and get on with their business. And after a year with Bowie as interim commissioner, everyone was quite pleased to continue with him on a permanent basis.

Things happen fast on the field. Events in your personal life often keep pace or move even faster. That was so for me in 1968 and 1969. First, Jane had some health problems that necessitated hospitalization. Shortly afterwards, I had what is known as pericarditis. Everyone thought at first it was a heart attack and I went by ambulance to the intensive care unit at White Plains Hospital in Westchester. While my condition was still undetermined, my oldest boy, Lee (who had been born in the blizzard in Toronto in 1942 and was now the general manager of the Reading Baseball Team—my first team and now a Phillie farm) was killed in an automobile accident driving home from a mid-winter banquet. There was much debate as to whether or how I was to be told. Jane insisted I know, and that she be the one to tell me. Our first born was buried in Baltimore. He left a little girl and a wife, pregnant with a son he would never see. All the family attended the funeral except for me (hospital bound) and Jane (who elected to stay with me). It turned out that my heart had suffered no permanent damage and after Jane and I had a few days together in Eleuthera to recoup physically and mentally from our problems, I joined the Yankees in Fort Lauderdale for spring training.

We opened the 1969 season in Washington with President Nixon throwing out the first ball. Mel Stottlemyre won 8–4 and Bobby Murcer, Roy White, Bill Robinson, and Jerry Kenney gave us four promising youngsters in the starting lineup. Murcer and Kenney hit back-to-back home runs but when someone—bursting with enthusiasm—asked me after the game how many home runs I thought Kenney would hit that year, I had to answer, "maybe three." And regrettably, we could not continue the progress in the 1969 season that we had shown in 1968, finishing in fifth place once more. It was the first year of divisional play. Mantle retired in March and that was an emotional wrench for all of us.* The team played well until September, but then pretty much fell apart. The pitching continued above par. Stottlemyre won twenty and Peterson seventeen. Jack Aker was excellent in relief, and Bobby Murcer and Gene Michael became regulars. But Pepitone disappointed—even going AWOL for three days—and Stan Bahnsen had an off year. We traded Tommy Tresh in June and Pepitone and Downing in December, so three more of the old Yankees were gone.

After the season, the American and National Leagues were again at loggerheads, this time over the designated hitter rule. The defense had been gaining the ascendancy over the offense in both leagues but particularly in the American League, where there was less artificial turf. Run production in both leagues was down. In an effort to put more offense into the game (and prolong the careers of some star players) the American League designed and suggested the designated hitter rule. The National League was immediately and unqualifiedly opposed and has remained so ever since. But the American League went forward with the rule change. Thus, today, the two leagues play under one different rule and advocates of both positions carry on a perpetual battle over the rule's plusses and minuses.

During spring training of 1970, Marvin Miller consolidated his control of the Players' Association and his unquestioned leadership of the players. An unimportant issue had come up with respect to the Pension Plan. It developed that there were funds available within the plan and the clubs wanted the money used to pay off the indebtedness of the plan's unfunded liabilities. Miller wanted the money to go for increased future benefits. A spring major league meeting failed to resolve the issue and Miller called on the players to strike during spring training to establish their position. The strike, from Miller's point of view, was really not so much about the issue on the table but simply to prove that the Players' Association and Miller had the clout to call a strike and make it stick. We were pretty shook up to think the players would really strike. I talked to the Yankee players and tried to get them to give consideration to the game, the fans, the office workers, and others. What the Yankee players told me, and I am sure other players told their clubs, was that it was not what the Yankees did that concerned them, but what some of the other teams did. And they struck during the last week of spring training, causing cancellation of

---

*We had a day for Mickey at the stadium in June to retire his number seven. Joe DiMaggio presented the uniform jersey to Mickey before more than 60,000 fans and his old teammates did their part by winning a doubleheader to help honor a great Yankee.

some of the final spring training games. Most important, it indicated that Miller now had the solid backing of the players for whatever strategy he might feel called upon to pursue. As the strike issue itself was not all that important, the strike was over in time for Opening Day 1970.

I used to like to schedule one short trip out of the country for the team during spring training. I felt it broke up the training grind and provided a little fun for the players, many of whom had never been out of the United States. It also helped defray some of the costs of spring training. The proposed Oriole trip to Havana had had to be aborted but other trips with the Orioles and Yankees to Puerto Rico, the Virgin Islands, and Mexico had turned out very well. When in Mexico City with the Yankees, Joe Iglehart and I had flown down to Acapulco on the invitation of the owners of the Mexico City Reds and had had a great day swimming and boating. Our hosts arranged for us to see the famous dive off the rocks for which Acapulco is famous. Our little boat sailed in close to the rocks and the crashing surf as we watched the diver, high up above the sea, preparing for his dive. At this point, the engine on our boat died and while our skipper kept trying to get our engine started we kept drifting closer to the rocks. Joe and I didn't know whether to concentrate on the diver or the rocks. We did see the beautiful dive, timed perfectly to coincide with an in-rushing wave. And then, fortunately, another boat came along, threw us a line and towed us out to safer waters.

In 1971 we arranged a trip to Venezuela with the White Sox, with two games scheduled in Caracas and one in Maracaibo. By now, Luis Aparicio was playing for the Red Sox. As Luis was a big hero in his native Venezuela, we got the Red Sox to let him go with us (General Manager Dick O'Connell came along to look after his shortstop). The financial arrangements for the trip provided that each team would receive a flat sum, paid in advance, in lieu of any share of the gate. On arrival in Venezuela, we were greeted by a representative of the American Embassy and we met the ambassador at one of the games. They were pleased that we were there and nothing was too good for us. We played the games to large crowds and everyone had a good time. The series over, the two teams were bussed to the airport and prepared to board our charter plane for the trip home. At this point, we were told that we could not depart as the admission taxes for the games had not been paid. In vain, I tried to reach the promoter of the games. In desperation I called the American Embassy. The ambassador was away for the weekend and now it seemed, when we needed them, no one had ever heard of us. I pleaded and tried to explain to the Venezuelan official holding up our departure that we had no involvement with the financial promotion of the games or the handling of the gate receipts. Finally, I was able to make a deal with him. They would let us go if each team would leave one representative behind as hostage. And so it was that Bob Fishel and Don Unferth, the White Sox traveling secretary, were left behind in Venezuela. The players thought it was a great joke and Mickey Mantle stood at the foot of the steps to the plane with his hat held out accepting contributions from everyone for Bob. I had my doubts about how long Bob could subsist on the players' largesse, so I also gave him a signed blank check, just in case. Fortunately, the taxes were paid the next day and we got Bob back.

Winning and losing is always very important and when you lose it is always a little grim, but we did try to mix some lighter moments into our daily baseball lives. One occasion on which a little fun was injected occurred while I was still with the Orioles, when the Yankees were playing in Chicago in the Bill Veeck era. Bill had just introduced his exploding scoreboard (which, of course, only exploded when the White Sox hit a home run). Bob Fishel orchestrated a Yankee counterplot. The Yankee players were all provided with small old-fashioned Fourth of July sparklers. When a Yankee hit a home run, all the Yankees then stood on the steps of the dugout and in line in the bullpen and held up their little sparklers as their home run hitter circled the bases. Even the White Sox fans had some fun with that one. Our reliever Steve Hamilton's contribution to a lighter approach was a facsimile of Rip Sewell's blooper pitch. He used good judgment as to when he threw it (when the game was not at issue) and grew quite proficient with it. It provided the fans with a laugh or two when we were out of a ball game.

Nineteen seventy brought solid encouragement. Thurman Munson was now our catcher and leader. Roy White had an excellent year. We had acquired Danny Cater in a trade with Charlie Finley for Downing and Fernandez and he contributed to the offense. Lindy McDaniel recorded twenty-nine saves, a club record. Youngsters John Ellis and Steve Kline were big additions. We won seventeen and lost only seven in June and went on to win ninety-three games and finish second. Ralph was selected as Manager of the Year. Our Triple-A team, Syracuse, won the Little World Series and we were starting to come up with some good young players from our farm clubs. The next year was not quite as upbeat. In the battle for second place that lasted until September, the club slumped at the end and dropped to fourth. There were still some encouraging developments, however. Bobby Murcer had an outstanding year, hitting .331 and finishing second in the league in batting. Ron Blomberg showed signs of filling the role we envisioned for him, hitting .322 in sixty-four games. We had acquired Felipe Alou the day after the season opened, and after a slow start he did very well. He was (is) an outstanding person as well. Our five starting pitchers recorded sixty-seven complete games. Unfortunately, the bull pen sagged and an erratic infield prevented us from finishing higher.

In the fall of 1971, I was asked to speak at a luncheon of a Swarthmore alumni group in Philadelphia. Actually, I was to substitute for my brother Bill, who had accepted and then was unavailable. Unfortunately, the date was November 18th, our wedding anniversary, but I promised Jane that I would get back in time to pick her up and we would drive up to Connecticut and stay overnight at one of our favorite inns. I made it back as scheduled and we had a nice dinner and night at The Stonehenge Inn, near Wilton, Connecticut. On the way back, she told me that she had had some pains in her chest over the last few days. I took her to the doctor the next day. He prescribed some medication, but a week later she became ill and had to be hospitalized. It didn't seem to be her heart or chest and the doctor was unsure as to just what was causing the problem. She was out of the hospital before Christmas and we had a very nice holiday with the children and my brother and sister. A day or two later, I was at the office meeting with Lev Pope of WPIX about our TV contract. Mike would normally have met with Lev but he had had an emergency eye operation and was in the hospital. I then got word that Jane had had an attack. She was hospitalized again and placed in intensive care, the same area of the same hospital in White Plains that I had been in just two years before. Things seemed to have stabilized but then on January 2nd she suffered a massive coronary attack and we lost her. I was now without my companion of thirty-three years. It was a desperate feeling.

For some reason Ralph Houk and Mike Burke were never too friendly. Cordial to one another on the surface, there was always an element of reserve—almost of distrust. Perhaps it was like two costars in a movie, jealous of who received top billing. In any event, during the 1971 season, Mike had gotten quite friendly with Billy Martin. I think they had had a few drinks together when Billy was in New York as manager of the Tigers. Billy could be a most charming rascal. Together they hatched a plot under which the Yankees and Tigers would trade managers. I really don't know how serious Mike was about it but he did call Jim Campbell, the Tiger general manager. Jim, knowing how close Ralph and I were, immediately asked if I knew about it and when Mike said no, Jim said he really couldn't discuss it. If the effort had been made, then Mike and I would have had a confrontation and I would have found out how solid the pledge was that I would have full responsibility on the field. None of this is in any way a reflection on Billy for, despite his occasional problems, I have always thought that he was an excellent manager on the field.

We kept struggling to improve our team. I have always believed that the best approach to building a contending team is to concentrate on your farm system and develop your own talent. I knew what that had done for the Yankees in the fifties and for the Orioles in the sixties. Now we were striving to make it work for the Yankees in the seventies. I spent a good portion of my own time visiting our minor league clubs and with our scouts in the field. But the world had gotten tougher. Free agency for professionals had not come yet and the free agent draft for amateurs pretty much limited you to your own share of the top amateur players. By this point all—not just a few—organizations were scouting extensively and spending freely to improve their teams. Also, you were never any better than your scouts. They were the people that put together the base from which you built and we were still trying to improve and rebuild our staff. Harry Craft and Darrell Johnson had joined me from the Orioles and I counted on their counsel in making important scouting decisions.

We had strengthened our scouting staff by adding Loren Babe, Don Gutteridge, Bobby Richardson, Sam Suplizio, Gene Woodling, and several others. Another important addition was Clyde Kluttz. Clyde started out scouting the southeast for us and eventually, after Johnny Johnson had gone, became farm director. It was because of Clyde that the Yankees were able to sign Jim "Catfish" Hunter in 1975, after Hunter was declared a free agent from Charlie Finley and the A's. Clyde had signed Hunter to his first professional contract with the A's and Jim had great confidence in his integrity.

The one advantage to finishing down in the race was an early pick in the free agent draft. In my first year there, because the Yankees had finished last the year before, we got the first pick in the country. It wasn't simple to determine your pick with different area scouts strongly plugging for the best player in their territory. We always tried to cross-check as much as possible and have several scouts, including Craft or Johnson, see the very top prospects. In 1967 we narrowed our choice down to Greg Luzinski, Ted Simmons, and Ron Blomberg. Unfortunately we picked Blomberg. Atley Donald, one of our very best scouts, was extremely high on Ron and there was no questioning his raw ability. He could run and had outstanding power; moreover, he was a left-handed pull hitter with the ideal Yankee Stadium stroke. He seemed to have a good temperament, showed great hustle, and really should have been a star. But it turned out that he was not willing to fully dedicate himself to his work. When he reached Triple-A, he had trouble hitting left-handed pitching and I had to fight with Frank

Verdi, his manager at Syracuse, to keep him from platooning Ron. He did not improve as he should have in the outfield and we decided to switch him to first base. We sent him to the Fall Instructional League team at Clearwater to concentrate completely on first base play, but he didn't want to field ground balls or work on the mechanics around the bag as he should have. He just wanted to hit. If Ron had developed to the limit of his potential he could have given us a big lift—but he didn't. In addition, he was so strong and muscular and ran so hard that he was constantly pulling something.

We had better luck with some of our other top draft choices. The best two were Thurman Munson and Scott McGregor. In drafting Thurman, the big question was whether he would sign or stay in college, and I went with Gene Woodling (who was now scouting for us in Ohio) to Thurman's home in Canton to discuss this with him. I was eventually able to convince Thurman that it was in his best interest to start his professional career right away. That would not mean that he could not continue his college work and get his degree in the off-season. This, I encouraged him to do. And what a player and what a competitor he was (and what a terrible tragedy it was when he was killed in a plane accident several years later). A few other high draft picks also worked out well, like Lamar Hoyt (outstanding until his later off-field problems), Terry Whitfield, Mike Heath, etc. Like most organizations, we had our successes and disappointments as there was no sure way to tell how a high school boy would develop physically or what was going to happen to him when he ran into the tough competition of professional baseball. Today, some players are spending time with drug counselors and psychiatrists. That was almost unheard of in the 1960s and 1970s. I only recall arranging consultation for one player. This boy was a fine prospect and was playing in the high minors when he was arrested for exposing himself to young girls. We were able to keep the incident from being publicized. He was basically a fine person with an attractive and intelligent wife. Either this was a once in a lifetime incident or the psychiatrist accomplished his mission for, as far as I know, he had no further problems and went on to enjoy a long and successful career.

As the free agent era was still in the future, the only other way to improve our team was through trades. In evaluating trades, I had the reports of our own scouts—plus I used to trade scouting reports with one or two other teams. Within our own league I relied mainly on the judgment of Ralph and our coaching staff of Jim Turner, Jim Hegan, Dick Howser, and later Ellie Howard. Again, if you think you can consistently outsmart other clubs you are only kidding yourself. The best you can count on in trading is to more properly balance your team (position-wise, left- or right-handed, place in the batting order, age, experience, or whatever). You can hope for a little luck and that the players you trade for progress well and don't get hurt. We did have a little luck with our trades. For example, we picked up Rick Dempsey in a minor league deal before he reached the major league level.

Another example: we signed Bill Monboquette as a free agent when Boston released him, mostly because he was a bear-down guy and we needed another arm. Bill pitched well for us—so well in fact that I was able to trade him for Lindy McDaniel. I had run into Chub Feeney in a hotel elevator during a baseball meeting. We both got on at the top floor and no one else was in the car. Apparently for some reason, Horace Stoneham had just told Chub to get rid of Lindy.

Top floor: Chub:	"Have you any interest in Lindy McDaniel?"
One floor down: Lee:	"Yes, we might. I think we could possibly fit him in on our staff."
Two floors down: Chub:	"Well, who would you give us for him?"
Half way down: Lee:	"We could give you either Monbouquette or blank" (another player, I thought if I named Monbo alone it would be too obvious).
Two more floors: Chub:	"Okay, we'll take blank."
Lobby level: Lee:	"Gee, I'm sorry, Chub, but thinking about it, it would have to be Monbo."

I got a glare but eventually he got back to me and said okay. I don't remember what "the other player" did (or even who he was, except that he was much younger) but Lindy was great for us. He was not only a fine pitcher but he was an outstanding human being.

We were also lucky with some of the veteran players we picked up in waiver-type deals. Here one looks primarily for someone who would help in a utility role and who also would help the team by his presence. Gene Michael came in that manner and turned out to be a better player than that. We also at various times picked up Dick Howser and Hal Lanier and drafted Bobby Cox. (I had done the same thing in Baltimore—Dick Williams, Whitey Herzog, Billy Hunter, Darrell Johnson.) There were others, of course, but it is amazing that all the men mentioned here eventually became major league managers. And I think I had something to do with getting almost all of them their first non-playing baseball job.

In the spring of 1972 the Red Sox became alarmed about their first base situation. They had traded George Scott to Milwaukee, planning to go with Cecil Cooper, but Cooper was having a bad spring. They worried that perhaps they were rushing him a little too fast and that he might need another year in Triple-A. At the same time, their relief pitcher, Sparky Lyle, had gotten in manager Eddie Kasko's doghouse because of a weight problem. Ralph Houk liked Sparky very much and I knew him because the Red Sox had drafted him from us while I was with Baltimore. We smelled the opportunity for a deal. I drove up to Winter Haven, Florida; sat with Dick O'Connell through an exhibition game; and drove back with a deal made for Lyle (Cater and an option to Boston to purchase Mario Guerrero, a young shortstop, from our Syracuse club). Ralph was elated and so was I. We felt Sparky could be a key figure in our rebuilding program. And he was outstanding—so outstanding that when he used to stride in from our right-field bull pen, Toby Wright (the Yankee Stadium organist) would play "Pomp and Circumstance." The fans and Sparky loved it. He did well for us in 1972, saving thirty-five games (breaking McDaniel's record) and contributing immensely to keeping us in the running until the final week of the season. (We floundered at the end and finished fourth.) Another colorful addition that year was third baseman Celerino Sanchez, acquired from the Mexican League.

Sometimes one position becomes a problem for a team. We had trouble with the whole infield. My blueprint for a pennant contender was that in addition to top pitching you needed a potential all star at every regular position. Horace Clarke did his best at second base but he wasn't of all-star caliber. Gene Michael finally filled the shortstop hole for us, and if he wasn't a potential all star he was close to it, but third base had been a nightmare to fill. In 1968 we had three good Triple-A third basemen fighting for the job—Mike Ferraro from our Syracuse club, Bobby Cox whom we acquired from the Braves' Richmond team and Len Boehmer, whom we also picked up from Triple-A—but they were all a little short in ability. We were still unsettled there in 1969. Finally, in 1970, we determined to fill the hole by trading one of our starting pitchers. I went after Don Money of the Phillies. John Quinn wanted Stan Bahnsen but I held out, offering to give them Steve Kline. I thought they would take Kline but I was wrong and they traded Money to Milwaukee. Next, we turned to the White Sox who had Rich McKinney, and when they wouldn't take Kline either, I finally gave them Bahnsen. This was the worst trade of my career. The mistake was made because I did not know McKinney well enough. He had a good bat, and although he had played second base for Chicago, we figured he could make the switch to third. That should not be an automatic assumption. But more important than that, for us, he simply did not have the aggressive bear-down temperament that we thought he had. Nor was the colorful, likeable Sanchez the answer. So when we went to the annual meetings in Hawaii in December of 1972 we were still looking for our third baseman. Cleveland had been after me throughout the 1972 season about some of our young players. At various times they had shown interest in Jerry Kenney, John Ellis, Charlie Spikes, and Rusty Torres. I kept telling them that any of them were available but that it would have to be part of a deal for Graig Nettles. (I had always remembered Billy Martin telling me once that if I could ever get Nettles for New York he would be a perfect hitter for Yankee Stadium.) We had a couple of sessions with Gabe Paul and Phil Seghi. Ralph and I were very anxious to make the deal but we did not want to appear too anxious. At one point, so we did not appear too eager, we asked for a recess while we went into the bedroom to caucus. We finally gave them a package of all four young players and we got Graig and Jerry Moses, a back-up catcher, in return. My comment to the press was that, "We had traded tomorrow for today." And after the trade we became favorites to win the American League East in 1973.

With our failure to contend for the pennant in 1971 and 1972, attendance had fallen off. It was further affected by the fact that the image of the South Bronx was at an all-time low and fans were concerned about attending night games. This was particularly true because we lacked adequate parking right around the stadium and people were forced to park blocks away on dark sidestreets. Moreover, the stadium was showing signs of age, with falling concrete and other problems. The New York Giants had moved from the Polo Grounds to Yankee Stadium in 1957 and had been a welcome and valued tenant. Now in 1971, both the Yankees and Giants were approached by individuals who wanted the teams to move to New Jersey. The plan was to build a modern sports complex with an ideal stadium for each team, with plenty of parking, near the New Jersey Turnpike and Lincoln Tunnel to Manhattan. Rental terms would be reasonable. Financially, of course, it was an attractive proposal.

The idea of the Yankees moving out of New York City was something I would prefer not even to contemplate and to Mike Burke's credit he felt just as strongly as I did. With the Yankee Board's approval (which meant CBS approval), Mike contacted Mayor John Lindsay. The city of New York had built a brand new stadium for the Mets. Shouldn't they be willing to do something to keep the Yankees and Giants in New York City? John Lindsay was sympathetic and anxious not to lose the sports teams. He talked in terms of appropriating an amount of money for Yankee Stadium equal to that which had been spent to construct Shea Stadium. Eventually, it was decided that the city would take over Yankee Stadium completely, refurbish it, improve the traffic patterns, and provide additional parking. The estimated cost was $25 million, though I assumed Lindsay and his people suspected that the final cost would exceed this by quite a bit.

Today, they say the total figure was $100 million, but that includes highway ramps, parking garages, and some improvements to the general area. It is not a figure out of line with the cost of other modern baseball stadia and, in my opinion at least, was a very wise investment for the city of New York. It would be tragic for New York to lose the historic stadium which has been the site of so much baseball history, the team whose name and deeds mean so much to so many New Yorkers, and one of the city's best tourist attractions.

The project and the refurbishing program were eventually approved by the Board of Estimate and planning went forward. Our aim was to provide as many improvements for the fans as possible— more and better traffic ramps off the expressway; perimeter parking around the stadium, including a new parking garage; improved entrances, escalators and elevators; improved rest rooms; better concession facilities; a better Stadium Club and dining rooms;* wider seats and aisles; new clubhouses; reorganized office space; and new public address and field lighting systems. At the same time we wanted very much to retain as much of the aura, flavor, and atmosphere of the old Yankee Stadium as was possible. We also wanted to make the playing conditions as ideal as we could, without entirely abandoning the old Yankee Stadium trademarks of a "short right field porch" and "death valley" in left center field. And we wanted to retain natural grass.

My role in the refurbishing was the responsibility for the playing field, bull pens, dugouts, clubhouses, etc., and for negotiations of the lease provisions with the city. Mike, Bob Fishel, Howard Berk, and I— plus our controller and lawyer—met together regularly to discuss ideas and plans. Out of these meetings came the idea to preserve the facade that used to grace the top of the upper deck and to place the plaques and monuments honoring Babe Ruth, Lou Gehrig, Miller Huggins, and others in a spot where they could be seen, and also on occasions visited by the fans.‡ I also attended many meetings with the city solicitor and his people in the city office building a block from City Hall. I was very favorably impressed by the caliber of the people that represented the city and by their care and concern for city finances. (In fact, it went so far that whenever we had a sandwich lunch during an all-day meeting at their offices someone came around and collected from us individually for the cost of our lunch.)

I think we ultimately negotiated a lease that was fair financially to

---

*My father had opened the original Stadium Club restaurant in Yankee Stadium.

‡There were actually five plaques and three monuments at this time, including one for Pope Paul VI who had spoken in Yankee Stadium, and ones for Mantle, DiMaggio, Ed Barrow, and Jacob Ruppert.

both team and city. In addition, we were able to retain control of the ground crew; to retain the natural grass surface; to keep the stadium measurements and layout proper for baseball (the fact that the Giants had gone through with the move to New Jersey facilitated this); to give the baseball schedule precedence and protect the field from the scheduling of events too close to baseball games; to arrange seating and fences in a way to best prevent interference with play on the field; and to make several other arrangements in the best interest of the team. It was an extremely interesting experience. The Yankees had to evacuate the stadium in 1974 and 1975 to permit the work to be done and to play those years at Shea, but I was most pleased when, on their return, things like dugouts, bull pens, clubhouses, etc., all worked out well. The credit for the original idea to refurbish the stadium and for the overall program of reconstruction belongs to Mike Burke and Yankee fans in the years ahead will be enjoying the fruit of his work and his dedication to the city. I was proud of the refurbished Yankee Stadium. I felt it was clearly one of the very best baseball stadiums in existence and so remarked at a luncheon in Toronto attended by Muriel Kauffman, wife of the owner of the Royals. I think I equated it to "the beautiful new K.C. Stadium, with its waterfalls and other attractions." Muriel took violent exception to the comparison—and has never let me forget it. Understandably, she does not think anything can compare to Royals Stadium. I can appreciate that, but I still believe what I said.

Sometime late in 1972, CBS decided to sell the Yankees.* I do not know what the thinking was behind their decision. It wasn't discussed at our Yankee Board meetings. It is possible they became discouraged over our inability to get the team back on top. Mr. Paley asked me a couple of times if we could not buy some star players but at that time no one was selling good players and there were no free agents available for the highest bidder. Ironically, that era started just two years later. More likely, they became concerned about the public reaction and their image, with New York City spending millions on the stadium on behalf of a major corporation. Or possibly it was simply a change in corporate strategy about diversification and non-broadcast

---

*The general impression of people today is that CBS did not provide good ownership—that it would not spend money to improve the team. Actually CBS did everything in its power—under the baseball rules in force at the time—to improve the club. Scouting and player development budgets were increased and it gladly would have purchased players had there been good players available for purchase. And actually, the team did improve. Nor was CBS any problem to baseball with respect to broadcast matters.

properties. They were also selling other subsidiary operations at this time. In any event, they started looking for a buyer. Mike Burke asked me if I would like to try to put a group together, but the only millionaires I knew already owned baseball teams. Joe Iglehart felt he should not become involved because of his connection with CBS and besides his heart and home were in Baltimore. I did talk to Del Webb about getting back into the picture and he seemed interested for a while but his financial people did not like the operating figures.

Toward the close of the year Mike became acquainted with George Steinbrenner. I am sure the contact came through Gabe Paul in Cleveland, although Mike was paid a finder's fee by CBS (a fact that later gave rise to a stockholder suit). Mike was also given five percent of the Yankee stock, so he came out of the deal in fine shape. Gabe was also part of the group and expected to be active in its management. This fact Mike kept carefully from me. Gabe later said that he asked Mike time after time if I had been told and stated that he would not be part of the deal if that would upset me and I wouldn't stay. I don't know why Mike wouldn't tell me. I finally learned about it the day before the sale was announced and I admit that I was shocked. Not that I had anything against Gabe—we were friends—but you didn't need two people running a team.

The announcement of the sale was made at a Yankee Stadium press conference. I remember George's remarks very well. He said he would be too busy with his shipbuilding business to be involved in the operation of the club; that he would leave this to the professionals—Mike Burke, Lee MacPhail, and Ralph Houk. Gabe was not present but another press conference was held two weeks later at the "21 Club." The announcement on this occasion was held up, literally, for half an hour while Gabe and Mike sparred on the precise description of Gabe's role. Mike finally told the assemblage that Gabe was planning to retire but would stay with the club for a year or two.

Although my contract with the Yankees had a couple of years to run, I felt a little bit like I did when Jerry Hoffberger took over the Orioles. I was uneasy in a situation where a new ownership had inherited me. I felt they should be free to pick their own man and if they wanted someone else running the team (Gabe for instance), so be it. It so happened that at that time I had some possible alternatives that might be open to me. Joe Cronin was talking about retiring as American League president and several members of the league (Gene Autry, John Fetzer, etc.) had asked me if I would consider becoming president. Jerry Hoffberger had also asked me if I would consider returning to the Orioles. I had told Jerry that I couldn't, but after the sale of the club and the announcement that Gabe was joining the Yankees, he had contacted me again. I therefore wrote Mike asking for some assurance in writing that the new ownership really wanted me to remain and fulfill my contract, and also seeking an understanding that I would have the right to move if things didn't work out. I received a written reply from Mike giving the assurances that I wanted.

We got off to a good start in 1973. We had pretty good left-handed punch for Yankee Stadium with Roy White, Bobby Murcer, Graig Nettles, and Ron Blomberg in the batting order and John Callison and Bernie Allen on the bench. Thurman Munson was our leader and the two Alous, Felipe and Matty (acquired from Oakland), gave us experience. The pitching was pretty good with Stottlemyre, Peterson, Medich, and Kline starting. Sparky Lyle and Lindy McDaniel were excellent as bull pen stoppers. I had picked up Jim Ray Hart early in the season from the Giants for a little over the waiver price to pair with Blomberg as a DH and he was doing a good job in that role. George and Gabe were worried about the pitching and before the trading deadline I was able to make a deal with Atlanta for Pat Dobson, a proven starter, and Gabe bought Sam McDowell from Horace Stoneham of the Giants. The season moved along toward the Fourth of July and we stayed up around first place, but on the Fourth we lost a doubleheader to Milwaukee.

From that date on, things began going downhill and as they did, George became more and more involved. There was an incident in Texas, when George was there, in which the players were clowning around. Hal Lanier had put half a weiner in the finger of Gene Michael's glove and when Michael got to his position and put on his glove he jumped a mile. As the team was losing, that was not the right moment for levity, but George's anger was beyond reason. He was also after me all the time about the salaries we were paying the veteran utility players such as Callison and Allen. (I personally like having experienced men on the bench backing up good young starters on the field, and the salaries he was objecting to were not out of line and by today's standards, were very, very low.) We had words once and I hung up the phone (hardly the proper thing to do with the owner of the club). Ralph, in the meantime, contrived to keep George out of the clubhouse. In all fairness though, George was not too unreasonable in 1973 and I got along with him satisfactorily. He was very knowledgeable and intelligent and, at times, could be charming and fun to be with. Nonetheless, as the season approached an end it became very apparent that working for the Yankees in the future would be quite different from what Ralph and I had been used to. You might say we had been spoiled. Certainly, we had each been fortunate in being given the authority to do what we felt had to be done in our area. We talked about it and both of us decided that it was time for us to leave. Finding a position would be no problem for Ralph. Any team needing a manager would be knocking at his door. In my case it now appeared that Joe Cronin definitely wanted to retire. (Earlier I had said that I would not be interested in being considered for the job as long as Joe wanted to continue.) Both Ralph and I had Yankee contracts running for another year or two. In my case, I had the letter from Mike Burke saying that I would be free to leave at the end of the year if I wished. Ralph seemed to feel that he had a verbal okay to leave but this was an issue that later was in dispute.

Once it became apparent that Ralph did not want to return in 1974, the Yankees put out feelers to see if Dick Williams would be interested in replacing him. Gabe approached Dick through a Yankee season box holder who was always around doing favors (like supplying cars) for the players. This man had Ron Blomberg under his wing and represented Ron in contract matters. I considered him on the shady side and told Gabe he should have nothing to do with him and that, if he had asked him to contact Dick, he should revoke any such instructions. When the season ended Ralph announced his resignation and the Yankees in a press statement wished him well. Shortly afterward, he signed to manage Detroit and shortly after that the Yankees tried to hire Dick Williams. But Dick was under contract to Charlie Finley at Oakland and Charlie cried halt. Both matters came before Joe Cronin. I found this a little embarrassing. I was still working for the Yankees and George and Gabe wanted me to serve as one of the team's representatives before Cronin. The Yankee position, however, I could support. I felt they should not contest Houk's leaving, but if he were free to go then it would seem they should be free to sign Williams. Cronin held to the contrary, however, ruling that Houk had verbal approval from New York, whereas Williams did not have the same from Oakland.

With Williams out of the picture George subsequently had a meeting with Gabe and me—and I think Bob Fishel was there—at the Carlyle Hotel, to discuss whom the Yankees should hire as manager. Many people were considered. I mentioned Frank Robinson but that didn't get too far. I then recommended Bill Virdon and it was decided to offer Bill the job. I was asked to reach Bill and have him call Gabe. That was almost, but not quite, my last assignment for the Yankees. I had been elected president of the league, but it was not effective until January 1st and George and Gabe asked me to attend the December meetings and represent the team in trade talks. The Yankees were looking for a right-handed hitting outfielder. This was like deja vu at Baltimore in December of 1965. Again I was fortunate in being able to make a deal and obtain our objective. Lindy McDaniel, for family reasons, wanted to return to the middle west and I was able to negotiate a deal with Cedric Tallis to send Lindy to the Kansas City Royals for Lou Piniella. And so the young high school boy that I recommended to George Selkirk at Washington many years earlier, and whom I had later acquired for Baltimore in a trade with Washington, now, as a seasoned major leaguer, became a Yankee. It was the last deal of my baseball career and not a bad one to quit on.

Postscript—The Peterson-Kekich Affair

In 1968, we had acquired Mike Kekich from the Dodgers for Andy Kosco. Mike was a left-handed pitcher with a strong arm and a free spirit. Mike and Fritz Peterson, another left-handed pitcher on our staff, became close friends. They were both very personable and likeable young men—and good pitchers. As time went by Mike and his wife and Fritz and his wife all became close. They lived near each other in New Jersey. The wives, both very attractive, went to the games together and kept each other company when the team was on the road. I have no play by play account of how the relationship transcended normal bounds, but eventually the individuals all came to the conclusion that they liked the other's mate more than their own. At what point that happened or whether they agonized over how to handle it, I do not know. In any event, they ultimately decided that each couple would get a divorce and then they would remarry. Obviously, a story like this could not be kept private and obviously there would be a lot of people trying to put the worst face on it that they possibly could. When the players told me the situation during spring training in 1973, I told them I thought we should simply tell the writers covering the team what the facts were and get it all behind us as quickly as possible. We did just that and the New York sportswriters handled the matter very maturely. That, of course, was not true of out-of-town writers and nonsportswriters in New York. There were all kinds of sick remarks such as "Who gets the dog?", but we did the best we could to keep the incident from adversely affecting the players' performances, and as a result the team's. Unfortunately, there was no way that it couldn't. Before the season was over we had to let Mike go on waivers to Cleveland, and Pete fell off from 17-15 in 1972 to 8-15 in 1973. They went forward with the divorces and Fritz and Mrs. Kekich were married, but Mrs. Peterson decided not to go through with it and she and Mike did not stay together. Today, Fritz Peterson does outstanding work for the "Baseball Chapel," a religious organization for active Major League players. Mike went on to earn a medical degree in Mexico and settled in the west. I hope he has not lost his verve and spirit.

10

Late Innings—League President

Although I was elected the day before my 56th birthday October 24, 1973, I did not officially become American League president until January 1, 1974. The American League office was in Boston because Joe Cronin lived there. It had previously been in Chicago because Will Harridge lived there. The National League office had been in Cincinnati (Warren Giles' home) when Giles was president and Chub Feeney moved it to San Francisco when he became president. Bowie Kuhn, however, was making a concerted effort to get all the baseball offices centralized—in one city to start with—ideally, eventually, in one building. This made sense to me; besides, although I liked Boston, I lived in New York. Consequently, I had told our clubs before I was elected that, if elected, it would be my intention to move the office to New York. This was fine with them, so we started to look for space in Manhattan. As long as the National League was not there I didn't think it would be proper to be in the same building as the commissioner but at least we would be close. Chub loved San Francisco and fought all suggestions that his office move to join us. (Eventually, however, his league members acquiesced in centralization and Chub was pretty much dragged, kicking and screaming, to New York.)

Until we could find proper space, however, the American League office remained in Boston. I stayed at the Copley Plaza during the week and took the Eastern shuttle home on weekends. It was a very uncomfortable feeling for me to go into the Boston office and take over Joe's desk. But before I even arrived, he had moved all his things into a smaller office down the hall. I was very fond of Joe. He had helped me when I was a young general manager at Baltimore and we had worked together through his years as league president for whatever appeared to be best for the league—things like divisional play and the designated hitter, which had met with some objections in the American League but primarily required a fight with the National League. We had lunch together pretty regularly, either at "Joseph's" or

"Jacob Wirth's" (Joe's favorite) until it was time for me to go to spring training.

During those first few weeks, I also got better acquainted with the American League staff: Bob Holbrook, who had come to the league after covering baseball for the Boston *Herald* for many years; Don Marr, the comptroller, who had just come a year before from Ernst and Ernst; and Dick Butler the supervisor of umpires; plus the ladies in the office. I told them all that they would be welcome to remain on and transfer to New York with us. None of the women did but Bob, Don, and Dick all did so and remained valued employees throughout my years as president. I was blessed to have them. Bob handled the schedule, a tough assignment, and still assists with it in a consulting capacity from his home in Wellesley, Massachusetts. Don not only handled American League finances but along about 1980, with our approval, he started doing work for the commissioner as well. Today, he is the chief financial officer for all of baseball. Dick worked out of his home in Fort Worth and was an unsung hero in scouting and bringing up good young umpires and in helping reshape the staff. To augment these three, and to replace the people we were losing, I got Jeanne Collins, my Yankee secretary, to come with me and, of course, asked the Yankees to let Bob Fishel transfer to the league staff. Bob was my alter ego and I was overjoyed when he was able to join us in New York in June. We hired two young ladies in New York to complete our lineup and really hit the jackpot when we picked Phyllis Merhige and Tess Basta. They are both still with the American League, Phyllis, as publicity director, and Tess doing Bobby Brown's work. Jeanne Collins had to leave when she got married and had a baby but around the same time we added Stephanie Vardavos, who had just graduated from Yale near the top of her class. Stephanie went to Fordham Law School at night while working for us and now has a law degree and is part of the commissioner's legal department. I was also fortunate to inherit the services of Jim Garner as league counsel. The Cleveland firm of Baker, Hostetler, and Patterson has represented the American League for many, many years. Their experience and Jim's legal expertise were invaluable. More than that Jim, the two Bobs, Don, and Dick became, and still are, my close personal friends.

In spring training, I was based in our own condominium in Delray Beach, on Florida's east coast, convenient to five training camps. I had purchased the spot in May of 1974 and it has proven to be one of my more inspired moves. It was perfect for spring training and also available to me or my family as a getaway spot when weather or business got too oppressive. A month or so after spring training, we were able to move into our new offices in the Bankers Trust Building at 49th and Park. They were small but convenient and only five blocks from the commissioner.

The first challenge for me, as league president, was to conduct league meetings. Imagine a group that consisted at various times of Bill Veeck, Charlie Finley, Vernon Stouffer, Calvin Griffith, Gene Autry, Edward Bennett Williams, Jerry Hoffberger, Danny Kaye, Bob Short, George Steinbrenner, Hank Greenberg, and a few others whose names are less well known nationally, but at times could be even more of a problem in meetings. The meetings had pretty much gotten out of hand in Joe's latter years, primarily because some people simply enjoyed hearing themselves talk. At one of my first meetings, I produced a three-minute sand clock and instituted a rule whereby the chair would interrupt any speaker who had not finished when the sand ran out. After a few meetings, people got the idea and I was able to dispense with the clock. The other difficult problem was keeping everyone's attention focused on the subject under discussion. We had fifty or sixty men who had a lot in common and who had not seen each other in a while and I had to keep the meeting from becoming a social get-together. Sometimes, I felt like an eighth grade teacher admonishing the students to stop talking.

At an early meeting I also brought up the problem of our miserable showing in the All-Star game. In the last ten games, the American League had been victorious once. It was crazy. About all of the games had been close. Six of the nine losses had been by one run; four in extra innings. But something always happened; like Willie Mays stealing home or John Callison hitting an extra inning home run. Always something. It hurt the league's image, and if it hurt the league's image, it also hurt our teams, especially those in two-club cities. Besides, it was just damn unpleasant to lose. I said I hoped to have some recommendations to make to try to turn things around. Later I suggested the league designate one starter from each club (pitchers who were apt to be chosen for the All-Star staff) and the club then would not be permitted to pitch that pitcher on the Sunday preceding the All-Star game. We would name the pitchers early enough so that managers would have a chance to adapt their rotation so that the named pitcher's turn would not come up that Sunday. We would then be assured of having top starters for the game who had at least two days rest. Of course, the managers did not like it but I thought it made a lot of sense—plus it protected some very valuable arms. The clubs went along with me for a few years but, unfortunately, we still lost and the rule was eventually dropped. I got through my first year without too many problems and Charlie Finley's Oakland A's won the World Championship for our league. I stayed in Oakland and rode in their victory parade before returning to New York—and getting married again, the day after my 57th birthday.

I married Gwen Dayton. She had been Gwen Brandt from Columbus, Ohio—growing up there at about the same time I did. Our mothers had played bridge together but I had never met Gwen as she was three years younger than I and went to a different high school. During the war, when I was on the USS *Turner,* Jane had taken our two little boys and had gone to Columbus to stay with my mother. Gwen had married a year after she graduated from Smith and, when her husband went overseas, she also returned to Columbus to stay with her mother. Jane and Gwen met and became friends and when Jane died, I received a very nice note from Gwen. Later, after she was divorced, I met her when my brother Bill brought her to a Giants football game at Yankee Stadium. And in the spring of 1972 I ran into her in Florida. We had a lot in common. She was very bright, attractive, and also liked baseball. And I had learned I did not like living alone. I was very fortunate to find her.

We had some serious problems to cope with early in my administration. First, we were being sued by the city of Seattle, King County, and the State of Washington because we had moved the Pilots (or acquiesced in their move) out of Seattle. Ever since the National League had deserted Milwaukee, Bud Selig and Ed Fitzgerald, two top individuals and ideal representatives of that city, had attended every baseball meeting, plugging for a franchise for Milwaukee. I was sympathetic to their problem, possibly because as assistant to the commissioner in 1966 I had been a first-hand witness of the circumstances under which Milwaukee had lost its franchise. (While still with the Yankees, I had supported a move to get some games played in Milwaukee. The White Sox agreed to play games there [one with each team] and drew very well. Chicago fans resented it, however, and the White Sox gave it up.) When the Seattle Pilots went bankrupt, the Federal Court judge ordered us to accept the best offer received for the team. That offer came from Selig and Fitzgerald and involved moving the team to Milwaukee. Ordered by the court or not, we were immediately sued for fulfilling the directions of the court. The suit began in Seattle but was moved to Bellingham, Washington on the grounds that this would be a less biased venue. No place in the State of Washington provided an unbiased venue, particularly when the case was to be decided by a jury. Right, we firmly believed, was on our side. I learned to my distress, however, that it was possible to be convinced that you were right and still not be sure of victory under our judicial system. How could we possibly win a jury decision in the State of Washington? So we settled the suit and agreed to place an expansion team in Seattle by 1977. Knowing we were obligated to Seattle, we looked for a combination franchise that would provide the most reasonable expansion solution possible.

There were other franchise problems in baseball, and the commissioner appointed a joint league committee to seek the best overall solution for them. This committee recommended, as one alternative, two thirteen-team leagues with the odd team in each league to engage in limited interleague play. From the American League point of view, this seemed to make sense for baseball but, as often happened, the National League pursued a course of what made sense for the National League. In this instance, this was understandable. As a league they opposed interleague play. Why should they adopt interleague play just to help the American League pull its chestnuts out of the fire? Once the National League turned down a joint approach, we looked for the best solution for the American League. The best territory available was Toronto. The people there had originally been interested in obtaining a National League franchise because that provided a natural rivalry with Montreal. The National League had considered Toronto as a replacement franchise for both San Diego and San Francisco but new ownership kept both of those franchises in place. We had agreed to stand by and let the National League have Toronto if they had immediate plans for it, but by now Toronto was tired of being romanced and dropped by the National League. The National League asked the commissioner to place a moratorium on any expansion moves not contributing to a solution of the Washington and Seattle problems. The American League opposed any moratorium and the commissioner therefore did not impose one. By now, the American League was intent on securing the best territory available to pair with Seattle and with the authorization of our league I inaugurated talks with representatives from Toronto.

At this point, we were running counter to the wishes of Commissioner Kuhn. He had a different objective—a franchise for Washington. He felt baseball had given assurances to political figures in Washington that Washington would probably get the next available franchise. He knew Baltimore would not permit an American League franchise to move into Washington as it was within their territorial limits. So his efforts for Washington had to be wedded to the National League. And the best way to get the National League to admit Washington was also to give it Toronto. This was not acceptable to the American League or to me. Our league did not feel that it was a party to any promises to Washington. I hated to oppose Bowie but the issue was crucial for our league and I had the 100 percent backing of our members. Bowie did not give up easily (and later actually threatened to resign because of the lack of club support on this issue), but the

American League owners and Toronto held firm and the city became a member of the American League. It was possibly the best thing I ever did for the league. If Washington deserves a franchise it should stand on its own and not go in on another city's shirttails. Nor would it have been fair to keep Toronto out until the National League decided someday to expand. (Eleven years later they still have not expanded.) I will give Bowie credit for this. When Seattle and Toronto opened their first seasons the next spring, he and I were there together for their openers. We watched a night game in Seattle and flew across the continent to see a day game in the snow in Toronto the next afternoon. I will confess that I was really tired but when I looked at Bowie he appeared as fresh as if he had not missed one hour of sleep.

An incident that ultimately had far-reaching effects was the 1974 application of Jim "Catfish" Hunter for free agency by release from his Oakland contract. That contract provided that Hunter would receive a total sum of $50,000 to compensate him for insurance covering his farm in North Carolina. Hunter had a valid complaint as Finley was delinquent in making these payments. But Charlie did finally make all the payments and, at his request, I sat with Hunter and Finley to attest to this. Nevertheless, a formal grievance went forward and an arbitrator, Peter Seitz, ruled that Hunter should become a free agent. We were shocked by Seitz's decision. We agreed that Finley had been wrong and should be assessed some sort of penalty but we never anticipated that Hunter would be declared a free agent. This was a case in which the penalty hardly fit the crime. We now had our first instance of an outstanding player being available as a free agent and the eventual impact was revolutionary. This should have been a signal to us, loud and clear, not to hazard any more major decisions with Seitz. Unfortunately, the signal was not loud and clear enough for us, as the same arbitrator ultimately voided our reserve clause. The Hunter decision was the first step down that path, for when he was free to sign with the highest bidder, the owners knocked themselves out making what were, then, unbelievable offers. Several owners flew to Ahoskie, North Carolina in their private jets to put their money on the line. Once the Players' Association saw how owners reacted to the availability of a top player and how much money was at stake, it was only a matter of time before they were able to set up an arbitration to test the reserve clause for all players.

Despite the fact that his performance as commissioner had found favor with a large majority of the clubs, Bowie Kuhn was almost defeated for reelection in 1975. The problem was the very stiff requirements of an antiquated rule for the reelection of a commissioner. The requirement was that there be an affirmative vote of three quarters of the teams in each league. Reelection was scheduled for a meeting in Milwaukee at All-Star time. Jerry Hoffberger had been turned off by Kuhn's somewhat imperial style. In his early years as commissioner, Bowie took himself very seriously. He had not yet developed that ability to laugh a little at himself which came later. Of course, Jerry had a natural ally in Charlie Finley but they still needed two more votes. Steinbrenner was under suspension by Kuhn at that time because of his indictment stemming from political contributions and was not at the meeting. He had indicated publicly, however, that his suspension would not cause him to vote against Kuhn's reelection. Even if he did, that would still leave three quarters of the clubs. I had no idea that serious trouble was brewing. There was a surprise defection, however, in the person of Brad Corbett, the new owner of the Texas Rangers. Brad, too, had been turned off by Bowie's style and the plotters found him fertile ground. When four negative votes surfaced at the American League meeting, we managed to get the matter tabled until the following day. I had brought my wife, Gwen, to the game and the meetings. We had been married for less than a year and this was her first exposure to a baseball event and baseball people, but I had to leave her pretty much on her own, because I spent most of the next twenty hours trying to get those two votes turned around. Others were also active. When I finally went to bed both teams had indicated to me that they would change their vote. I hadn't been asleep more than an hour when the phone rang. It was Finley and Gene Autry. They were suggesting that I become commissioner. I am not sure how many similar calls they had made to others they considered potential candidates, but I did know that they had had a few drinks. I told them that we should reelect Bowie. And the next morning we were able to do just that.

The next problem we had to come to grips with was the issue of whether or not Kuhn had the right to stop Charlie Finley from selling the contracts of key players Vida Blue, Joe Rudi, and Rollie Fingers. The commissioner's position was that he was preventing an owner from undermining a franchise by selling off its top player assets. In his opinion, the moves were bad for baseball and could be stopped by him under the clause in the Major League Agreement that gave the commissioner the authority to take any action he deemed was "in the best interest of baseball." I was concerned about this ruling, as there was no existing baseball rule that prevented Oakland from assigning these contracts. The players were approaching the date that they could become free agents and Finley obviously would not be able to re-sign them. When Finley sued, however, and the issue had come before a judge in a Federal Court in Chicago, I could testify without reservation that I believed, right or wrong, the commissioner clearly had the *authority* to take the action he did. This was the judge's ruling in what was a landmark case for baseball. That decision reaffirms the commissioner's power to do anything he wishes providing he considers it to be "in the best interest of baseball" (anything, apparently as long as it does not conflict with player rights in areas covered by the Basic Agreement with the Players' Association—but that is another issue).

The American League Constitution lists the duties of the league president as follows: The president shall be the executive officer of the league and shall manage all of its affairs subject to the supervision of the Board of Directors. It also spells out the powers and responsibilities of the president. One of the additional "powers" conferred upon the league president was the handling of the transfer of ownership of a franchise. (During my presidency eleven of the fourteen franchises in the league changed majority ownership.) To assist me in this, I appointed a "Long Range Planning Committee" of John Fetzer of the Tigers, Ewing Kauffman of the Royals, Bud Selig of the Brewers—and to have someone with a general manager's background, Harry Dalton, then with the Angels. This committee was very helpful to me. I used it almost as one would a Board of Directors. (The League Board was not too useful as membership rotated annually and it only met at the annual meeting.) It was the Long Range Planning Committee that devised a so-called "60-40" rule" that has become official in both leagues and provides, in general, that an owner must have sixty percent of his financing in cash or the equivalent and that only forty percent of the funds required may be borrowed. This guideline was originally set in 1975 in the American League and was to apply only to new ownership. And the first person to run afoul of it—attempting to purchase the White Sox from John Allyn—was Bill Veeck. The league ruled he exceeded the debt limit and told him what would have to be done to pass muster. When Bill came back some months later, having done what he had been told to do, a few clubs still did not want to admit him. As a three-quarter majority was required, this threatened to block his approval. I argued that the league could not honorably refuse to approve now that he had done as instructed. I was having tough sailing but John Fetzer came to my aid and Bill was finally approved.

A few of the league president's responsibilities, enumerated in the Constitution, sound routine, but are actually fraught with discord. At one time, making the schedule was a pretty straightforward matter. There were only eight teams, all in the same division, none west of the Mississippi River, playing 154 games. Now the American League has fourteen teams, spread from coast to coast and in Canada, divided into two divisions, playing 162 games in not more than 178 days, and with a myriad of scheduling restrictions negotiated with the Players'

Union. (No night doubleheaders before day games; a day off required for travel on many trips; no split doubleheaders; a scheduled day off every twenty days; etc.) Moreover, there was a basic disagreement between the clubs as to the type of schedule desired. The Eastern teams wanted to play an unbalanced schedule, with more games against teams in their own division. This reduced travel for those teams and gave them more games with their traditional rivals. The Western teams (many of them expansion teams or in new areas) wanted a balanced schedule, with all teams playing all other teams an equal amount. This gave them more games with the established and better drawing Eastern teams. The American League schedule is basically balanced; the National League tends a little more toward a non-balanced format.

But the real bugaboo in making up the schedule stems from the fact that the clubs' overall costs have increased so much that it is mandatory that they get in as much revenue as possible. As both the average attendance and the per capita from the gate is higher today than in the past, it becomes paramount to play as many home dates as possible and to play them in that part of the season more favorable for drawing customers (June 1 to Labor Day). Strangely, the clubs seem to think that somehow they should be able to play most of their home schedule in that June-Labor Day period and should be able to play their better drawing opponents on the most attractive dates. We did everything we could think of to make sure we were doing the job of scheduling as efficiently as possible. We had the clubs advise us on which dates they preferred to be home and away. (Seattle didn't want to be home during the Water Festival; Cleveland wanted to be home July 4th, other clubs did not; Boston had to be home Patriot's Day; Toronto had to be home on Canadian holidays; Baltimore wanted to avoid a conflict with the Preakness; some clubs wanted to open at home, others did not, etc.) Moreover, teams sharing a city had to be away when their counterpart in the other league was home. We used computer experts to correlate the data. We had a management organization analyze the way we were doing the job to see if it had any suggestions (it did not). We used a committee of good baseball operators to work with us in putting the schedule together. Whatever we tried, some clubs still howled bloody murder, partly on the theory that the squeaky wheel gets the oil. My friends, Bud Selig and Gabe Paul, were the worst of the complainers. Bob Holbrook got the brunt of the criticism. At one schedule meeting that I could not attend because of a player negotiation meeting, some of the owners themselves attended by design (schedule meetings usually were attended only by the professionals) and jumped all over Bob Fishel. It was one of the few times that I was really mad at our people.

Equally troublesome was the matter of umpiring. Umpires are human and they do miss calls, though the percentage of correct calls is higher than we have any right to expect. When your team is losing, however, every close call that goes against you appears a bad call and "bad" calls (right or wrong) are hard to take with equanimity. And then situations develop between an umpire and a team, or a manager, or a player—Joe Brinkman with Kansas City, Kenny Kaiser and Eddie Murray, and Larry McCoy and Billy Martin were just a few examples. Sometimes umpires, as a group, develop a defensive way of thinking and it gets to be the rallying cry within the profession not to take any guff from anybody. To managers, coaches, and players this translates as an over-aggressive, chip-on-the-shoulder type of attitude. Although it has to happen in some instances, I didn't like to see people get thrown out of games—especially pitchers. I liked to see umpires walk away from trouble and not have "rabbit ears," picking up every little barb from the dugout. This was one of the many things Dick Butler and I talked to our umpires about, both in meetings with the entire staff and in smaller meetings with just the crew chiefs. I didn't make any friends with our umpires in trying to sell this approach. I realized that I was asking them to be a little more than human, but that is what a good umpire has to be—a little better than human.

The two major leagues finance an Umpire Development Program, designed to train and to promote young umpires up through the minor leagues, just as the clubs bring up young players through their farm systems. There are several umpire schools run by active (or former) major league umpires for people who want to become umpires. A limited number of the best graduates from these schools are chosen to go to a special camp run by the Umpire Development Program. A few of the best people from this camp are then signed to professional umpiring contracts at the lower minor league levels. The program is run by a former umpire and he is assisted by a staff of regional supervisors. Minor league umpires are scouted and graded by this staff and the better umpires are advanced to higher classification leagues. When they reach AA or Triple-A they are scouted by the two major leagues and may be selected by either major league and gradually worked into that league's umpiring staff. Dick Butler and his supervisors did this work for the American League while I was there and did an excellent job in picking talented young men. John Stevens and Nestor Chylak, two fine veteran umpires, assisted Dick most of my ten years with the league, but neither are alive today. (Today, Marty Springstead has taken Dick's place and Dick, Larry Napp, Jerry Neudecker, and Hank Soar serve as area supervisors.) We made many changes and, of the umpires on the American League staff when I took over, about fifty percent of them were gone when I left the league. I am surely prejudiced, but I think the American League has some very fine young umpires today. The key to a good crew, though, is the veteran crew chief, as he is the captain and sets the tone for his group.

It is definitely a shock to go from being a general manager of a team and trying to maintain a rational outlook about umpires to being the president of the league and worrying about umpire miscalls. Seldom it seems does an umpire blow a call to give a team an extra out and have the next man pop out to end the inning. It seems that when an umpire errs it often leads to the game-winning run. You knew which clubs you would hear from on every controversial call, which managers would go crazy on the field, and which owners would go crazy on the phone. Weaver and Martin easily led the managers in that regard, and Steinbrenner won going away among the owners. (Once George called me in New York from Tampa in the middle of the game to scream about a call. I knew the game wasn't being televised in Tampa and asked him how he knew the umpire had been wrong. He said he had been listening to Phil Rizzuto on the radio.) Steinbrenner also used to send tapes down to our office on a regular basis—tapes that were supposed to show umpire errors. In ninety percent of the cases the plays were so close you couldn't tell from the tape whether the umpire was right or wrong. This was true even after viewing it over and over on slow or stop motion. George was not alone however. Calvin Griffith could also get worked up, but he never called you. He saved it until he saw you and then recounted a whole series of questionable decisions. Buzzie Bavasi was known to call and on one occasion Gene Autry interrupted a discussion on the budget at a league meeting to complain about an umpire.

This is not to say there were not umpire decisions about which the clubs had a right to be upset. The day after opening day in Milwaukee one season (I had attended the opener but fortunately left the next morning), Don Money of the Brewers hit a grand-slam home run in the ninth to beat the Yankees—or so it seemed. Unfortunately, the umpire had called time-out just before the pitch. (I had had the same thing happen in my favor when a crucial Ted Kluszewski homer against Baltimore in the sixties was nullified.) And there were others. One of the most embarrassing umpiring incidents happened in Baltimore, and involved Earl Weaver and Bill Haller, an excellent umpire. Haller, without our knowledge, had agreed to be taped by a local radio station. Late in the game, they got into a long heated argument over a play. The words of both men were faithfully transcribed and later broadcast by the station. They sounded like two little kids arguing. I was embarrassed for them, for our league, and for the umpiring profession.

Other duties of the league president related to the game on the field and I regularly had decisions to make in this area. The league president is the final authority on playing rules and, as a result, rules on protests and forfeits and imposes discipline wherever and whenever necessary. We had many protests, many of them frivolous. Bill Veeck was always looking for some minor infraction, hoping that the outcome of the game would be reversed thereby. One protest claimed that the White Sox opponent had violated the rule requiring teams to be dressed in similar uniforms. The other team had acquired a new player who had just joined them and his name was not yet on the back of his uniform. (That one was rejected in a hurry.) It was my feeling that, whenever possible, games should be decided on the field and not by unimportant technicalities. I did not uphold many protests, though the one I did uphold—Kansas City's protest over the elimination of George Brett's home run—generated plenty of attention, notoriety, and controversy. (More about that later.) On the other hand, I did back the umpires in forfeiting three games. One was played at Comiskey Park in Chicago (several things that happened there created problems during my presidency) on what Bill Veeck billed as a "disco demolition night." There was disco music and the stands were jumping. The White Sox had given out records to fans as they entered and by the middle of the game fans were sailing them on to the field. It was actually dangerous. Nestor Chylak was chief of the umpiring crew and he stopped the game to give the Sox security people time to restore order. When the game started again, so did the sailing discs. Nestor stopped the game again and had the PA warn the fans of the danger of forfeiture. Veeck rushed to the umpire's dressing room and they got me on the phone. After listening to Bill, I then heard Nestor, and told him I would back him in whatever action he took. When the third attempt to play was no more successful, Nestor forfeited the game.

A similar problem occurred in Cleveland, when the Indians scheduled a "Beer Night." There was a full moon and too much beer and young fans got out of hand. When there was a scuffle between players during the game, fans poured onto the field and some actually threatened the visiting players. The Cleveland players then came to the visiting players' aid, and helped them get safely to their dugout. When order could not be restored, the umpires, quite properly, forfeited the game. Both of these forfeitures were the result of ill-advised promotions that resulted in stadium security breaking down. When that happens the safety of fans and players must take precedence over the game.

The third forfeit I had to uphold involved an Oriole game in Toronto in September of 1977 and my friend Earl Weaver. When rain started falling during the game, the ground crew covered the bull pens and put planks on the tarps to hold them down. Weaver objected that this constituted a hazard which could cause an accident to a player. An argument ensued and some changes were made, which still did not satisfy Earl. The game was stopped by rain, but when the rain stopped, Earl refused to bring his team back on the field unless the bull pen tarpaulins were arranged to his satisfaction. Marty Springstead (who had not yet succeeded Dick Butler as league supervisor of umpires) was the crew chief and he ordered the Orioles to take the field. When they did not do so within the time required in the rules, he forfeited the game. The Orioles protested. As I was due in Baltimore to attend ceremonies at a night game honoring Brooks Robinson, I agreed to hold a hearing on the afternoon of the game. Since the Orioles had been well behind when Earl ordered his team not to take the field, and because they had to catch a plane prior to midnight (which was fast approaching) to take them back to Baltimore or, as an alternative, make a long bus trip to Buffalo to get a plane, some people thought this was a factor in Earl's behavior. In any event, the umpires had ruled field conditions were safe. I had to take their judgment over Weaver's. I denied the protest. Of course, the Baltimore fans learned about the decision immediately and, as the game was important in the pennant race, they were livid.

Memorial Stadium was jammed for Brooks and as part of the ceremonies, I was to make a presentation to him. Chuck Thompson, the master of ceremonies on the field, knew there might be a problem. When he introduced me, he made a very flowery little speech about how much I had done for Baltimore while there, etc.—but it was of no use. When I stepped up to the microphone 55,000 people booed—and loudly. You should have 55,000 people boo you someday. It is, to say the least, an unusual experience. I made a couple of efforts to start but if anything the boos grew louder. I was standing there trying to decide whether to give up or just plow ahead, a la Spike Eckert at that dinner in Chicago. And then, running out onto the field from the dugout, came Earl Weaver. He ran right out to me, put his arm around me, and said into the microphone, "Don't boo this man"—and there was quiet. It was like the Red Sea parting and I made my little speech and my presentation to Brooks. That is the way it was with Earl; he would stand up for you one minute, battle you the next. He would go three months without being thrown out of the game, then get thrown out four times in one week. A season or two later, he pulled the same stunt again. He had an argument with an umpire during a spring training game in Fort Myers, Florida, took his team off the field in protest, and wouldn't let them come back out. This time I suspended him for three days and he thanked me publicly for getting him three days off in spring training. I don't know who led in suspensions and fines—Earl or Billy Martin—but it must have been very close. Martin's favorite trick was kicking dirt on the umpire. Weaver's was getting nose to nose in an argument, then bobbing his head so the bill of his cap banged the umpire in the face.

I had one unusual, as well as unfortunate, problem with Billy Martin. A young woman reporter for the *New York Times* came into the home clubhouse at Yankee Stadium hours before game time. Only a few players had reported at the time. The facts as to what happened are in dispute but the reporter left in tears and said she had been treated improperly by Martin, who she said had used obscene language in addressing her. Naturally, the *Times* reacted aggressively in backing up its reporter. The Baseball Writers Association also filed a protest. George Steinbrenner and Billy were not getting along too well at that time and George asked the league to investigate. I think his intention was, if the reporter's story was borne out, to get rid of Martin. I tried very hard to get the facts and interviewed everyone that was in the clubhouse, including, of course, Martin. Not surprisingly, none of those people said that they had heard or seen anything improper. When I tried to talk to the young lady, the *Times* would not let me do so. I learned later that this was the paper's policy but I am not sure I understand it. In any event, I could uncover nothing and reported so publicly and to George, who seemed genuinely pleased that that was the case.

As far as player discipline goes, we seldom had suspensions of more than two or three days, generally for bumping an umpire during an argument. You had to draw the line somewhere and we drew it to outlaw physical contact of any sort. If there was no physical contact but the argument was too long and the language unacceptable, the player was fined a nominal amount ($500 or less). That didn't seem to be an unreasonable fine when you consider the salary most of the players were getting, but the way some of them reacted you would have thought the league was bankrupting them. (I had one player bring his pregnant wife with him to a hearing to help plead his case.) Often, however, all the player wanted was a chance to complain to someone about what he considered unfair treatment and after talking to him, if I felt he was sincere, I sometimes reduced or cancelled the fine. Phyllis Merhige, who handled the umpire reports in our office, the TV tapes, the letters to the players, the minutes of the hearings and everything else having to do with player discipline, used to get irritated with me for not being tough enough. And I must admit that on one occasion when I scrubbed a player's fine when he told me it was the first time he had been ejected, she was able to produce records that showed I had been naive. It wasn't always the player who was fined. In a few cases I fined umpires but we did not publicize umpire fines because I thought it would make their job on the field even more difficult.

If the player, manager, or coach thought that he had been unfairly disciplined he could ask for a hearing. The hearing was held before the league president—the same person who had fined him—whose decision was final. Although this may not seem like a very fair judicial system, we had had enough experience with outside arbitrators to make us determined not to let incidents on the field involving umpires and games get out of the hands of someone who at least had had experience with what occurred on the field. Nor could we afford to have these things put on hold, waiting for an arbitrator to fit a hearing into his busy schedule and finally make a decision. Sometimes, a fight between teams was involved and it was important to be able to move quickly. The Players' Association used to complain about the league president being judge, jury, and appeal judge but I think they understood, and because the discipline was reasonable, they never fought too hard against the procedure.

The aspect of player discipline that was most difficult involved the so-called "brush back" pitch. Pitchers maintain that they must be able to pitch inside to move a hitter back off the plate and to prevent him from "digging in" in the batter's box. The hitters naturally complain if they feel they are being thrown at, particularly if the ball is up around their head. We had devised the best rule we could to stop this but no one was completely satisfied with it. The rule provided that if an umpire thought a pitcher was throwing at a hitter, he was to warn the pitcher and his manager and if it occurred again they were both to be ejected. Further, the rule provided that the other pitcher also be warned. Some people thought this unfair. However, we could not permit the second team to "get even" and maybe end up hitting someone in the head. It was hard to get some umpires to invoke the rule. They said "we're not mind readers," but it was my experience that when the rule was invoked at the very start of an altercation it generally proved effective, even though the pitchers complained that we were taking the bread out of their children's mouths. Otherwise, what often happened was that an infuriated hitter charged the mound; a fight broke out with the entire personnel of both teams eventually becoming involved; and ended up with someone getting hurt.

There were always issues pending in the league office that had to be contended with—different events or issues took center stage at different periods. Should female reporters be allowed in the clubhouses? Should the league be divided into three, instead of two, divisions?

Should the use of electronic equipment be permitted to communicate on the field? Should clubs be allowed to record the time between pitches on their scoreboards? Or the velocity of the pitch? Should the league schedule opening days and early season series in "warm weather" cities and in cities with domed stadiums? At one point my energies were directed at trying to mitigate a Red Sox crisis caused by a late tender of contracts to Carlton Fisk and Fred Lynn. At another, in trying to steer Jerry Hoffberger, whose family had decided to sell the Orioles, to Bill Jovanovich of Harcourt Brace and Jovanovich, who was interested in buying. At another point I was trying to ameliorate a charge brought by a Baltimore writer against Ralph Houk, then the Tiger manager, for striking him. (During our Yankee days, Ralph's wife Betty and I had always worried that Ralph's temper might result in his hitting an umpire, but he was always careful to control himself with umpires—not so with sports writers or night club singers.)

On one occasion I stuck my nose in where it did not belong—and to no avail. I knew Steinbrenner was upset with Martin and I also knew that Veeck was thinking about letting his manager, Bob Lemon, go. I also knew George liked Lemon and that Billy was the type that would appeal to Bill. I therefore suggested to both that they consider a trade of managers. For whatever it was worth, it would also be sure to generate a lot of publicity. Veeck was all for it but George, at least for the time being, changed his mind about Billy. Martin later found out about it and I think he was a little irritated with me. Although I was only trying to do something to help everybody, it wasn't really my proper role.

The league presidents regularly serve on countless committees; I think baseball must have more committees than any other existing organization of comparable size on our planet. And finally there was the issue of the reelection of the commissioner. At the annual meeting in Hollywood, Florida in December of 1981 a block of nine clubs surfaced that announced their opposition to the reelection of Kuhn. This was most serious because, as noted earlier, the Major League Agreement provided that a commissioner must have three-fourths of the vote of each league to be reelected. Much of our time and thought from that date forward for several months was directed toward finding a solution to that critical problem (see Chapter 12).

I saw many baseball games during my term as league president, making sure that I got to each city once or twice during the regular season. In addition to many regular season games with incredible plays and occurrences you had never seen before, the post-season games were generally packed with high drama. Carlton Fisk's home run at Fenway in the 1975 World Series against Cincinnati; Bucky Dent's home run in the Boston-Yankee one-game playoff to decide the American League East in 1976; Reggie Jackson's four consecutive World Series home runs on four consecutive at bats. (The last is probably the toughest feat to match that I have witnessed.) Of course, for me our one-sided All-Star win at Comiskey Park in 1983 ranks very high. I had been president for nine years and we had lost nine All-Star games. This game represented my last chance for a win and the sight of Fred Lynn's grand-slam home run, which started the runaway victory, is something I will never forget.

The league presidents are in charge of the League Championship Series (LCS); the commissioner the World Series. I had just a couple of worrisome problems to cope with in the League Championship Series. The first was a rain problem in the California-Milwaukee series in 1982. I insisted we play when some thought I was making a real error. But many things, such as pitching rotation and readiness for the World Series, can be affected by an LCS postponement. This time I was lucky and we got the game in under satisfactory playing conditions. Milwaukee was down 0–2 in that series, but came back to win three games to two. (Though the league president must be neutral—and I wasn't sorry to see Milwaukee win—I felt very sorry for Gene Autry and Gene Mauch.) The other problem I had with an LCS occurred at none other than Comiskey Park. There had been one of those "brush back" wars and a fight on the field. The White Sox pitcher, Richard Dotson, admitted throwing at an Oriole hitter and there were threats of retaliation. I talked to the two managers (Joe Altobelli and Tony LaRussa) individually before the next game and made it clear that there was not to be any more throwing near hitters or fighting on the field. The managers can control things if they really want to and they did. I fined Dotson and said a decision on a suspension (effective in 1984) would be made after the season. Tony LaRussa said, "If you are going to fine my pitcher, you should fine me too." I replied, "Fine Tony, you have just been fined $1,000."

In addition to the games, there were some very special events for which I feel privileged to have been on the scene. Al Kaline and Carl Yazstremski's 3,000th hits; ceremonies to retire the uniform numbers of Yaz, Joe Cronin, Ted Williams, Hank Greenberg, Charlie Gehringer, and many Yankees—including Mantle, Berra, Dickey, and Martin; a dinner to honor Joe Cronin in Boston, attended by a score of Hall of Famers; the opening of many new stadia—Anaheim, Atlanta, Kansas City, Toronto, Seattle, Minnesota (not to mention Jarry Park in Montreal and the refurbished Yankee Stadium). And the honor of presenting Hall of Fame rings to Mantle, Whitey Ford, Brooks Robinson, Luis Aparicio, and other great American Leaguers. I also enjoyed presenting the "Larry MacPhail Promotional Trophy" at the National Association banquet each year. Bill Veeck had originated this award and named it for my father and I was pleased that Johnny Johnson delegated the presenter's role to me each year. And finally, to balance the nice things, I got to testify in too many court cases—Finley v. Kuhn in Chicago; a tax case in Washington on behalf of Charlie Finley;* a Milwaukee tax case; Ted Turner against Bowie Kuhn in Atlanta; McGregor Cos. v. Rawlings Cos. with respect to the Official American League Baseball; Shapiro v. Kauffman in Kansas City; and more. That is the life of the league president—not the same as running a team, but at least closer to the game on the field than the commissioner's job, and certainly not boring. Each daily telephone call had the potential of a new experience.

So we came to 1983 and my last year in office, which I thought was also the last year of my baseball career. I had told the clubs in mid-summer that I did not wish to be reelected. I had served two five-year terms. I thought it was time I change my life a little bit. I like to change things every seven to ten years. I thought it was important to do something different; to get a fresh outlook. Even if it was retirement—for that would be the biggest challenge of all. I also felt that it would be good for the league to get someone younger, with a new approach to the job. The clubs were very gracious. They made it plain that I could stay on, with any term contract I wished, even if on a year-to-year basis; but my mind was made up. The job now was to finish out my final year and help the league find the right replacement for me.

---

*When I was on the witness stand in the Finley tax case, in the middle of the proceedings, someone entered the courtroom, went up to the judge and gave him a slip of paper. Everything came to a standstill. The judge read it and sent it over to me. It said "Call Bowie Kuhn." I couldn't believe it. I later told Mary, the commissioner's secretary, that I thought that if I was adrift on a raft, in the middle of the ocean, with sharks all around me, someone would still come swimming out and hand a note out of the water saying, "Call Bowie Kuhn."

11

Last of the Ninth—1983

There was still much ahead of me in 1983, my last year as league president. A look at my little datebook for the first three months of that year gives you a feel for the life of a league president. Here in part is what it showed:

1/4   complaints received from clubs re: shares they were receiving from New York Yankees' pay TV

1/4–7   problems with Players' Association and teams with regard to spring training reporting dates

1/12   Brooks Robinson and Juan Marichal elected to the Hall of Fame; attended press conference

1/17   finalized spring training dates

1/20   problems re: White Sox compensation selections (Jenkins and R. May)

1/21   schedule meeting

1/22   NYBBWA dinner, made presentation to George Bamberger

1/24   Hall of Fame Board meeting

1/26   Executive Council meeting (subjects: Pay Cable, sale of Pirates, Steinbrenner problems, report of Commissioner Search Committee, etc.)

1/26   pinch hit for Joe DiMaggio at Eunice Shriver Charity Event at Sotheby's

1/27   E.B. Williams talks to me about taking commissioner's job if Bowie cannot be reelected

1/31   Finance Resolution re: club operations, passed by clubs

2/1   black tie dinner for President David Fraser of Swarthmore College

2/3   talked to Mantle per request of Kuhn re: casino involvement

2/4   Players' Association files grievance re: Finance Resolution

2/8   letter to me from Steinbrenner blasting Finance Resolution

2/10   meeting re: Seven-Game League Championship Series

2/10   Cancer Society press conference re: Bill Kunkel film

2/16	Executive Council meeting (subjects: Steinbrenner and Finance Resolution, TV negotiations, Seven-Game LCS, Montreal-Toronto broadcast conflict, Commissioner's Search Committee, etc.)
2/16	dinner with umpire crew chiefs
2/17	meeting with umpire crew chiefs
2/17	Ewing Kauffman decides not to sell to Michael Shapiro
2/18	conferences with Restructuring Committee
2/18	problems re: improper players in spring training camps
2/18	meeting with Stephensons on 1984 schedule*
2/22	meeting with Hadden and Feeney on litany of subjects
2/23	meeting with Grebey and group re: Seven-Game LCS
2/24	angry call from Richie Phillips, umpire counsel
2/25	depart for spring training
3/1	gave long deposition in West Palm Beach regarding the ownership of broadcast rights to the games, resulting from a controversy with the Players' Association on this subject and resulting legal action
3/10	meeting with general managers and Player Relations Committee (PRC) staff in West Palm Beach
3/11	Caribbean Confederation party for Kuhn (St. Petersburg)
3/11	Governor of Florida's dinner for baseball
3/13	good meeting with Steinbrenner in Fort Lauderdale
3/15	my wife Gwen's appointment at University of Miami Eye Institute
3/17	meeting and dinner with Richie Phillips re: his grievances
3/19	dinner with Bob Howsam—discussion of Grebey problem
3/22	Gwen falls and breaks arm
3/23	Kuhn advises Grebey to resign
3/25	Executive Council conference call re: TV negotiations and Grebey
3/28	PRC Conference call re: Grebey
3/31	Galbreath, Selig, Feeney and I meet with Grebey

That's a slice of what goes on in a league president's life. The most pleasant thing about those three months were the exhibition games I was able to attend in Miami, Fort Lauderdale, Pompano Beach, West Palm Beach, Tampa, St. Petersburg, and Lakeland. (There is nothing quite like a baseball exhibition game in the spring.) And the openers that followed close behind in Boston, Detroit, Milwaukee, and Yankee Stadium. In Milwaukee, I got to present the 1982 American League pennant to the Brewers before the start of the game. And a few weeks

---

*Holly and Henry Stephenson are the American League computer schedule makers.

later I had the chance to take Mike Burke to a game as my guest at
Yankee Stadium. It was a nostalgic afternoon for both of us and I
know Mike was secretly thrilled both by how great the Stadium looked
and also by how many people—ticket-takers, ushers, ground crew,
and fans—greeted him warmly. It is hard for me to realize he is no
longer with us.

A major concern on club owners' minds early in 1983 was the question
of the leadership of the clubs' Player Relations Committee, the organization representing the twenty-six teams in their negotiations with the
Players' Association. The last agreement, reached in 1981 after much
bloodshed, would expire after the 1984 season and the majority of the
clubs, although concerned about the economics of the game, did not
want another long strike. They felt that part of the problem in the
previous negotiation had been the bitterness that grew up between
Ray Grebey, head of the PRC, and Marvin Miller. Grebey had been
hired in the late 1970s prior to the negotiation scheduled for 1980.
He came to baseball from General Electric and was an experienced
labor negotiator, very personable, and very bright. He had done a
good deal of excellent preparatory research during his first year on
the job and was the first to warn the teams about the economic path
they were following with their player contracts. I really don't know
why Ray should have had problems with club people, but he did. I
think part of it was his own lack of confidence and a concern for his
security. At times, he would seem almost paranoid. His feelings were
sometimes hurt when there was really no intention on anyone's part of
hurting them and he had a terrible habit of talking about people to
other people in the business.* Whatever the reasons, a growing group
of club owners were coming to the opinion that a change should be
made. When I found out about it, I did my very best to turn it off.
Chub Feeney helped me—as did Barry Rona, legal counsel to the
PRC. Bowie Kuhn had lost faith in Ray—the two men never really got
along from the start—and there were several members of the Executive Council who shared Bowie's feelings. Bowie took an informal

---

*I always felt remarks by Ray had caused a misunderstanding between Jim
Campbell of the Tigers and Harry Dalton, who by then was with Milwaukee. The
misunderstanding led to a break in the relationship between them. These were
two of my favorite people and I took it upon myself to try to be a peacemaker. I
talked to each man separately and then got them together and asked them to
shake hands. I was shocked when one of them knocked the proffered hand of
the other away and the second strode away from the scene. What I didn't know
was that the earlier talks I had with each individually had straightened things out
and that they put on the dramatic confrontation just to shake me up.

poll of the twenty-six clubs and found that more than half wanted to let Ray go. As a result, Bowie advised Ray to resign. Based on that poll, the Player Relations Committee made the decision to remove Ray and Danny Galbreath (owner-head of the PRC) and I got the unhappy assignment of advising him of the action. He was very bitter and though baseball was quite generous in its financial settlement with him, he remained bitter. Happily, he later made a good connection with Pan Am and was given responsibility for its labor program.

After the long and bitter player strike of 1981, Marvin Miller decided to retire (although it turned out to be a very active retirement). To replace him the players turned to the man who had served as federal mediator during those negotiations and had tried to find solutions for the problems and to avert a strike and later to get play resumed. This was Ken Moffitt, an attractive and personable man in his forties. The players who occupied key leadership positions during the negotiations had a lot of exposure to Moffitt and were impressed by him. From my own point of view, I did not think he had played a very effective role in settling the strike and was too friendly with the players' side. We were surprised (a few people shocked) when prior to the 1983 season he was elected to be their new director. Nevertheless, he was obviously more moderate than Marvin and the clubs viewed his election (and it was so represented by some of the players) as a gesture of peace. Some of the owners thought it important that the clubs accept the olive branch and select someone to represent them who was moderate and respected by the players. However with Ray gone, Chub, Barry, and I had a meeting with Moffitt in early April with respect to our request to the players that they go along with a best of seven (instead of best of five) League Championship Series. The answer, which was no—unless they received a portion of the TV money—was disappointing. Plus there were other indications that Moffitt might be having trouble with Don Fehr and Mark Belanger, top officers of the Players' Association, and with Miller.

The umpires' chief representative during the late seventies and eighties was Richie Phillips. Richie insisted on calling himself the umpires' legal counsel, not the director of their association. He loved publicity and was not above turning umpire negotiations into a twelfth-hour crisis, and in the process enjoying the resulting personal exposure in front of TV cameras. We had been through a tough strike with him in 1979 but there should not have been any major problems in 1983. He manufactured one over the treatment of a young umpire named Bill Emslie. The National League had been interested in Emslie, who was in the minors at the time of the umpire strike. During the preliminaries to the strike, Emslie played a very active role on the side of the union. When he wasn't brought up to the National League

in the years following the strike, Phillips claimed he was being per-
secuted for his strike activities. Actually, his abilities seemed to have
tapered off and he had too aggressive an attitude on the field. The
American League reports on him were not particularly good and the
National League had lost interest in him. Nevertheless, Richie made it
a cause celebre, probably because Emslie had close friends among the
major league umpires who were influential in the union.* The two
major leagues went along and subsidized Emslie's salary in the International League but would not be pressured into bringing him up to
the majors. The Umpires' Association filed an NLRB charge. This was
just one of the issues causing friction between us in 1983. In any
event, I made a trip to Philadelphia in May and had lunch with Richie
and told him he was using the wrong tactics. A little later in the
month, Chub and I met with Richie and umpire Paul Runge, who at
that time was president of their association. Paul is the son of Ed
Runge, a former American League umpire. He is an intelligent and
reasonable young man. Although we didn't get all the problems
solved, we at least got things back on the right track.

In 1982 there was a split in the partnership of the Red Sox and a battle
for control was brewing. Buddy LaRoux, who had once been the
trainer of the team, was one of three general partners and had a
group of limited partners that he had brought in with him. On the
other side were Jean Yawkey, Tom's widow, and Haywood Sullivan, as
general partners, and another group of limited partners. LaRoux's
group had engaged James St. Clair as its attorney. (St. Clair had been
President Nixon's attorney during the Watergate hearings.) At some
point during the season, he came to New York to see me to discuss the
problem. I had written both groups advising them that either party
gaining control would have to be approved by the American League.
St. Clair was not happy with this letter as he knew that the general
sympathies of baseball people were with Mrs. Yawkey and Sullivan.
Buddy's group were mostly people from outside Boston. His number
one backer was a coal miner from Kentucky, who knew and cared
nothing about baseball, and was only looking for a return on his
investment. St. Clair asked me if I would be willing to arbitrate the
dispute and I replied that I would if both sides desired it. I heard no
more about that idea and eventually the dispute went to court. When
called upon to testify in court in Boston, I reiterated my position that
any transfer of control would require the approval of the American
League. This pretty much blew Buddy's group out of the water. St.
Clair tried to ridicule me (one Boston writer said he played with me

---

*In 1988, Emslie was named traveling secretary of the Yankees.

like a cat with a mouse). In any event, I think I got the important point of required league approval across and the Yawkey group eventually won the court case.

At that point in time it seemed that the Yankees, as an organization, could not stay out of controversy for any significant period of time. I had had a good meeting with George Steinbrenner during spring training. I had gone to a game in Fort Lauderdale; met with him in his office-trailer before the game and sat with him in his roof box during the game. It was all very friendly and I thought I had made some progress with George. My message had been that he could and should help provide constructive leadership for the league and for the game. I also stressed that the Yankees, as a well respected organization, should do the same and he was the one who set the tone for the club. He was certainly bright enough and forceful enough to fill that role. The season wasn't even under way, however, before George had questioned the integrity of the National League umpires during an exhibition game and was hardly under way before Billy Martin had called an umpire a liar. George's act was Kuhn's problem as it occurred during an interleague exhibition game. Billy's act was my problem. Both were fined but Billy was lucky. Bowie fined George $50,000. Billy's fine was probably $\frac{1}{100}$ of that amount. I had another meeting with George but that was to look at the Yankee pay TV contracts and verify that their payments to the other teams were correct (which they were) and we only touched on their umpiring transgressions. But Billy was right back at it before the month of April was over, this time kicking dirt on an umpire. For this I suspended him for three games. In May it was a squabble with Henry Hecht of the *New York Post,* whom he ejected from his office in the clubhouse. I required an apology and reinstatement of his clubhouse visitation rights. Then George was off again, this time publicly calling one of our young umpires, who had worked during the umpire strike, a scab. By then I had had it with the Yankees and I suspended Steinbrenner for seven days. To my knowledge it is the only time a league president has ever suspended an owner. I know the effect was largely symbolic, but it represented the displeasure of the league office and the other clubs over the Yankee actions, and at least re-sulted in more circumspect behavior for a couple of months. In August Billy erupted again—this time against Bill Kunkel—and phys-ical contact was involved. Once again I suspended him, this time for a week, and this time he appealed necessitating a hearing.

The hearing was held in the American League office and in addition to Billy and myself (plus Dick Butler and Bob Fishel) there were seven others present, all lawyers. The Yankees had three lawyers there including Roy Cohn. Billy had his personal representative,

Eddie Sapir, a judge from Louisiana, in attendance. Richie Phillips was on hand to represent the Umpires' Association. Don Fehr, legal counsel for the Players' Association, sat in. (Why I am not sure—maybe just to watch the three ring circus.) And I had Jim Garner, American League counsel, with me. The proceedings lasted for more than three hours and we heard everything from constitutional rights to law-suits. I would have liked to have given them an immediate decision, then and there, upholding the suspension, but I restrained myself until I had received and reviewed the testimony from the court reporter. After going through all this I had to get up early the morning after the hearing to fly to Chicago in order to testify *for* the Yankees in a grievance hearing brought by Rick Reuschel, alleging that he was being improperly carried on the Disabled List.

I was having personal problems of my own that spring. My wife was having a tough year—cataract implants, a broken arm, and general health problems. As for myself I had grown aware of a strange feeling in my head which came and went. It wasn't pain, more of a feeling of fullness, but when it started occurring more often it began to worry me. Just about that time, Bowie called me to say that Danny Galbreath was in town and asked if the three of us could have lunch together. I should have foreseen what was coming, but I didn't. They asked me to take Ray Grebey's place as head of the Player Relations Committee. It was the last job that I thought anyone would think me qualified for. I had no formal labor experience. I was not a lawyer. I was not the world's toughest negotiator. I had planned to retire and this job unquestionably meant a couple of years of real turmoil. Plus I was worried about my wife's health and my own. I did my best to turn them off but they were dogged in their approach. I finally said I would think about it and write them a letter. My follow-up letter asked them to please try to get someone else—but that if they honestly could not get someone satisfactory by the end of the season I would talk to them again.

Before the month ended the PRC (six owner representatives and the two league presidents) met in New York and naturally Grebey's replacement was the key issue on the agenda. At this meeting they all put pressure on me—Bob Howsam, Joe Burke, Eddie Chiles, Bud Selig, and Danny. They came down on me pretty hard. The importance of the job at this time for baseball; I was the only one who could do it; etc. I told them to give me ten days to consider it. I said that, knowing that ten days would cover an upcoming medical exam and CAT scan on my head. My doctor had told me my problem could simply be the effects of too much caffeine. That seemed too simple and too good to be true. But the CAT scan bore him out; there were no serious problems. I told Gwen what I had been asked to do. Actually I asked for her concurrence for my taking the job would have a major impact on her life as well as mine. She was great about it. I then wrote Danny Galbreath saying I would accept to serve only until the negotiations were completed, but on one condition—that I be requested to do so by all twenty-six teams. The negotiations had been a shambles in 1981 and the clubs had not supported the PRC. I wanted no part of that and thought that if each club played a part in my taking the job, I would be in a better position to exact their support. Also I thought that if any opposition to my selection surfaced, it would be a graceful way out for me. On the other hand, if all twenty-six teams thought it was important that I do this, then I could hardly refuse. Baseball had been too good to three generations of MacPhails* not to try to help when called upon. Miraculously, all twenty-six teams (including the Yankees) went on record asking me to accept the assignment. Although I would continue as league president through 1983, I was to commence my PRC duties immediately as well. This was not as burdensome as it might sound for Barry Rona and his staff would handle the routine work of the office.

I had a friendly call from Ken Moffitt and we started meeting informally. We were having a drink together when he brought up the drug problem. I had just been through an FBI drug seminar and it was also much on my mind. It was quickly apparent that he was very concerned about the possibility of drug use in baseball. After a couple of more meetings, we began to think about attacking the problem in unison, a joint drug program of clubs and the Players' Association. In August we had a meeting with Bowie and other top people from both sides. On September 1st we agreed to try to put a program together and to submit it to both players and clubs for ratification. I was enthused. This was a problem that had to be met head on and a unified approach was obviously what was needed. I also felt that if we could successfully work together on drugs, it would do much toward constructing a better overall relationship between the parties and help in the coming negotiations. The challenge was to work out a program that would be acceptable to both sides. We went right at it. Roy Eisenhardt of the A's and John McHale of the Expos, two of the best executives in baseball, agreed to join Barry and me in representing our side. Ken had Don Fehr and Mark Belanger, plus two attorneys from Washington that he had added to their staff. It was quickly apparent that there would be stumbling blocks and that both sides

---

*Plus a fourth generation—my grandchildren, Kathy and Lee IV, have each worked for the Orioles in an intern position.

would have a tough job selling any compromise to their own people. But where there is a will there is a way.

In July I had to take my wife, Gwen, to Florida to the Bascom-Palmer Institute at the University of Miami for an eye operation. I had just come back from the hospital when my son Allen called me from New York to find out how things were going. Before he rang off he said, "I think you ought to know that George Brett hit a home run with two outs in the ninth in the game today to put the Royals ahead, but that the umpire threw out the home run and called Brett out for having too much pine tar on his bat." I knew right then that we had a hot potato on our hands. That was July 24th. I was back in New York on the 26th and found the media had really zeroed in on the story. I also found that an expected protest from the Royals had been filed and was on my desk. I listened to both sides. I talked to Steinbrenner in Tampa and suggested that the Yankees file anything they might wish me to consider before I ruled on the Kansas City protest. I talked to Dick Butler and Bill Haller, our umpire supervisors. I talked to some members of the Rules Committee to be sure I understood the intent of the committee when the rule was last amended. And, of course, I studied the rule itself and all regulations and precedents that related to it. I then sat up at home until about 3 a.m. writing a draft of my decision. It was not a hard decision for me to make for, in my opinion, the rule, the intent of the rule, and past precedents clearly indicated the umpires had erred. (I felt bad for the umpires for the rule was not well written and is confusing.) Just as important, as far as I was concerned, was that my instincts told me that it simply was not right to erase the home run. Pine tar did not aid in propelling that ball out of the ballpark. George Brett did it and it would be wrong not to recognize it and to take a possible victory away from Kansas City. It was a case again of trying to see that games were decided on the field and not by technicalities in the rules. My decision reinstated the home run and made the game a suspended game with two out in the top of the ninth and Kansas City leading 5–4. The teams would have to play four more outs to finalize the game. The next day, I polished up the draft of the decision and released it to the clubs and the press that afternoon.

I was amazed at the size of the turnout at the press conference and apparently some members of the press were amazed at my decision. I was aware that, whatever I did, many people were going to be very unhappy. The New York press was mixed; the out-of-town papers generally supportive. Some Yankee fans were livid. I felt sorry for the poor people in our office who took their calls and were subjected to a lot of irate and obscene language. Steinbrenner was off the wall and told the press that I might have to move from New York City to Missouri. In any event, I was satisfied I had made the proper decision and I can report today that three New York law schools made the play and decision a study project in their classes and all agreed with my findings. But if I thought that the pine tar matter was all behind me, I had an unhappy surprise ahead (see Chapter 12).

Many other events occurred during the course of 1983, my last American League year—some fun, some not fun, some just the normal course of business. In April we had a little farewell party for our office at 280 Park Avenue. We had been in it for nine years and were sad to leave it. Bob Holbrook came down from Boston, Dick Butler came up from Texas, Jeanne Collins (now Mrs. Ron Bill) was there. The move marked the end of an era for our people. In May I spent an afternoon in Washington where the president was on hand to honor Amateur Baseball. They played a Little League baseball game on the White House lawn and the Marine band played "Take Me Out To The Ballgame" from the balcony. That was one of the fun things. I also had an enjoyable lunch with Bowie and Luisa Kuhn and Chub Feeney at the Japanese Consulate, when the Japanese Baseball Commissioner was in New York. And Governor Celeste of Ohio sent a plane for Bowie and me and flew us to Columbus, where we had lunch at the Governor's Mansion in Bexley. Mayor Voinovich and the head of the Cleveland City Council were also there and we discussed the need for a new baseball stadium in Cleveland and ways to make sure that the team would not move. In a similar vein, I had a visit from some Minneapolis businessmen. Calvin Griffith had received an offer for the Twins from a group in Tampa and they were concerned. I later made a trip to Minneapolis and met with a civic group that was determined to try to keep the team there. Carl Pohlad was among them and it was he who later bought the team. Sadly, that ended the long period when it was owned by the Griffith family but it made certain that the Twins would remain in Minnesota. Other club transfers were taking place. Ewing Kauffman sold forty-nine percent of the Royals to Avron Fogelman and John Fetzer sold the Tigers to Tom Monahan. While Fogelman and Monahan were fine new owners it made me unhappy to see John and Ewing beginning to move out of the picture and it underscored the fact that my time and my era were coming to a close. Unhappily, my last year was also marked by little progress in getting Bowie Kuhn reelected.

Much of the year was spent grappling with the structure of the office of commissioner, and with who would occupy it. (See Chapter 12.) Although most of us were most anxious to keep Bowie in office, a

Restructuring Committee and a Commissioner Search Committee were busy throughout the year and I was in regular touch with both. Bud Selig, chairman of the latter, asked me if I would contact Bart Giamatti, president of Yale, for him. The committee was interested in speaking with him. I had gotten acquainted with Bart when, on his election as president of Yale, he had told everyone that he was surprised; that all he had ever wanted to be president of was the American Baseball League (he was a Red Sox fan). When I read this, I jokingly wrote him offering to trade jobs and received a humorous reply. That led to a lunch in New York with Chub Feeney and myself and we both liked him and enjoyed his company. Another year-long controversy was the manner of sharing the new network TV revenue. The National League (twelve teams) wanted to split it evenly between the two leagues. The American League (fourteen teams) wanted to share it equally between the twenty-six teams. When the leagues (the league presidents plus a committee on each side) could not resolve the matter* we finally referred it to the commissioner for a decision. As we all anticipated, he pretty much split the difference.

As the end of my term as league president neared, the New York baseball writers had a little luncheon for me at Gallagher's Restaurant in Manhattan. It was an unusual and thoughtful thing for them to do. Many of them were long-time associates and friends and it meant a great deal to me. It made me realize how fairly the media had treated me, not only in New York but elsewhere throughout my career. I may have been criticized on occasion, but I don't think it was ever mean or unfair.

My final responsibility to the league was to help it find a good replacement for me as president. Some of the people I thought would be good were not interested. They did not want to leave their clubs and the competitiveness of the game on the field. Finally, however, we were very fortunate in getting Bobby Brown to accept the position. Bobby had been a Yankee third baseman. Actually, my father had signed him, while he was attending Tulane Medical School, to his first professional contract. Bobby had been with the Yankees while I was there in the fifties so I knew him and respected him. After his baseball career, he became an outstanding heart specialist in Fort Worth, Texas. He had gone back into baseball in an executive capacity when Brad Corbett bought the Texas Rangers, to serve as president of the

---

*On-field competition between the leagues was friendly but always intense. Off the field, however, the two leagues worked very well together and disputes were rare. Chub and I were friends, and now that centralization of the offices had been achieved, their fine staff of Phyllis Collins, Katy Feeney, and others worked very closely with our American League people.

club, but after a year had returned to his medical practice. He, too, was looking to change his life and anxious to trade the pressures of critical heart problems for lesser pressures of a more pleasant kind. The Commissioner Search Committee, in seeking a successor to Bowie Kuhn, had interviewed Bobby and its members were impressed with him. I made a trip to Fort Worth toward the end of the year and talked to Bobby and his wife Sara and we had our man. It was a solid choice. With Bobby in charge of the American League, I could now focus all my energies on my new assignment.

Although Bobby would not actually be able to physically report for duty until some time after the new year and, as a result, I would still look after things in the league office for a while, December 31, 1983—New Year's Eve Day—was my last official day as American League president. It was late in the afternoon of that day when my secretary said there was a call for me from Mr. Steinbrenner in Florida. A sudden thought flashed through my mind that George might be calling to say, "Look, we've had our disagreements and I don't agree with some of the things you have done, but I just wanted to call and say let's let bygones be bygones and I want to wish you a happy new year and good luck in your new job." I don't remember exactly what he did say but that was not the tone of the message. The message was that although he would have to maintain business relations with me in my new assignment, he preferred not to have any social contact with me, and he would appreciate my not coming to the stadium except on business. I simply said, "Fine, George, if that is the way you want it." But I was disappointed. We had had a pretty good relationship most of the time and I didn't like to end the year and my time with the league on a down note. Despite all the problems we had had, I appreciated his plusses—his generosity to educational institutions and charities and his loyalty to former employees. And I understood his intense desire to win. But what will be, will be.

12

Bad Hops—Nine of Them

Baseball can be a strange game. A batter can hit a ball 420 feet to center field and it is an out. Or he can hit a scorching line drive right at the third baseman for an out. He can also hit a little pop fly that falls between the first baseman, second baseman, and right fielder for a hit. Balls can be lost in the sun, seeing eye ground balls can somehow just get through the infield for a hit. Or what should have been an out can take a bad hop! Nothing is more exasperating to the defense than a bad hop. Artificial turf is supposed to reduce the chance of bad hops but balls still hit seams on the edge of turf and dirt or bounce high in the air over infielders' or outfielders' heads. (When I was president of the American League, it seemed the National League was often getting those artificial turf, high bounding hits against us in the World Series or All-Star Games.) What can you do about a bad hop—an ordinary bad hop on a grass and dirt infield, not one of those that occur on artificial turf? A very quick and adept infielder can sometimes adjust and field it cleanly. That is the difference between a normal player and a very gifted one with quick hands. But sometimes even the best of players can only knock the ball down and keep it from rolling down the foul line or to the outfield for a double. Sometimes that scratch hit hurts, but these are the breaks of the game; like a bad call from the umpire or a rainout when you have a four-run lead in the third.

Some of the things that have happened during my career I put in the category of "bad hops." Some of them affected me or my job greatly, others had an impact on baseball itself. Some of them were tough to take at the time but, once past, were easily forgotten. Others you simply did not get over, though there was no recourse to be had. They were part of the game—an unfortunate part, but part of the game. Following are nine "bad hops" that occurred during my nine innings, listed chronologically after 1974. There were others, but for reasons of time and space I have confined my list to those that occurred after I became league president. They range from those causing discomfort and distress at the time to others causing lasting regret.

1976. The first "bad hop," which was monumental (it could be compared to a double bad hop, the first over an infielder's head and a second over an outfielder's for a home run inside the park), was the loss of baseball's Reserve System. As I have noted, the system as it existed was actually too restrictive of player movement; it was too much in the club's favor. It had been legally protected by a Supreme Court ruling of Justice Oliver Wendell Holmes' in 1921; reiterated by the Court thirty-one years later in the Toolson case; and again in the Curt Flood case as recently as 1972. The Players' Association, once it was directed by Marvin Miller, was constantly designing attacks upon it. They had tried negotiations; they had tried the courts; now they tried the Grievance Procedure—agreed to by the clubs and the association in their 1970 Basic Agreement. Although it had been understood that the Basic Agreement did not cover the matter of free agency, nevertheless an arbitrator ultimately ruled that the matter could be decided by arbitration.

The Uniform Players Contract contains a clause giving the club the option to renew a contract, if by March 11th the player has not signed for the ensuing year. When the contract was renewed it contained the same option clause for the following year and thus in effect the contract was perpetual. The Players' Association took the position that a contract could be renewed only once and, when renewed, it did not continue the option clause. They then got two players, unsigned but renewed for 1975, to contest the renewals of their contracts for 1976. The players were Andy Messersmith of the Dodgers and Dave McNally—formerly of the Orioles, more recently with Montreal, but then retiring. A grievance was filed in their behalf and taken to Peter Seitz, the permanent arbitrator, who had recently declared Catfish Hunter a free agent from Oakland. The clubs maintained the Grievance Procedure did not cover the Reserve System and that the arbitrator lacked jurisdiction to rule and went to the Federal Court in Kansas City to establish this. Judge John Oliver instructed them to go forward with the arbitration but, if not satisfied with the result, to come back to him. Not a very encouraging ruling.

The PRC (as league president I was one of its members) now wrestled with the question of whether to proceed with the arbitration before Peter Seitz or to dismiss him, as was the right of either party, and have the matter arbitrated by a new arbitrator. The arguments for firing Seitz were his decision in the Hunter case and a general feeling that he was pro labor. The arguments for retaining him were as follows: (a) the facts of the case were strongly in the clubs' favor and firing Seitz would worsen the relations with the players and damage the clubs' image unnecessarily; (b) having ruled against us on Hunter, Seitz might be less inclined to rule against us in Messersmith; and (c) Seitz's record as the arbitrator for the National Basketball Association had been good and, if he was replaced, one never knew who one would get in the grab bag-type selection of a replacement. (The American Arbitration Association would provide a list of approximately nine names and the PRC and Players' Association would strike names alternately until one remained.) I must confess I leaned toward the arguments for retaining Seitz. Also, as a relatively new member of the PRC and because of my limited experience in this area, I was inclined to follow the lead of John Gaherin, our PRC director, and Ed Fitzgerald, owner-chairman of the PRC. Bowie Kuhn sat in on the meeting and said little but did caution about retaining Seitz if we had any misgivings. When the vote was taken (three club representatives from each league and the two league presidents), the vote was 7–1 for retaining Seitz—the one negative vote was cast by John McHale of Montreal. Bowie now stated he thought we had made a mistake and asked us to reconsider. After much more discussion a new vote was taken and the vote was still 7–1. In retrospect this was a grievous error. Seitz heard the testimony—including Bowie's (and mine)—and then suggested the matter would be better settled by negotiation between the parties than by arbitration. So we in the PRC had another chance, but the thought of negotiating with Miller with Seitz standing in the wings was not appealing to most of our members. Nor did we think that in a relatively short time frame we could produce an agreement acceptable to both parties. I think I would have given it a try but I don't remember arguing the issue very strongly. Ed Fitzgerald and most of the committee members were strongly opposed. So things went forward and Peter Seitz issued his decision completely abolishing the Reserve System. The option clause in major league contracts was to be good for one year only. The PRC returned to Judge Oliver to no avail and then appealed to the Federal Appeals Court, losing there in a close 2–1 call. This was a "bad hop" of major dimensions.

Fortunately, at this time we also had to negotiate a new Basic Agreement for the 1976 season and thereafter. The PRC now took a strong position (or at least strong in view of having lost the arbitration) holding that a satisfactory compromise on the reserve issue must be a sine qua non for a new Basic Agreement. Although there were many matters to be covered in negotiations for the new agreement the Reserve System clearly became the most important. We held that the clubs were spending large amounts on player development—to the player's benefit. We also held that something must be done to maintain competitive balance, otherwise the rich clubs would simply outbid the poorer ones. We proposed a reentry draft for players becoming free agents with selections being made in inverse order of the clubs' finish in the preceding pennant race and with only a limited number of clubs eligible to bid on each player. We also proposed that there be compensation to a club losing a player and that once a player had been able to elect free agency he should not be able to do so again for several years. (This was in response to the Players' Association's original argument that players should at least have the right to sample free agency *once* in their career.) This was known under the term "repeat rights." Those were our demands and we refused to open the spring training camps, stating that they would be opened only when there was satisfactory progress toward constructing a new Reserve System. In fairness, the Players' Association adopted a moderate stance. They recognized that there was logic in some of our arguments; plus they wanted the camps opened, the season started, and free agency established for the future. There were a score of other issues but the key one related to the clubs' position on free agency, to wit: (1) a period of club control before free agency; (2) compensation for players lost; (3) a reentry draft; (4) a period before the player could then elect free agency again.

John Gaherin was a very skilled labor negotiator, but he disliked speaking to the press. In our negotiations, there were always scores of media people waiting outside each meeting room door expecting (and deserving) to be updated. To take the load off John, the PRC asked Chub Feeney and me—as league presidents—to take over this function and we used to handle it together. Chub always accused me, however, of giving him the short end of this assignment. Once in St. Petersburg (he regularly reminded me) I had monopolized the mike for my ten minutes and then turned it over to him for equal time. However, right at that moment, one of our PR people came in the room and started handing out the prepared press release. There was a stampede by the writers to get it; then a rush to the telephones; and Chub was left standing at the microphone in an empty room. On another occasion, in Philadelphia (he also regularly reminded me), I grabbed the mike and made all the routine announcements. Then when a writer asked, "What is the commissioner's role in all of this?"— the favorite and toughest topic of the day—I said, "I'll let Chub answer that question," and handed him the mike.

We recognized that we must open the training camps in time to provide at least the minimum workout period before the scheduled start of the season. It was not our plan to delay the start of the season. The strategy, therefore, was to use the closing of the spring training camps to gain as much leverage as possible, knowing that ultimately the camps would have to be opened. The Players' Association recognized this but at the same time was getting pressure from players who wanted to play and who had some sympathy for the club position. It acceded to all our major points in principle but bargained hard on the exact terms of each. It would not consider a ten-year period prior to free agency, but wanted something closer to four or five years. In addition, from a political point of view, the association had to give all current players an immediate one-time shot at free agency. It would not consider a professional player as compensation to a club losing a player. It accepted the theory of "repeat rights" but tied the number of years to the length of the original waiting period. All was close to resolution with the two sides fighting the last battle over whether the waiting period was to be seven or six years.

At that juncture, Commissioner Kuhn ordered the camps opened. There was consternation and some bitterness in the PRC ranks as the move came as a complete surprise to most of us and few, if any of us, were notified before the move was announced publicly. There were some people on the PRC who believed (and still do) that if the commissioner had not opened the camps we would have been able to achieve a seven-year eligibility period. I did not (and do not) share that view. Most of our committee felt that the commissioner had yielded to pressure from a few influential owners, such as Walter O'Malley. Years later, the commissioner stated that he never would have opened the camps if John Gaherin, the director of the PRC, had not concurred. Kuhn's book *Hardball: The Education Of A Baseball Commissioner,* recounts this fact. It is unfortunate that many people blamed him for a long time, perhaps without cause, although Gaherin has never agreed that he concurred. When it was all over, however, we had come out with what appeared to be a fair and reasonable Reserve System. It has not worked as it should have but much of the blame for this must rest with the owners themselves. Even granting that the desire and public pressure to win puts owners in a very difficult position, the lack of self-discipline and financial responsibility in dealing with free agency and its ramifications has been disastrous for the game.

1979. The second bad hop was an umpire strike. In 1979, Richie Phillips and the Umpires' Association went all out to force the leagues to increase umpire salaries. Up to this time, the leagues had negotiated salaries individually with each umpire, within limits determined by the umpire's years of experience. The Umpires' Association actually had no right to take any concerted action at this time as their agreement with the leagues had another year to run. Nevertheless, Phillips simply advised each umpire to "act individually" in refusing to sign his contract. Both Chub Feeney and I regarded this as completely irresponsible. We were willing to negotiate a new agreement to commence when the old one expired. We were not willing to be unfairly (and we believed illegally) pressured into negotiating a new one prematurely. The stalemate ended in a Philadelphia Court before Judge Joseph McGlynn. It was a bizarre trial. Every umpire who testified was described by the union as "one of the five best umpires in baseball." The judge finally said, "We will now hear testimony from the 19th of the five best umpires in baseball." We were also treated to the spectacle of Richie Phillips on the witness stand. He was lamenting the case of umpire Bruce Froemming, who had earlier testified that, although he lived in Milwaukee, he could not afford to send his son to Marquette, a local private college. Richie literally managed to produce tears and when told he could step down shuffled off sobbing and wiping his eyes, but "the drama" turned to comedy when he tried to go out the wrong door and ended up in a broom closet.

When he ruled, Judge McGlynn in effect said the leagues were right and the union could not legally strike but one could not prevent a man from individually withholding his services. Not unexpectedly, therefore, the umpires all "individually withheld their services." Not unexpectedly, we refused to give in. We recruited the best amateur umpires we could find in each area to work our games. These men were well qualified but we needed people with professional experience to serve as crew chiefs for each crew. We therefore invited the best young umpires in the minor leagues to work in the majors. Each one would head up an amateur crew. We needed seven in the American League and six in the National. We promised them that if their work justified it they would be maintained on major league contract when the strike was over, with our amateur umpires and the young professional crew chiefs officiating. There were no serious problems. Actually, there were fewer fracases over umpire calls, probably because the players and managers were more tolerant than they normally would be. We were concerned, however, that other unions— electricians, ground crew, etc.—would strike in sympathy, but Phillips was careful not to invite this. He knew that if the games were stopped and the clubs suffered serious economic losses, given the questionable legality of the strike, he could be responsible economically.

The umpires went on the picket lines and the union distributed cartoons of "MacFeeney and MacFailure" in caricature. There was some public sympathy for the umpires but the only support they got from the Players' Association was verbal. Finally, outside pressures brought both sides to the bargaining table and a reasonable deal was concluded. The individual umpires actually lost money. With one exception, the clubs had supported Chub and me very well. The exception was George Steinbrenner, who at that time was a personal friend of Phillips and who also might have figured that he was gaining some "brownie points" with the umpires themselves. The real "bad hop" of the entire affair was the impact of the strike upon the young umpires that worked at the leagues' request. It was natural that there should have been some feelings against them, even though legally they were not scabs. The treatment accorded them, however, was scandalous and continued year after year. It abated more quickly in the American League than in the National, but in both leagues the treatment was stupid and inhuman.

1979. The third bad hop was a Comiskey Park field that was unplayable. On the evening of August 24, I got a call from an enraged Bill Veeck. The umpires had just called off their game against the Orioles at Comiskey Park because they said the field was unplayable. Chicago had had a lot of rain and the Comiskey Park drainage system was poor. Veeck had been promising to do something about it each year, had tried, but had not solved the problem. (He blamed it on the city, saying water backed up from city drainage.) A concert or some event had recently been held at the park while the team was on the road which tore up the field. Much of the outfield had been resodded and the sod had not taken hold. The umpires were warning that tomorrow's game might also have to be called off. Bill wanted me to fly out there, see the field myself, and talk to the umpires. I told him that I would be on an early morning plane. I then called John Stevens, one of our umpire supervisors, and asked him to go to Chicago, meet with the umpires, and I would see him there. I was in Chicago early the next morning. It was a nice day and I cabbed directly to Comiskey Park. When I entered the park I went right down to the playing field and could see the problem immediately. Underneath the new sod were three or four inches of muck. It wasn't drying out very fast. What amazed me was that no one was working on the field, nor was there even a ground crew anywhere in evidence. When I found Gene Bossard, the head groundskeeper, he said he was waiting for some truckloads of sand. Actually, I don't think they knew what could be done to speed up the drying process.

John Stevens was there and we debated as to what should or could be done. John was for removing the new sod, removing the muck, and letting the dirt dry out. Roland Hemond came down from the office. He obviously recognized the seriousness of the problem but was going along with his boss' position that the field was okay—that games had been played on worse fields than this one. Finally, Veeck appeared. He argued vigorously that the field would be all right. They had a good advance sale and could not afford to lose a second gate. About this time a call came through from Jerry Hoffberger in Baltimore for me. He had received reports from Earl Weaver and others with his club and was in an uproar. His people said the field was still clearly unplayable. He didn't want one of his players injured playing on the muck that covered the outfield.

We gave the field all the time we could. The gates were opened and the crowd came streaming in, thoroughly expecting to see a game on this balmy summer evening. The players knew we were considering playing and both teams met in separate team meetings. The White Sox were not happy about things but they had not said they would not play. The Orioles, however, announced that they simply would not play. All were in accord on this—the owner, the manager, and the players. I walked around the field with Stevens, umpire Ron Luciano, the groundskeeper, and Weaver. The fans were now aware of what was going on and watched our actions with interest. Weaver wasn't too bad. He obviously didn't think that the field was fit to play on, but he wasn't necessarily going along with the players if we ruled the game must be played. There was no thought of trying to take batting or infield practice, but the White Sox players were warming up, playing catch, on the sidelines. As we got closer to game time, the fans were getting louder and more verbal in voicing their feelings that the game should be played. It wasn't the fans who would get hurt, however, should we try to play. We called the game. Because their drainage was improper and possibly because they scheduled other activities on the field too close to a scheduled home game, another White Sox gate went "down the drain."

My son, Andy, was working for the Cubs at that time and I stayed overnight with him in his North Side apartment, not too far from Wrigley Field. It was a good hideaway. I didn't need to talk anymore to Hoffberger, Veeck, or the press about the problem. The umpires knew where to reach me. We got to work on the field early the next morning, removed the worst sod and did what we could to dry up the problem spots. It was still touch and go and we went through the same routine of testing the field as game time approached. This time, although the Orioles were unhappy, we gave a go-ahead approval for the game. Games had been played under conditions just as bad. The infield was fine, the outfield was still bad in some spots. I sat with John Stevens and hoped for infield outs and no problems when a ball did go to the outfield. We were getting along fine when, all of sudden, trouble of another sort developed. Luciano, who was behind the plate, was having trouble with the Orioles on ball and strike decisions. Finally, Ron and Weaver really got into it and Weaver accused Luciano of deliberately calling all close pitches against the Orioles. It was a bad performance. Luciano ejected him and I sent word to him by Phil

Itzoe, the Orioles' travelling secretary, that he was suspended. But that is another story.

The "bad hop" was the field problem. It wasn't a bad "bad hop" like the players' strike. On the other hand, although we got through the game all right, it was bad in my mind because it was a thoroughly uncomfortable experience for me. Walking the mucky field; the fans yelling "play ball"; the two teams holding separate meetings and phone conferences with the Players' Association as to whether or not they would play; Hoffberger and Veeck's exhortations strongly impressed upon me; concern for possible player injuries much on my mind—it was not a happy experience.

1980. The fourth bad hop concerned Oakland. Bad hops should never happen and yet they do—with ground balls on the field and with developments off the field. Bad hop number four involved our attempts to move the Oakland franchise. It never should have happened because the franchise should not have been permitted to move there in the first place. I never did learn exactly what happened that night in 1967 that changed our solid bloc of no votes that had prevented Finley from moving to Oakland, to yes votes. It was short-sighted and unfair to the San Francisco Giants and the National League. At the time, the American League wanted Seattle and if the National League had been willing to give assurances that this territory would be left open, it is possible the American League never would have gone to Oakland. Nevertheless, the American League should not have gone there anyway. It is true that San Francisco and Oakland are separate cities and have trouble thinking of themselves as a united area. They had separate Triple-A baseball teams and they compete for things like port facilities. Yet with the economics of baseball today— and we should have been prudent enough to see the way things were going—you must have a large metropolitan area, both to draw from and for a broadcast market. Two teams in the same area means dividing the fans, competing for publicity, playing against the other team's broadcasts and telecasts, and having one team's broadcasts and telecasts compete with the other team's games (not necesarily head to head, but the problem is just too many games).

Actually, after the A's moved to Oakland, total attendance for the Bay area was not a great deal better for two teams than it had been for one. The Giants were drawing around 1.5 million fans in the ten-year period before the A's came. From 1968 through 1973, the two teams together drew approximately the same figure. In 1974, despite the fact that the A's won their fourth straight American League West title and third straight World Series, their attendance fell below one million and the Giants drew only half that. The A's won their fifth straight title in 1975 and got just over the million mark. And when they finished second in 1976 the attendance fell to 780,000. In 1977 it fell further to 495,000 and by 1979, with a non-contending club, it went down to 306,000. Finley had started trying to sell players for cash and he was as thoroughly disliked by the fans in Oakland as he had been by the fans in Kansas City.

I started working on the problem shortly after becoming league president. Finley, Bob Lurie (the Giants' owner), and Bowie Kuhn were convinced one team had to go. There were times when it appeared the Giants would move, but Bob Lurie was a San Franciscan and his heart was there. Something always happened to keep the Giants there. We couldn't control what the Giants did. Our goal therefore was to move the A's. We had the spot (Denver) and the owner (Marvin Davis). Davis was fabulously wealthy and had inherited a love for baseball from his father while growing up in Brooklyn. If he got the team, Marvin was prepared to build a new Kansas City-type baseball stadium. It was an ideal situation, but to move there we had to get the A's out of their long-term lease in Oakland. When the team moved to Oakland it was required to sign a short lease only but at the press conference, strictly for showmanship and the dramatic effect, Finley tore up the short-term lease and voluntarily suggested a long-term lease. Obviously, it wasn't going to be easy to get Alameda County and the city of Oakland to agree to let the A's go. Our only chance was to make the Giants an area team. That plus money.

Our plan was to have the Giants play a portion of their schedule in Oakland and to change the name of the team to the "Bay Giants" or something of that nature. Lurie was willing. He would be eliminating the competition from the A's; plus the Oakland Coliseum was actually a better place to play than the Giants' Candlestick Park and was easier to reach by the new subway from downtown San Francisco. Bob was willing to do whatever was required, including contributing his share of the money needed (it looked as if we would have to pay around $4 million). The rest of the money would be contributed by Finley, the American League, and Marvin Davis. In November of 1979 the American League voted to contribute one-fourth of what would be needed, up to a maximum of $1,000,000 but, in no event, more than Finley provided. Chub Feeney stubbornly refused to have the National League contribute, but otherwise was behind the plan. The problem was getting approval from the city of San Francisco to the name change and the reduction of games from the Candlestick schedule. With this objective, Kuhn, Feeney, Lurie, and I met with Mayor George Mosconi of San Francisco. Things seemed to be progressing well. Bowie worked very hard to help work out the problems. He had a good relationship with Bob Nahas who, at the time, was the head of the Alameda County Coliseum Commission. He also had a special reason for wanting to see the transfer go through, for it meant that Charlie Finley would be selling his team to Davis. Finley and Kuhn had been bitter opponents.

We had many characters in baseball at that time. Bill Veeck was certainly one; Gene Autry was also, in a different way. In fact most baseball owners were what people generally looked upon as "characters." They were people who had been enormously successful in their work and as a result had a great deal of self-confidence and assurance. Call it ego, if you like. As Ewing Kauffman put it, "Baseball ownership is made up of twenty-six egomaniacs and I am one of them." Charlie Finley may have been the character of all characters. I often did not agree with positions he took but we got along pretty well. He seldom caused the league office any trouble. He never complained about umpire decisions or other regular league functions. He could be charming and a lot of fun. He could also enjoy himself at your expense. (When Gwen and I were married after my first year as American League president and slipped off to our new condominium in Florida, he somehow found out where we were going and fifteen minutes after our arrival had delivered to us a dozen quarts of milk and a dozen cartons of frozen oysters.) But I could talk to him about league problems and generally get his support. Perhaps I wasn't a big enough cheese to really attack. He saved his energy for Bowie. Bowie reciprocated the personal disrespect and nothing would have made him happier than to be able to put together a program that was good for baseball and at the same time got rid of Charlie.

Our efforts proceeded over several years and required many trips to the Pacific Coast and many meetings. At times, things looked promising but then bogged down when we ran into roadblocks. Mayor Lionel Wilson of Oakland liked baseball and hated the thought of the A's leaving his city, but understood the situation. The Oakland *Tribune* was the same. Marvin Davis was marvelously patient. At one point, when things looked promising, I took Frank Cashen out to meet Davis. Frank was out of baseball at that time and anxious to get back in. That meeting went well and either Frank or Al Rosen, both excellent baseball men, would have headed up Marvin's organization. In the middle of the 1979 World Series, Bowie and I left Pittsburgh and flew to Oakland to try to nail down some loose ends and push the deal along. Everything looked very good and then came the bad hop.

Al Davis, owner of the Oakland Raiders, announced his intention of moving his team to Los Angeles. When the National Football League voted not to give him permission to move, he decided to defy the league and move his team anyway. It was incredible considering the fact that the Raiders had sold out for many, many consecutive games. Davis was looking for increased capacity and luxury boxes. It is sad that some people can be so greedy that for additional profit they will go against their league and desert an area that had supported them magnificently. Or maybe I see it wrong because it upended everything we were trying to do. There was no way that Alameda County or the city of Oakland were going to see both major league sports teams leave their area. They tried their best to stop Al Davis and couldn't. They knew we would fulfill our agreed obligations. Our move to Denver was off, at least for the foreseeable future. We lost a fine city and a fine owner. Baseball was left with a serious problem that still exists. Hopefully I will be proved wrong and the area will support two teams (and 1987 attendance was encouraging), but a lot of hard work and hard-won cooperation went down the drain in trying to solve the problem. It was personally very, very disappointing. Everything, it seemed, was finally working out and then an uncontrollable outside occurrence intervened. In my mind, it certainly was a bad hop.

1980. Bad hop number five involved Edward DeBartolo. It also involved Veeck. Bill had a way of shaping events in ways that did not follow normal procedures. This time a messy situation arose following his decision to sell the team. Bill's health, never good, was a serious concern and the White Sox, saddled with an aging Comiskey Park, were having financial problems. Bill entered into negotiations with different groups. The White Sox were owned by a syndicate with more than forty limited partners and it seemed a local buyer would materialize from among them. Then Edward J. DeBartolo entered the picture. DeBartolo was immensely wealthy, having made his money primarily in constructing and operating shopping centers. (His son operates the San Francisco Forty-Niners football team.) DeBartolo lives in Youngstown, Ohio and this, in itself, was disturbing, as the league had determined to try, wherever possible, to steer new ownership to local people. We wanted owners who lived in the same city as the team and who had a natural commitment to that city. We felt this was the best way of ensuring responsible ownership and of eliminating attempted sales for profit to new cities. We recognized that if local ownership was not available there was no way we could prevent an owner from selling to someone else. But if good local ownership was available, without involving financial sacrifice to the seller, then we felt the league was within its rights in insisting that such local ownership be given preference. Such was the situation with the White Sox. Moreover, we knew that DeBartolo was heavily involved in horse racing, operating two or three tracks, and Commissioner Kuhn was dead set against any linkage between baseball and professional gambling—be it casinos or race tracks. This was bound to be a stumbling block. When Jerry Reinsdorf became interested, it appeared the problem could be avoided. Jerry was a Chicagoan, had attended Northwestern University, was a law school graduate, and appeared to be a most desirable owner. He had been very successful as a real estate developer and was financially able to operate a team.

With Veeck in the hospital, negotiations for the sale of the team were nominally being handled by a committee headed by Andy McKenna, though Bill was steering the ship. In August of 1980, I went to Chicago at Andy's invitation and had dinner with him and two other members of the committee at the Chicago Athletic Club. We had an early dinner in the club's immense, old dining room on Michigan Boulevard. Outside of another table about fifty yards away, we were the only people in the room. I told them that, in my opinion, DeBartolo would not be approved by the league. The next day I went to the hospital with Andy and visited Bill. He was a tough and gutsy guy and despite all he had been through and was going through, he was chipper. We had a good visit during which I told him I did not think that DeBartolo could possibly be approved by the league and urged him to go with Reinsdorf. For some reason, which I do not know, but probably because he would continue in a major role if DeBartolo bought the club, Veeck was strong for going ahead with DeBartolo despite the position of the league. It was almost as if it were *because of* the feelings of the league, for Bill loved to accept a challenge and do battle with the constituted authority at any time.

When I got back to New York, I brought Bowie Kuhn up to date on developments. He knew about DeBartolo's racing connections and was determined not to let him become owner of the White Sox. At the same time, we did not want to publicly embarrass DeBartolo by having the league turn him down. We decided that the most sensible approach was to meet with him and explain to him exactly what the problem was and what we foresaw happening if he went forward. I had been talking with Paul Martha, who represented DeBartolo. Paul was a former University of Pittsburgh and Pittsburgh Steeler football star. He seemed very sensible and I liked him. Through Paul, we set up a meeting at a hotel in the Pittsburgh Airport. Andy McKenna joined Paul and DeBartolo, Sandy Hadden came with Bowie and the six of us sat together in the living room of a small suite.

Bowie outlined the problems in a very frank, straightforward, but possibly brusque manner. I simply stated that I concurred with Bowie's analysis and felt certain the majority of the club owners in the league would so vote. DeBartolo was furious and his remarks bordered on the insulting. I could see Bowie getting very hot and he replied in kind. Bowie told him that if, by some chance, the American

League approved him, he could be certain that the commissioner would not. DeBartolo threatened litigation. It was a very tense situation. I tried to create a little more constructive atmosphere and Andy McKenna did the same. Gradually things cooled down and we got around to analyzing the problems and looking for solutions. DeBartolo was willing to sell one race track but not Louisiana Downs, which apparently was a big money maker for him. We then lunched together in the suite. I suggested that he meet with our league's Long Range Planning Committee so he would be familiar with ownership thinking, not just Bowie's and mine, and I later set up two such meetings for him. I cannot say our meeting ended on a cordial note but it at least ended better than it had started, and DeBartolo agreed not to go forward with the purchase if, on review, the White Sox did not desire to.

Unfortunately though, things did not get better, in fact they got progressively worse. The meeting that I set up with John Fetzer and Bud Selig did not turn out well. DeBartolo's aggressive manner and his comments about Kuhn irritated John Fetzer. Without Fetzer's support, he was going to have a tough time selling other American League owners. Nor did his later meeting with Ewing Kauffman make a convert of Ewing.

Somewhere in this time frame, the Committee of White Sox Limited Partners met to review its position. Veeck, of course, was angry at our actions and determined to force the DeBartolo sale. In the middle of the meeting, my old friend Bill DeWitt, who at this time was one of the Limited Partners, called me. I gave Bill the same message I had given everyone else. I don't know what he reported to the rest of the committee—or if it cared. In any event its decision was "damn the torpedoes, full speed ahead." The committee voted to go ahead with the sale to DeBartolo.

DeBartolo did much better when he appeared before a full league meeting in Chicago in September. He acted and spoke reasonably. He had the Chicago press solidly behind him. It appeared that, if he would only sell the rest of his gambling interests, he might conceivably be approved. When the league voted a month later, however, he had not done so and he received only six (of fourteen) affirmative votes. Still, we did not close the door entirely and told him that we would review his application at our annual meeting in December. In those remaining weeks, two things occurred which decisively ended his chances. First, he apparently tried to bring outside pressure on some of the owners who had voted against him. When word of this got around, all the clubs were angered. Second, one of his spokesmen, Vince Bartimo, said publicly that the only reason that DeBartolo wasn't being approved was that Bowie Kuhn was anti-Italian. The remark was both ridiculous and stupid. I can't believe DeBartolo himself had prior knowledge of it. Still it was the final straw. When the league voted in Dallas the vote was eleven to three against.

This whole incident was certainly a bad hop. You don't like to be forced to turn people down. There was much ill feeling and no one came out of it looking very good. The publicity was bad for baseball, Kuhn, the American League, the White Sox, Veeck, and DeBartolo and it never should have happened.

1981. Bad hop number six was a Player Strike. An umpire strike is bad, but you can play games without professional umpires. A player strike is something quite different. The impact of free agency in combination with salary arbitration on club salary structures had been more dramatic than had been anticipated. The clubs also still believed that teams losing star players should be compensated with more than just a free agent draft choice. They felt this was important to maintain competitive balance, but that it was also what was fair and right. The Basic Agreement negotiated in 1976 had been recognized as experimental and this fact was expressly stated in the language of the agreement. The new agreement had created economic problems for the clubs and was causing them to lose money. The industry, overall, had operated at about a break-even level through the seventies, but was now sliding dangerously into red ink. Therefore, the clubs approached the 1980 negotiations intent upon moderating the effects of free agency. The clubs proposed that a team losing a free agent be allowed to pick a lesser player from the signing team. There were, again, many other issues but compromise solutions were found for them. The compensation issue, however, found both sides dug in and uncompromising as the start of the season approached. Grebey brought in the Federal Mediation Service and Ken Moffitt, the Services' top mediator, was assigned to the case. Then Miller moved to apply pressure on the clubs, announcing that the players would not finish spring training; would open the season; but if there was no solution by May 22nd, would strike. He did not believe that the clubs would stay united in the face of the strike threat and issued the strike challenge even though, in the past, we had regularly played and negotiated at the same time. In 1976, it had been July before an agreement was reached and it had been Miller who was urging us to play and negotiate. There were many bargaining sessions but no progress and May 22nd approached. The clubs were prepared to take a strike at this point. Commissioner Kuhn then assumed a more active role in an effort to avert the strike and in an all-night session, with the PRC standing by, Kuhn and Grebey made an agreement with Miller that postponed Armageddon for a year. In the meantime, it was agreed, a Joint Study Committee was to be set up to try to work out the problem. If this did not result in a settlement, the clubs could then impose their last compensation proposal and the players could accept or strike.

I appointed Harry Dalton as the American League representative on the Joint Study Committee. Frank Cashen was the National League representative. These two men were intelligent and reasonable.* The Players' Association appointed Bob Boone and Sal Bando, two more excellent men who were fair and had a feel for the game. I felt a surge of hope as I thought these four, if left alone, might really accomplish something. The trouble was they were not left alone. Miller and Grebey insisted upon attending all the sessions and as a result the committee had no real authority to do whatever was required to fashion a compromise settlement. Nor is it clear that either side really wanted its Study Committee members to move off its own position. The club position was that when a "top" free agent (determined by how many teams drafted him) signed, the signing club would compensate the team losing the player with a contract of a professional player. Miller's position was that they would absolutely not agree to any additional compensation from the signing club, as he feared this would significantly affect free agency. So the battle lines were drawn. In retrospect, the clubs would have probably been better off to have resolved things one way or another in 1980, rather than postponing strike day for a year. First, there were other issues at that time that could have been used in seeking a compromise solution. It is very dangerous to allow a negotiation to be reduced to a one-issue crisis. Second, if there had been a strike in 1980 it probably would have been of shorter duration than the one that occurred in 1981, when the two sides were well prepared and determined to have an all-out fight. I say all these things in hindsight for I, as did almost all of us on the PRC, welcomed the temporary solution and applauded the work that Bowie and Moffitt had done in staving off a strike decision.

There were a couple of skirmishes in 1981 before war began. First the Players' Association went to the NLRB, complaining that clubs were using their financial status as an argument in negotiations and thus committing an unfair labor practice. It asked that the clubs be required to furnish financial statements for 1978, 1979, and 1980. The NLRB issued a complaint and the matter moved to the Federal District Court in New York. The judge was Henry Werker and the case was heard in Rochester. The judge decided in the clubs' favor, describing the Players' Association action in filing the complaint as a

---

*They also could work together. They had shared the top administration of the Orioles after my departure in 1966.

"bargaining tactic." The result of the judge's decision, however, was to force the Players' Association to make a decision—accept the implemented change with player compensation or strike. We argued and pleaded with the Players' Association that the change related only to star players; that the impact on free agency would not be severe; and the result would be fairer and more acceptable to the clubs. For either side to insist on a system that the other side finds basically unfair is dangerous and poisons the basic relationship between the parties. But Marvin was never that concerned with the relationship between the clubs and players. This was simply the way he felt and thought as a traditional labor zealot. And so the strike was called. It was the first real strike in baseball. It turned out to be the longest strike in professional sports history.

Marvin thought the clubs would not stand together and would give in quickly. He was wrong in this. The PRC had been provident enough to get strike insurance and this mitigated club losses. On the other hand, the Players' Association incorrectly believed that we would not bargain in good faith as long as the strike insurance continued and, therefore, it simply refused to compromise and held its ground until the coverage ran out. For a considerable period Miller even refused to sit at the bargaining table. His announced reason was that club owners and Grebey had said that it was he who was preventing a settlement; therefore he would step aside and let the clubs negotiate with Don Fehr, Mark Belanger, and Dick Moss.

When a compromise is inevitable, it makes sense to go to work to achieve a solution as quickly as possible. Both sides were remiss in not doing this. Finally it became apparent that the time was fast approaching when it would be too late, and would no longer make sense, to resume play at all in 1981. If that happened it meant we would all have to undergo a fall and winter with the pall of an unsettled strike hanging over our game. If you were concerned about the game itself, this was unthinkable. Unfortunately, management is the only side that must always be concerned for the game itself. The players are, in a way, but they are primarily concerned about what happens to them in the course of their careers. The Players' Association, unfortunately, on most occasions, has been concerned only with getting the best conditions and the most money it can for the players. It is too bad really that the clubs' compensation proposal could not have been tried. Surely it created a more equitable situation as far as the clubs were concerned. Also, as the proposal was finally written, I do not feel the impact on salaries would have been too great—and some leveling off of salaries, if that occurred, would have been in the game's best interest. It is possible that, had the Players' Association accepted the clubs' proposal in 1981, in addition to avoiding a long disastrous strike, the system would be working better today and the two sides would not still be at war with one another.

Small cracks began to appear in club unity before the strike was a week old. First, there was an ominous dinner meeting between Edward Bennett Williams and Kuhn. Bowie brought me along because he had anticipated the subject, but it was quickly apparent that Ed was not happy about my presence and I left immediately after eating. The next day Williams, Steinbrenner, and Eddie Chiles went to Bowie's office for a meeting. Again, I was there at Bowie's request, as all three were American League club owners. Chiles launched into a tirade. He accused us of doing nothing to settle the strike; made it clear he considered us his employees, obligated to do his bidding. (Bowie told him off in a manner that reminded one of Kenesaw Mountain Landis.) The other two were more polite and reasonable but you had a pretty good idea who had put Eddie up to his histrionics. These three were a minority. The great majority of the clubs were still determined and supportive and a major league meeting held in New York gave the PRC unanimous backing. The clubs also adopted a "gag rule" to discipline anyone speaking publicly against the PRC position. (To me this was as offensive as it was ineffective.)

As time wore on, however, a group of owners developed who favored a settlement by binding arbitration and I'm sorry to say most of this sentiment was in the American League. I myself was looking for some kind of solution that would end the strike but that would at least improve compensation to some extent. Arbitration, given the genesis of the problem, didn't seem to be the way for us to go. It was absolutely clear, however, that Miller was not going to accept compensation from the "signing club" unless forced to do so. To force him to do so would require a year-long strike, plus the clubs holding firm well into the 1982 season. That perhaps would have broken the union, but we had no desire to break the union. We simply wanted better compensation for clubs losing top free agents and a strike into 1982 would have been disastrous for the game. Lou Hoynes and I began to kick around ideas of how we could provide the clubs increased compensation, but divorce it from coming from the signing team. The final idea was to create a pool of players, provided by all the clubs, that a team losing a free agent could select from. We argued with our own PRC members that it was time for us to consider this approach. The game could not stand the strike running well unto 1982, nor could we expect the clubs to stand behind us much longer. At a special American League meeting in July, Ed Williams urged that we seek binding arbitration. Steinbrenner backed him, Roy Eisenhardt moved it, and Gabe Paul seconded it. I pleaded for a little more time and got them not to take a vote. (Any meaningful vote would have had to be taken at a Joint League meeting anyway.) In addition, there was pressure from Congress and individual Congressmen to break the impasse. Later that month, Labor Secretary Raymond Donovan came to New York and talked to both sides. He then asked us to meet in Washington the following week.

Much bitterness had developed between Miller and Grebey. They clashed at the bargaining table and criticized each other in the press. It was apparent to all of us that this situation was making it harder to work things out between us. Bowie Kuhn, under great pressure to resolve the problem and end the strike, started asking me to talk to Miller. Actually, Marvin had already given me some indication that he would like to talk to me. I was reluctant to assume this role. First, it was not fair to Grebey and, second, I had no desire to push anything the PRC itself was not behind. But when other members of the PRC urged me to act, with the PRC's and Grebey's knowledge, I arranged to meet with Miller. We met at the Helmsley Palace Hotel in Manhattan and had a workmanlike discussion of the problems that separated us. By now, the issue of players' service time for free agency, salary arbitration, and pension purposes had come up. Would the players get service time for the period of the strike? When the meeting was over, I had a pretty good idea of just how far Miller might be willing to go in attempting to reach a solution. I reported this to the PRC and to Bowie. I must also say for Ray Grebey that, at least at the time and at least to me, he did not show any resentment over my role.

When the PRC moved down to Washington, as per Secretary Donovan's request, Bowie established his own headquarters there and also had the Executive Council convene there. Consequently, we had all the people on hand required to make a decision for baseball. We restructured our position in the light of what I had learned from Miller and put out feelers in this direction in our Washington meetings with the Players' Association. I was shocked when they were not met receptively. Unsuccessful, we returned to New York on July 25th. The problem, apparently, was that Miller needed to run the framework for the proposed solution by his Executive Committee before moving forward with it. He called a meeting for the night of July 27th in Chicago. He talked to me on the phone early that morning before he left New York. On his return, he asked for a private meeting and one was set up for July 30th. We met in the National League office with Marvin, Don Fehr, Ray Grebey, and myself in attendance. In the meantime, of course, all the details had been gone over with the PRC and the commissioner. The players would get service time. The clubs would get an extra year's duration of the Basic Agreement. The players would go along with a split season—or any plan the clubs adopted—for the balance of the 1981 season. Compensation would come from a pool, not from the signing club. An understanding reached, a meeting of the PRC and Players' Association followed immediately and at 5:30 a.m. on July 31st we, at last, had an agreement.

As is often the case, no one benefited from the long strike. The clubs did not get what they wanted in the way of compensation. Though the compensation was good, no one had any enthusiasm about it coming from a non-signing club and it did not have as much impact on salaries as it should have. The players lost millions of dollars in salary. The game suffered with its fans. The commissioner suffered, as people had expected him to wave a magic wand to settle the strike. Also some clubs and fans criticized him for the split season. Ray Grebey eventually lost his job. So no one gained. Mark Belanger looked at me at the news conference announcing the end of the strike and said, "Lee, we can never let this happen again." I agreed, and we did prevent it from happening in 1985. But given recent developments, I am not all that sanguine about the future. Anyway you look at it, the 1981 player strike was a very bad hop.

1983. The seventh bad hop involved George Steinbrenner. One of the responsibilities of the league presidents is to rule on protests. It was the Kansas City club's protest of the game of July 24, 1983 that resulted in my reinstating George Brett's ninth inning home run at Yankee Stadium. For me this was not a difficult decision. As I regularly attended meetings of the Rules Committee, I knew the intent of the rule the umpire cited in calling Brett out. The intent of the rule was to curtail the excessive use of pine tar and to stop it from getting on the baseball. The rule provided that the bat be cleaned up or not used. As pine tar did not affect the way the ball traveled after it was hit, it was not the intention of the rule makers to nullify such a hit once it had occurred. The intent was simply to provide a means of eliminating excessive pine tar. I was also cognizant of other league decisions with respect to pine tar on the bat that provided a precedent for my ruling. Making decisions of this nature was part of the job. No bad hop here. What followed the decision, however, was wrong, inappropriate, and definitely qualifies as a "bad hop."

Quite expectedly, Steinbrenner was furious at my ruling. At first, with his encouragement, the Yankee players were not going to finish the game. I knew that in the final analysis they would play the game, as they were still in the pennant race. If they didn't play they would lose the game by forfeit. What developed next, however, was that the Yankee management took a position that the game not be played until after the end of the season. This was not satisfactory to me. I did not want our League Championship Series held up while we played unfinished games to determine a division winner and it was conceivable that either New York or Kansas City could end up in that position. This could affect the outcome of the League Championship Series and could also put the eventual Amerian League World Series entrant at a disadvantage. I insisted that, in accordance with American League regulations, the game be finished during the season and surprisingly the Players' Association backed my position. Fortunately, August 18th was an open date for both teams with Kansas City conveniently in the east and I scheduled the game for that date. This brought on a fight with George. He eventually yielded on the date but then insisted that the game be played in the afternoon. This was impossible, as Kansas City was scheduled at home the night before and scheduling rules prevented an afternoon game following a night game when significant travel time was involved. I explained this to George and his comment was "F___ Kansas City, we're playing a day game." I pointed out to him that it was the league that scheduled the replaying of such games and that we had no alternative but to play this one at night. He immediately proceeded to announce it as a day game anyway. I overruled him and announced the game would be played at 6:00 p.m. At this point, he publicly grieved for the thousands of kids the Yankees had intended to have as their guests at a day game, who could not attend at night. The league and I personally were being unfair to these children.

When two Yankee season ticket holders brought suits on August 16th, two days before the game date, maintaining that rainchecks must be honored for the game, we supported the Yankee's position and met with their lawyers—including Roy Cohn. It struck me then that something odd was going on. They didn't seem interested in using the material we gave them explaining why rainchecks could not be honored for the completion of protested games. It almost seemed as if they wanted to lose the case—and in fact that was indeed their strategy. When the case came to trial the next day, the Yankees joined with the plaintiffs in a stipulation to enjoin the game. The case was brought before a judge in the Bronx County Court House, a stone's throw from the stadium. As the office of our American League counsel was in Cleveland, the National League law firm of Willkie, Farr, and Gallagher graciously came to our assistance. Lou Hoynes and Bob Kheel did a great job for us. Together we quickly produced an affidavit and filed it in time for an immediate appeal, should we lose. Time was a key factor. We did lose in the Bronx Court, with Yankee people testifying that 55,000 people would attend and there was great danger of riots and violence should the game be played. But with the Kansas City club standing by at Newark Airport, we won in the Appellate Court in the afternoon of the same date. At last the way was cleared to go forward that evening with the completion of the game.

Though the Yankees had done everything they could to play down publicity on the completion of the game, even refusing to sell tickets until shortly before game time, there were a few thousand people on hand—but no 55,000. Plus the fans were very orderly. All the dire Yankee predictions of crowd control problems were proven to be insincere. But the Yankees had still another trick up their sleeves; this a little skullduggery on the part of Manager Billy Martin (who played a lineup with a pitcher in centerfield and a left-handed throwing rookie first baseman at second).*

The umpires who had worked the game on July 24th, in which the incident occurred, were working games on the West Coast. It was not practical to bring them back for four outs, so we had Dave Phillips' crew on hand. Billy knew there would be different umpires, so as soon as play resumed he had the ball thrown to second, ran out and protested that Brett had failed to touch second base in running the bases after his homer. We were one jump ahead of him. One of the Yankee officials had asked us if the same umpires would be there. That started Bob Fishel and me thinking. What could they possibly concoct based on the original umpires not being there? Missing a base was the obvious one, so we drew up a statement confirming that all bases had been touched; had all the original umpires sign it; had it notarized; and gave it to Dave Phillips, the August 18th crew chief. When Billy came dashing out Dave simply pulled out the notarized statement and showed it to him and the game then went forward for the final four outs. The Yankees did not threaten in the bottom of the ninth and it was over. I got booed quite lustily as I left the stadium but I expected this and it didn't bother me. I wrote our clubs and chronicled without comment everything that had happened. It was this letter, perhaps, that angered George more than anything. The "Brett" game was finally behind us, or so I thought. There was still one more chapter left to be recorded.

Bowie Kuhn was angered about the Yankee activities throughout the entire affair—Steinbrenner's public statements about me, their stated refusal to play the game as scheduled, their position in the court case. He scheduled a hearing, with George on hand, to consider the possibility of a fine or suspension. (George responded by filing suit to prevent any such discipline.) I appreciated Bowie's support but I really didn't want the matter to go further. I could do battle with George on my own and I would have preferred to write finis to the entire episode. Bill Shea, George's counsel in most baseball matters,

---

*Ron Guidry and Don Mattingly, respectively.

called me and asked if I couldn't sidetrack any disciplinary action on the commissioner's part. I did try. I asked Bowie if he couldn't just drop it, but he was not willing to. Then at the hearing, I did my best to assume as tolerant and non-accusatory a position, with respect to the Yankees' actions, as I could. I did that until I became angered by the aggressive position the Yankees were taking. Unfortunately, Bill Shea did not represent George at this hearing. If he had been there the penalty assessed by Bowie (a $300,000 fine) might not have been that severe. I found out later that the statements and questions that irritated me were being suggested to the Yankee attorney by notes from George. If Shea had been there he might have ignored them. In any event, this was the final act of the affair—except for George's hostility to me, which continued long after the "last out and the last fine." To me, all the post-decision events and the personal hostility were a bad hop. Again they never should have happened.

1983. Bad hop number eight occurred when Kuhn's reelection was blocked. The commissioner's term was seven years. It was a little less than seven years after the attempt to unseat Bowie in Milwaukee in 1975 that they were at it again. This time there was a group of nine who had signed a letter stating that they would not support Kuhn for reelection. Once again, a Baltimore owner was one of the instigators. Edward Bennett Williams had purchased the team from the Hoffberger family in 1979. He had parted with Kuhn as a result of the 1981 player strike, feeling the commissioner should not have permitted the strike to occur, or at least to go on as long as it did. Other clubs signing the letter were the Yankees, Rangers, Mariners, Cardinals, Cubs, Reds, Astros, and Padres. Although Ted Turner had not actually signed the letter there was a concern that because of his clashes with Kuhn (including a lawsuit over broadcast privileges) he too could be negative. I got wind of the plot a day or two before it was revealed, from Bud Selig, who had been sworn to secrecy about it. When Peter O'Malley also learned about it from one of the letter-signing clubs, some of us gathered late at night in my suite at the Diplomat Hotel in Hollywood, Florida, where our annual meetings were taking place, to consider what action we might take—Bud, Peter, Chub Feeney, and several more of Bowie's supporters. We finally decided to wake Bowie and at least alert him to what was coming up tomorrow.

There was turmoil in that meeting room the next day and it was finally decided that one owner from each club would meet separately as a committee to try to thrash out the problem. The antis, whatever their real reason for opposing Kuhn, focused on the need for a more businesslike approach to industry problems. The pros tried to turn the revolt away from Kuhn to a restructuring of our administrative procedures, thereby accommodating the antis' grievances without sacrificing Kuhn. As often was the case, John Fetzer was the leader in working for a compromise solution. A "Restructuring Committee," headed by Roy Eisenhardt and Peter O'Malley, but also containing people opposed to Bowie, now took center stage, working for several months on the problem. It did a good job, accomplishing some needed reforms for baseball, including changing the voting requirements for the reelection of the commissioner. The anti-Kuhn bloc would not agree to this provision becoming operative, however, until after the issue with respect to Kuhn had been settled. Another idea that was put forward was to divide the job and create a chief operating officer for business affairs—COOBA, the proposed office came to be called. The fight then involved how much independence such an officer would have from the commissioner. This change was not really needed and would have resulted in an unwieldy structure. It eventually was dropped. Moreover, the objective of restructuring in order to get the opposition off Kuhn simply was not achievable. The antis didn't really want restructuring, they wanted to dump Kuhn.

Throughout this period, many, many efforts were made to change the minds of the recalcitrants. Ed Williams quickly reversed course and became one of Bowie's strongest supporters. Ballard Smith and the Padres also shifted over to the Kuhn camp. The other people, however, with Lou Susman of the Cardinals quarterbacking their strategies and John McMullen of the Astros providing a tough base, simply would not budge. It would appear at times as if the Reds or the Cubs, or even the Cardinals, had an open mind but that was not really true. These clubs, plus the Astros and Braves, stuck together despite many one-on-one meetings and the most able appeals. Peter O'Malley exercised the main oar on Bowie's behalf and Peter, plus others, urged Bowie to hang in there and fight.

No one wanted to see Bowie retained any more than I did. I thought that he had improved remarkably and steadily during his tenure. I thought the rule requiring a three-quarter majority in each league was archaic. (If the President of the United States gets sixty percent of the vote it's a landslide.) I felt Bowie had all the good qualities that a commissioner needed. He was honest, straightforward, hardworking, intelligent, and fair. Most important, he loved the game and put that before anything else. He was a good representative for baseball—both in Washington and internationally. There was no assurance that we could find someone as good to replace him, plus any new commissioner would have to be educated in office. Kuhn's years of experience would be wasted. It was very frustrating to have the personal feelings of the few come before what we felt was the best interests of many. I was all for the effort to change peoples' minds or to find some compromise solution. And in August of 1982, at the summer meetings in San Diego, the American League (by unanimous resolution) made a compromise proposal to the National League. The two leagues would reelect Kuhn for a three-year term. An assistant for business affairs would be selected to work under the commissioner, and the commissioner could be removed at any time by a majority vote of the twenty-six teams. The National League rejected the proposal.

When it started to become apparent that minds were not going to be changed and that more than one-quarter of the National League—in fact perhaps one-half of the National League—was still in opposition, Bowie's supporters started plotting other ways to retain him in office. The general idea was that they would block any new candidates from being elected and the Executive Council would therefore simply keep Kuhn in office. Bowie was all charged up for the fight and he embraced this approach. I thought this was wrong. We might not like the three-quarter rule, but that was the rule. We had no right to circumvent it. We had no right to deny to those clubs opposed to Kuhn rights that were theirs under the Major League Agreement. I voiced my opinion at an Executive Council meeting. I told Peter O'Malley and Ed Williams (who were behind this effort) in a separate private meeting exactly how I felt; I told Bud Selig, chairman of the Search Committee, that in my opinion he must conduct the search honestly and diligently; and I told Bowie exactly how I felt. In the final analysis, the Executive Council realized it must recognize the rights of the minority. The other people on the council who finally accepted this and, despite any personal feelings, led the council in making this difficult decision were Danny Galbreath, Bob Lurie, Peter O'Malley, and Chub Feeney. When Bowie heard the council's position, at an all-day session the day before the crucial major league meeting in Boston in July of 1983, he realized that the issue was resolved against him. The next day, he told the Joint Meeting of the clubs that he would not be a candidate to succeed himself. It was a tough spot but he handled himself superbly.

So we lost our commissioner—an able, upfront man, with many years of valuable experience. This was a bad hop for me personally because Bowie was my friend and I had to take a position that hurt him. It was also, at that time, a bad hop for baseball because we lost a very fine and dedicated man as our leader without knowing who might be available to replace him.

1984. Bad hop number nine was the Joint Drug Program. Baseball had always had a problem with alcohol. It was always accepted as part of the macho-male syndrome. We were all aware of the alcoholic legends about Ruth and Waner, etc., and we used to laugh when Mantle hit a home run, despite a gigantic hangover. And it was not confined to the playing field. There was always lots of drinking at baseball meetings or whenever baseball people got together. It was considered an important part of the job to be able to drink and still function well. Many trades were made after the fourth or fifth round of drinks. Fortunately in later years there has been improvement in this area. People now recognize how dangerous alcohol can be. And although I will not maintain that baseball is now a bastion of abstinence, the general approach to alcohol is far more enlightened. In the past, baseball also had a problem with "greenies" or "uppers" (amphetamines-barbiturates) and at one stage they were even available in some clubhouses from the trainer. These things were bad, but no one gave too much thought about doing something about them unless the players' ability to perform on the field was affected, and then the solution was generally to simply get rid of the player. Then in the seventies, other problems began to surface. It was difficult to be sure of exactly what was happening but there were some drug incidents and a suspicion that other problems might be drug-related. At first few people thought it was widespread and if someone brought up the problem, the general managers would always maintain that no drug problems existed on *their* club. And they believed what they said. We did try to conduct drug education seminars for our players. The commissioner had organized these as early as 1971 in conjunction with the club doctors and he had also made use of the FBI in conducting annual clinics in our clubhouses.

Gradually, however, it began to sink in that the situation was not only dangerous but that it could be getting more so. If drug use existed to a great extent in our society at the high school and college level, it was obvious that some of the young men coming into our game would be bringing their problems with them. We had always thought that we were protected in a way by the fact that you could not be on drugs and perform acceptably on a baseball field but we found out that was not necessarily so—at least for a period of time. It was true that if a player persisted in drug use it would eventually eliminate him, but there could be a period of time before his performance was that adversely affected. We did not really know how bad the situation might be. We did understand the factors that made players prime prospects for drug problems: they had plenty of money; they had too much leisure time on the road away from their families; and they were under constant pressure. It became obvious that we should be trying to find out just how bad the situation might be; that we should be doing even more to keep our people drug free; that we should try to make certain that no active players had drug problems; that we should be getting players who needed help into treatment. The commissioner required all clubs to have EAPs (Employment Assistance Plans) in place for anyone seeking help. Unfortunately, those who needed help simply did not seek it and serious problems surfaced in Kansas City, Montreal, and Pittsburgh and with Ferguson Jenkins, Darrell Porter, Lamar Hoyt, Steve Howe, Alan Wiggins, and others. As I was now acting in my new capacity as president of the Player Relations Committee, these problems were of direct concern to me.

From the beginning, Ken Moffitt, the new head of the Players' Association, and I had a good working relationship. As previously related, we often met for lunch or a drink and discussed our mutual problems. Drugs were on the top of our list of concerns and we both decided that the only way to attack the problem was through a joint unified effort. The players wanted to eliminate the evil and to remove the pall over the game that reflected on the great majority of players who were non-users. At the same time, they had concerns as to what would be done and how it would be done and what use management would make of any information received. There would have to be a lot of give and take and the program would have to have safeguards for the players. Ken and I decided that what was needed was a formal program that spelled out in writing when players should be placed on a restricted list; what kind of medical treatment they should receive; who would pay for it; what would happen with respect to their salary; whether or not they would eventually be allowed to sign with other teams, etc. We decided to go to Bowie Kuhn with our suggested approach. Bowie convened a meeting in August 1983 in his conference room. Barry Rona, Chub Feeney, Sandy Hadden, Ed Durso, Bowie, and I were there and Ken Moffitt had three or more people from his staff, mostly new people that he had brought with him from the National Mediation Service in Washington. (Ken it seemed was not hitting it off too well with Don Fehr and Mark Belanger, holdovers from Marvin Miller's regime.) It was a good meeting and we decided to put together a joint committee and see if such a committee could come up with a program satisfactory to both groups. I appointed John McHale, president of the Montreal Expos, and Roy Eisenhardt, president of the Oakland A's, to join Barry Rona and me as the management representatives. I later added Sal Bando of the Milwaukee Brewers, a former player who had been influential in Players' Association circles, and a top man as well to our group. Moffitt was enthused and said that he had the support of the key players in the association hierarchy.

The first major decision of our Joint Committee was that we needed medical expertise to help us. We agreed to mutually select three doctors or scientists with extensive experience in the drug field to serve as a neutral advisory body and, for some purposes, a decision making body. We interviewed several very qualified people and eventually selected Dr. Donald Ottenberg as chairman, Dr. Joel Solomon, and Dr. George DeLeon.

With our medical-scientific trio on hand to advise us, we started working on the provisions of the program. It quickly became clear that the players wanted the program to concentrate on cocaine—our deadliest enemy—and not to cover other related areas such as alcohol, marijuana, and amphetamines. We agreed to this as a starting position, but with express language providing that other problems would be addressed in the future. I talked several times with Dr. Rob Pandina, who was the commissioner's advisor on drugs. Although he was not always in exact accord with where we were coming out, he was in general accord with our approach. After the World Series, I attended the general managers' meeting in Palm Springs, California and brought them up to date on what we were discussing. This was a tough group. They wanted a no-nonsense, "strict mandatory testing" type of agreement. This was fine, but not obtainable. I realized that any Joint Drug Program would contain elements that clubs would not like and would not be tough enough to please them, but I was confident that I could sell them on going forward on any plan that John, Roy, Barry, and I would recommend. You had to start somewhere and all of us expected the original agreement would need constant amending and improving.

Things were progressing as well as we could possibly hope. Then a case involving Steve Howe of the Dodgers and the commissioner's role as disciplinarian began to cause complications. Marvin, Don, and Mark used this as an excuse to air their concerns about Moffitt with the player leadership of their association. They also attacked him because of the staff he had brought with him from Washington. It was very possible that another charge was that he was working too closely with the clubs. Working closely with the clubs was not Marvin's way of doing business. He now exerted his influence and showed that, retired or not, he still exercised control. On November 22nd, Moffitt was fired. All our club people were shocked. I was stunned. I had been selected for a very difficult assignment because the clubs felt the players, in their appointment of Moffitt, were demonstrating a desire to work together. Now he was summarily dismissed. It appeared that prospects for our new Joint Drug Program were down the drain or, at the very best, on hold. If revived, clearly there would be tougher negotiations over the terms of the program.

Our annual meeting of 1983 was in Nashville. The Players' Association met at approximately the same time in Hawaii. I would have loved to have been privy to their discussions. We did get an update from Marvin and Don later in December after we all got back to New York. Don had been elected acting director. He is a bright man. His demeanor could put you off at times but basically I felt he was fair and inclined to be reasonable. Also, he and Barry Rona were good friends and this provided an extra avenue of communications.

When we sat down with them we found they were still negative on expanding the LCS from three out of five to four out of seven, unless they benefitted markedly from the TV revenues. On the other hand, much to my surprise, they wanted to resume negotiations on a Joint Drug Program. We wasted no time in getting back to the table and our first few sessions went well. (I did threaten to walk out on one occasion when they started insisting that the commissioner have no power to discipline in drug cases.) Dr. Ottenberg was very helpful in acting as the moderator between the two sides and, one by one, we agreed on the provisions of an agreement. We were finally down to one major issue and that was the matter of the amount and type of drug testing that would be included in the program. At a meeting in Scottsdale, Arizona, in the spring of 1984, they refused to include any kind of regular mandatory testing in the program, stating that the players themselves would not accept this. We finally resolved this, as well as we could, by providing for testing at any time if directed by the Joint Drug doctors and also providing that the issue of testing would be reexamined after a year's experience and mandatory testing instituted if the Joint Drug doctors thought it desirable. I had to warn the Players' Association that the lack of more testing made it questionable that the program would be ratified by the clubs. We needed the affirmative votes of fourteen teams, with at least five in each league. My warning was both sincere and realistic. The players quickly ratified the plan but, as a meeting of the clubs for that purpose grew close, I knew we did not have the votes and got the meeting postponed.

There was no problem in getting support in the American League. The only clubs opposed appeared to be New York, Texas, and Seattle. Some of the others were lukewarm but they knew I not only believed in the plan but I wanted it to be a first step in building a better relationship with the Players' Association, so they went along. Things were quite different in the National League. The only clubs that appeared to be behind it were Montreal (because of John McHale), Pittsburgh (because of Dan Galbreath), and Philadelphia. So I had some work to do. We finally got the Executive Council to approve, though Bowie was not for it, nor were some other members. I then had personal meetings with the remaining National League clubs, looking for at least two other affirmative votes. I badly wanted more as I wanted the program inaugurated with good support. Nelson Doubleday, Ted Turner, the Cardinals, and San Diego were hopeless "no's." So was Peter O'Malley, on the advice of Dr. Tennant, the team's drug adviser. I had hopes for Houston, Cincinnati, San Francisco, and Chicago. Al Rosen told me he felt sure he could get John McMullen's support, but called me back a few days later and said he had failed. Bob Howsam and Bob Lurie would generally go along with me on issues, but in this case I could get no assurances. My meeting with Dallas Green and Jim Finks of the Cubs was also non-conclusive, so when we finally had the meeting the result was far from predetermined. At the end, Bowie came around and supported the plan and I got good support on the floor from Ed Williams, Danny Galbreath, and a few others. We also had Dr. Ottenberg there. The Reds had sent Bob Howsam, Jr., Bob's son, and he had talked to me at some length the night before. His vote and that of the Cubs turned out to be pivotal yes votes.

In the end we got the majority of the National League clubs to approve and the Joint Drug Program was in business. It did not accomplish anything sensational in those first few months, but we had not expected miracles. On the other hand, we were working together on the problem and the Players' Association was being constructive. We weighed plans to try to find out how widespread the problem was in baseball. The only cases that we knew about were old ones that had existed prior to the program. We did find that the clubs were reluctant to come to the Joint Drug doctors when they were concerned about a player. They wanted to be tough on drugs but they did not want to be involved in any way in confronting their own players.

By this time, Peter Ueberroth had been elected commissioner but because of his Olympic duties he could not take over until October 1st. Bowie Kuhn had agreed to continue until that time. I talked to Peter a few times by telephone to keep him abreast of what was going on. He had had considerable experience monitoring drugs in the Olympics. It was an area in which he felt he had some expertise. It was clear that he wanted to be involved on this issue and he made it plain that he would prefer it if we did nothing until he became active. We had gone too far by then to turn back, but I did assure him that the program could be revamped, or if it did not work to our satisfaction, the clubs could void it. I was convinced in my own mind that it was the only way to go. I had seen Bowie Kuhn consumed by trying to handle all the various drug matters. Whenever he tried to discipline a Howe or a Blue, the Players' Association filed a grievance, and we generally lost the grievance. The Joint Program recognized the commissioner's right to discipline in accord with the principles of the program. Moreover it eliminated ninety percent of the adverse publicity, which was largely created over attempts at discipline. Finally we were hopeful that our neutral panel of three experts would eventually sanction additional testing procedures. At the very least it was a start.

Once Peter Ueberroth took office, he met several times with Don Fehr and tried very hard on his own to get the Association to accept more testing. Peter is an extremely intelligent, personable, likable, and persuasive man. I am sure there had been very few times in his career when he had tried to win someone over to his way of seeing things and not been successful. When he could not win Fehr and Company over, it really turned him off on Fehr, Miller, Belanger, the Players' Association, and the whole idea of working and cooperating with them in the drug area. Moreover, the Pittsburgh drug cases had now reached the courts and the publicity was very bad for baseball. Although all these cases had existed long before our Joint Drug Program, it made it appear as if baseball was soft on drugs. The NBA had a program that looked very tough. In substance it was questionable, but from a public relations standpoint it was excellent for them. Peter steered the clubs away from the Joint Drug Program. The clubs came to believe that they could insert clauses in the players' individual contracts requiring testing and that this was a better way to go. At a meeting held in St. Louis in the fall of 1985, at a time when the relationship between players and clubs was in turmoil because of other problems, Peter raised the issue of the continuance of the Joint Drug Program. There were few defenders. Everyone knew my position. Roy Eisenhardt did his best, but even John McHale seemed on the fence. When a vote was called there was little doubt as to the outcome and everything we had worked for went down the drain. This was a real bad hop for me personally and I truly believe a bad hop for the game. The best weapon against drugs is peer pressure. The best way of achieving this is through a Joint Drug Program. Someday baseball will realize this and reconstruct a joint program and erase this particular bad hop.

13

Extra Innings—Player Relations

I conducted my last American League meeting in Nashville (coincidentally, the city of my birth), in early December of 1983. As was our practice, we had a Board of Directors meeting the afternoon before and I think it was quite appropriate that in the course of that meeting George Steinbrenner (New York was on the board in 1983) let loose a final salvo at me about the umpires. It was helpful to me in a way because it made leaving easier. More important the board voted unanimously to recommend Bobby Brown as president and Bob Fishel as vice president, and approved the financial arrangements suggested for each. (In fact, I think George suggested increasing Fishel's salary.) And the next morning the league had a little breakfast for me and a few members said some nice things. They had arranged for my brother Bill and son Andy to be there and I was very pleased that Joe Cronin was also there. At the regular American League meeting that followed, Bobby was introduced to the members and officially elected and afterward introduced to the press. Everything went fine. (The only slight reservation I had was when Bobby told the press he wasn't sold on the designated hitter rule.) Although my time as president would not end until the last day of the year and although Bobby could not physically come to New York and take over until sometime in February, my real league responsibilities were fulfilled.

It was now time for me to concentrate on my new office as president of the Player Relations Committee and to start preparing for the 1984–1985 negotiations for a new Basic Agreement with the players. Fortunately the PRC staff was good: two young lawyers (John Westhoff and Lou Melendez), Sandy Dengler (our computer expert), Wendy Selig (doing her pre-law internship), and Eleanor Mieszerski (who ran the office and did the important administrative work for Barry Rona and me). I was particularly fortunate to have Barry as my aide, as he was experienced, able, practical, and maintained his sense of humor throughout it all. We worked together very well.

It was generally recognized—for several reasons—that the coming negotiations would not be easy. Any hopes that we were in "an era of good feelings" (a la the days of President James Monroe) were dispelled with the firing of Ken Moffitt. We knew that Marvin Miller was going to be most influential in his new role as consultant, and that Don Fehr, whose title was "acting director," was on trial. In other words, he was going to have to produce. On the clubs' side, there were also strong feelings as to what must be accomplished. The economics of the game had become alarming. From a time as recent as the late seventies, when the industry was roughly in a break-even position, costs had been rising annually at so rapid a rate that by 1983 eighteen of twenty-six teams were losing money. Most of the owners had no real thoughts of making substantial money from their baseball team, but they did want to break even. And some of them were losing sizable sums—anywhere from five million to ten million per year. The clubs blamed free agency and salary arbitration, as most of the increased costs were due to player salaries. They were the two bug-a-boos and they wanted something done to lessen their economic effect. Finally, a big new issue had developed that clearly was going to be very difficult for both sides. This was the question of the amount of the annual club contribution to the Players' Pension Plan.

Miller and the Players' Association had, in recent negotiations, claimed that the size of that contribution should equal one-third of the amount the clubs received from their national television broadcasts. The clubs had always steadfastly refuted this and there had never been an agreement of such a nature, but their contributions had actually been close to that amount under recent Basic Agreements. The players had also used the cost of living as an argument for increases in the contribution. It had turned out that in practice in recent negotiations both arguments resulted in a comparable increase. In 1983, however, Bowie Kuhn and his TV negotiating committee of Bill Giles of the Phillies and Eddie Einhorn of the White Sox had managed to reach agreements with ABC and NBC bringing very substantial increases in national TV revenues to baseball. The Players' Pension Plan was already excellent (the best in sports), and to put additional funds of staggering proportions into the plan at a time when most of the clubs were losing money and were looking to these increased revenues to assist them economically, was, in the opinion of the clubs, unthinkable. On the other hand, the Players' Association was going to be equally determined not to give up their sacrosanct one-third formula. These and other issues were what confronted us. Some of the issues were not major but would require delicate negotiations; some were very important financially; others were emotional issues.

One thing we had was time. The present agreement ran through the 1984 season, so we had all of 1984 and until opening day 1985 to complete an agreement. Of course, everyone said, "Why let things drag on until the last minute and risk the chance of a strike?" But in practice, at least in negotiations of this type, neither side was going to uncover its hole card until late in the game. Although the Players' Association leaders used to chide us in the press and urged us to make early offers to achieve an early agreement, both sides knew there was no way a settlement could be reached without the pressures of a deadline. The constituents of each side would be convinced their negotiators had settled for less than could have been obtained if any agreement was concluded months before necessary. Someday, hopefully, that will not be the case, but the economics of the game will have to be more settled (or satisfactorily encompassed in the agreement). And the two sides will have to have a better, more trusting relationship and a more mature approach to their problems. Both sides knew that situation did not exist in 1984.

With some leeway as far as time, we were at least in a position to do some advance planning and to try to get our organization and our own people prepared for difficult negotiations. The previous negotiations had been a disaster and we had to learn from our mistakes. The clubs had already started this process by letting Ray Grebey go. I knew far less about labor negotiations than Ray, but I did have the advantage of knowing our own people better. (I also had the advantage of not being viewed by the players as some tough labor figure brought in from the outside to beat them down at the table.) We were determined to do everything in our power during the first half of 1984 to get ready and we started holding regular discussion meetings amongst ourselves very soon after I became head of the PRC in June of 1983. Those meetings were attended by Barry Rona, legal counsel of the PRC; Chub Feeney, National League president; Lou Hoynes, National League counsel; Jim Garner, American League counsel; and myself. We five had been through much of the past negotiating history together. We were friends, respected one another, and did not hesitate to express our own opinions. After Bobby Brown came on board, he became a sixth member of our group. The Player Relations Committee itself had consisted of eight members—the two league presidents and three owner members from each league. In the 1980–81 negotiations the league representatives had been Ed Fitzgerald (Milwaukee), John McHale (Montreal), Bob Howsam (Cincinnati), Clark Griffith (Minnesota), Joe Burke (Kansas City), and Dan Galbreath (Pittsburgh). It was the custom to have an owner representative serve as chairman and Ed Fitzgerald and later Dan Galbreath had performed this duty. By 1984 some changes had been made in the membership of the committee. It was a seven-man group consisting of four owners—Bud Selig (Milwaukee), Ed Williams (Baltimore), Peter O'Malley (Los Angeles), John McMullen (Houston)—the two league presidents, and myself. I was pleased when Bud was made chairman, as we had always worked well together.

In the 1981 negotiations, one of the chief complaints of the clubs was that they were not kept properly informed. I didn't think it was really a valid criticism but we determined that this time we would use the time at our disposal to fully brief them in advance and to give them a chance to express their views. We decided to do this through regional meetings and later to update them in the same manner. In addition I decided that—even before the regional meetings commenced—I would try to have a "one-on-one" meeting with each team individually to see just how they felt, how tough they were going to want us to be and what their priority issues were. This was going to take much time and work but hopefully it would not only pay dividends in creating club unity but would be helpful to me personally. I was able to accomplish this, for the most part, during the last few months of 1983. I believe my last such meeting was in Montreal in February of 1984, when I had lunch with the full Board of Directors of the Montreal club.

The first few months of 1984 were devoted primarily to the Joint Drug Program, but we did have several Joint PRC-Executive Council meetings, plus separate Executive Council meetings on PRC matters. We also had many planning and discussion meetings of our inner group of six (two league presidents, myself, and three legal counsels). And after the All-Star Game in San Francisco (in which the American League reverted to its losing ways), we started holding the regional meetings. Each meeting was attended by between five and seven clubs. Barry and I were always there for the PRC, plus at least one league president and one league counsel, and from one to four members of our PRC Executive Committee. When these meetings were concluded, every club had now had a chance to voice its complaints, concerns, and objectives before we started preparing our position. In addition to meeting with owners and general managers in this fashion, I arranged separate meetings to brief and listen to club PR people on one occasion, club controllers on another, club doctors on a third. I also set up an advisory panel of club PR people, as press relations had been another big complaint of the clubs about the previous negotiations. At the same time, club PR directors—who talked to the press on a daily basis—were complaining that they never knew in the past what the club position was. How could they help get our arguments and our story out if they didn't know what it was? I drafted Bob Fishel (on loan) from the American League to handle our media relations. I particularly wanted Bob's help because of his low-key, professional approach and because he was greatly respected by the baseball press people all over the country.

One more advisory panel was composed of club lawyers and negotiators who dealt with salary arbitration to see what procedural changes they might suggest to make this program work more favorably for the clubs. These moves were all helpful, especially later when we got into the pressure of daily negotiating meetings. Finally, I appointed an informal "Kitchen Cabinet" of four knowledgeable professionals with whom I could converse and off whom I could bounce ideas. The four were Jim Campbell (Detroit), Joe Burke (Kansas City), Hank Peters (Baltimore), and Bob Howsam (Cincinnati). When Bob retired, Frank Cashen took his spot. These were the people who actually ran teams and struggled with the day-to-day operations and I wanted to be able to turn to them to discuss the advisability of proposals and the pitfalls of changes.

We tried again to get strike insurance, meeting several times with representatives from Lloyds of London and also with Larry Rhea (our old Kansas City Blues radio announcer) about coverage by American companies. We could have secured it but the cost—because they had to pay off last time—made it impractical. In addition, as I have noted, it had impeded the 1981 negotiations. That was not the approach we wanted to pursue in 1984. At this point I was hopeful that the Joint Drug Program would help provide a better spirit between the two parties and assist us in working things out together.

One suggestion made by several of the clubs during our first round of regional meetings was that we hire an outside, experienced, labor consultant to advise us. As businessmen, I guess they were a little uneasy about having their negotiations carried on by an amateur. It is true that I was an amateur in the labor field, but I did not consider that our three lawyers were. Barry had worked for the NLRB before he came to baseball; Jim Garner did a lot of labor work for his firm; and Lou Hoynes was bright enough for any field. Moreover, those three—plus Chub and myself—had had more experience with baseball negotiations than anyone on either side. However if the clubs were uneasy on this score, we had no problem with hiring someone to fill this role and we eventually made an arrangement with George Morris, who had recently retired from General Motors where he had been in charge of labor relations. The clubs were reassured and George was valuable to us, though it was very difficult for him, not having the background of baseball labor negotiations and not being involved on an everyday basis.

There were, of course, other things going on in baseball in 1984 other than our preparations for the negotiations. The Orioles, who had been selected to make baseball's bi-annual trip to Japan, after apparently agreeing to go, voted not to go unless there were significant changes in the economic package. This was the doing of the Players' Association. It had never gotten closely involved in arrangements for this trip in the past, but had really jumped in now and, as a result, I had to have many meetings with Mark Belanger and phone conversations with Hank Peters of the Orioles before we finally got it worked out. I think the voices of reason in this case were Scott McGregor, the Orioles' player representative, and Ron Shapiro, who served as agent for many Oriole players.

In February, I had yet another confrontation with the Yankees when Oakland selected Tim Belcher in the "Compensation Draft." Oakland was entitled to select from a pool of players provided by all clubs, as they had lost a free agent (Tom Underwood) to the Orioles. Their choice of a player without professional experience surprised everyone, but the Yankees had not protected him and the A's selection was clearly within the rules. I sympathized with the Yankees, but actually, it was their own error that brought about the loss as there had been no need to sign him and put him on the roster in time to expose him to selection.

The Search Committee had recommended Peter Ueberroth as the next commissioner and he was elected at a meeting in March, but was not to commence his duties until October. There were the memorable Hall of Fame ceremonies at Cooperstown in July with Luis Aparicio, Harmon Killebrew, Pee Wee Reese, Don Drysdale, and Rick Ferrell—all special people for me—being inducted. There was a nostalgic night at Fenway Park in May, when Joe Cronin's (5) and Ted Williams' (9) numbers were retired, but a most unhappy date in September on Cape Cod when I served as an honorary pallbearer at Joe's funeral. When Peter Ueberroth came aboard and the League Championship Series began, the umpires greeted the new commissioner by striking. Richie Phillips planned his timing well and his union made a significant financial gain before going back to work for the World Series.

And then the World Series, with the Tigers trouncing San Diego. Unfortunately, all hell broke loose after the final game at Tiger Stadium. Uncontrolled pandemonium resulted in cars being overturned, burning, and rioting. My brother Bill and I walked back to the hotel through the thick of it. It was dangerous to be in a car, but walking, wearing a Tiger cap, and holding up your finger to represent "we're number one," made you part of the wild throng. It was not a good night for baseball but the real destruction and rioting was not carried out by baseball fans but by gangs of youths looking for any excuse to riot.

Our negotiations commenced in November and we met twice in New York that month. We agreed that we would use any meetings in December for both sides simply to raise and give their views on issues that they felt should be addressed in the negotiations. We then proceeded with our second round of regional meetings with our clubs because, having the initial input from the first round and being better advised as to what the players demands were likely to be, we were ready to start refining our own position. We held meetings in Los Angeles, Chicago, and New York and these were immediately followed by the annual major league meetings in Houston. I took advantage of the fact that there were always many press people in attendance to hold my first formal press conference on the coming negotiations. I tried to present a reasonable, low key, optimistic attitude and the response was good. Four more meetings with the Players' Association followed—two in New York and two in Los Angeles—before the year ended. Many players attended these meetings, particularly in California, and each side outlined its concerns and what it hoped to achieve. The preliminaries engaged in during the last two months of 1984 were now behind us and it was time to get down to hard bargaining.

It was very clear from the start that we were far apart on many issues and our feeling that it was to be a difficult exercise was proving to be true. Clearly the biggest issues were the players' demand for one-third of the national TV revenue as the Benefit Plan contribution and the clubs' determination to try to do something to halt the out-of-control increase in player costs. There were still other matters that were not going to be easily resolved. The players wanted to change the procedures governing termination pay if a player was released, to provide a full year's salary regardless of the date the player was released. The players wanted any player assigned outright to the National Association to have the right to opt for free agency. And the players were complaining that the clubs were violating a clause in the existing Basic Agreement which prohibited concerted action by the clubs in dealing with free agents. Of course, they routinely wanted a major hike in the minimum salary as well. We wanted the players to go along with a seven-game LCS. We wanted the clubs to be able to bring players up in September, at the close of the season, without their being credited with service time. We wanted players to be able to agree in their contracts to waive rights that gave them the ability to demand, or prevent, a trade. And we wanted to be sure that a fair portion of any increase in our pension contribution would be credited to older, retired players. We had our work cut out for us.

Before we even got started we ran into a major crisis. John McMullen, an outspoken owner of the Houston team and a member of our PRC Executive Committee, told the press that "the players should get rid of Miller and Fehr" and that "the economic position of the clubs had to be considered at the bargaining table." The Players' Association was furious. The first statement was certainly injudicious and not defendable. The second, although I personally agreed with what John was saying, brought up an argument that was a major issue in the 1981 negotiations. The players had complained that economic objectives were a factor in the clubs' bargaining tactics and that they should therefore be privy to team financial information. They filed a complaint with the NLRB demanding such financial information for the years 1978–79–80. The clubs had always maintained that their position was not based on their "ability to pay" and had consistently refused to give the association financial information. And in 1981, the court supported the club position. McMullen's statement had re-opened this whole can of worms and the Players' Association refused to bargain further until it received an explanation of McMullen's statements. Barry and I had an informal lunch with Don, Mark, and Gene Orza—apologized for John's first statement—and told them we would not be arguing "ability to pay." Eventually, after the exchange of a couple of letters, we got the negotiating meetings back on schedule.

That fire was no more than put out when a new controversy arose over the Dodgers putting drug clauses in the contracts of some of their players. This was contrary to the provisions of our Joint Drug Program and we had to get the Dodgers to rescind these contracts (this did not please our new commissioner). But finally, on February 7th, we were back at the table in Chicago. There were players present and when players were there the association representatives always seemed to feel they had to put on a show. This meeting became strident. It was discouraging. I remember lecturing myself that it was essential "to hang patiently tough," but the key question remained: How were we going to convince them to give up their claim to one-third of the national TV revenue? We needed to be able to give them some valid reason for such an important step, one that involved millions of dollars. That reason was the financial state of the industry. This was not a bargaining stratagem. It was the truth.

We took three days off for another round of regional meetings—in Los Angeles, Chicago, and New York again. Some of the clubs, especially those at the California meeting, understood the problem and strongly urged the release of financial information. If done, this would be a revolutionary step. Many clubs guarded their financial statements closely—even the league offices and the commissioner's office were not privy to them. On the other hand, the situation called for revolutionary measures and we started debating this course in our staff meetings. All of us, except Chub, were convinced that giving the Players' Association the financial information was the only means we had of convincing the players that they should take a more moderate position with regard to the pension contribution. Although the Players' Association had demanded our figures in the past, it did so knowing the clubs would not give them up. Marvin had said to us several times across the table, "If you truly have economic problems come to us and we will sit down together and try to find reasonable solutions." I am paraphrasing, but that was the substance of his remarks. I think he believed that the clubs were making substantial amounts of money and that when we pleaded financial problems it was just a bargaining ploy. If that were so, we naturally could not give them the financial figures. In my mind, the fact that the Players' Association did not think there was truly a problem in this area was the real reason it was most important that they see the operating numbers. After one of our staff meetings, we had a telephone conference call with our PRC Executive Council and told them how we felt about releasing the financial information. They were very upset— especially John McMullen. I guess we had sprung this on them without proper advance preparation but at least now the seed was well planted. Barry and I then went to apprise Peter Ueberroth of the action we wanted to take.

It is difficult to accurately and fairly portray Peter's role throughout the entire negotiations. I guess there are three main points I would have to make. First, with Barry and me personally, he was exceptionally supportive. No one could have asked for a better one-on-one relationship. He was always ready, in fact seemed eager, to back us in any disagreements we might have with any of the clubs over our policies or actions. Second, he was far more concerned with the PR aspect of everything than we were. At times, it seemed that the publicity and potential press reaction was as important to him as the substance of the issue. In fairness, his position required him to give a great deal of consideration to this aspect of the negotiations. He was very bright and very quick and had disciplined himself to always think one step ahead newswise. He thought in terms of what headline he would like to read in tomorrow's paper. Third, to some degree, he was an unknown factor in the beginning. You could never be absolutely sure what his reaction to something was going to be or what he might do on his own that would come as a surprise to you. Several incidents of this nature had happened (or were about to happen) that caught me, at least, by surprise. The more we worked with him, however— and I guess as we all got to know each other better—this was less of a problem. I think Barry and I came to understand what we could count on and what we couldn't. This was not true with our people on the PRC Executive Committee and as a result misunderstandings did later arise between them and the commissioner. On the other hand, especially as the negotiations got down toward the end, Barry and Lou Hoynes and I pretty well knew where Peter stood.

When Barry and I related to Peter our conclusion that we needed to give the association (and the public) our financial figures and the reasons for our conclusions, he was in complete agreement and assured us of his backing. In fact, he told us that if the clubs would not willingly accede to our request, he would order them to do so. We then were assured of the ammunition we needed. We could go to the Players' Association, and even more important to the public, with our troubled financial picture. We could then rightfully argue that, although individual clubs might have their financial ups and downs, the industry as a whole, over a period of time, should at least be able to break even. It would then be our objective to work out with the Players' Association, over the course of the negotiations, a fair and reasonable system of club-player relations that would provide this. The NBA had done something similar to this. If their players were willing to accept this approach why shouldn't ours? So at a major league meeting in New York on February 26th we requested that the clubs permit us to use club financial information in the negotiations and to supply us with their financial statements and all the back-up material we would need for the purpose. The clubs voted to do so, but some preliminary statements by Ueberroth clearly had a bearing on the votes cast by some of them. It is doubtful that we could have achieved concurrence without Peter's help. There were also some Peter-type surprises at this meeting. He simply announced that there would be no more regional meetings; no meetings of the PRC Executive Council; that Barry and I—with the advice of the league presidents and counsel—would have the authority to do whatever we thought best. I was not really in accord with this. On the surface that made our job easier but I still believed firmly in having the clubs well advised and with us each important step of the way. In any event, at a negotiating meeting on February 27th, we told the Players' Association of the change in our position and that we could not continue with the negotiations without introducing, as a factor, the financial condition of the game. We now had a completely new ball game.

The Players' Association appeared to accept our shift in gears rationally, but it was quickly apparent that it would not settle for consolidated industry figures or the like. It wanted individual financial statements, even if not expressly identified, and when it received this the association asked for all kinds of explanatory, back-up, financial information. The negotiations pretty much came to a standstill while first, we gathered and supplied the information it demanded;

then second, while it took the necessary time to analyze it. By now we were in spring training and were holding meetings in different spots to accommodate the union, as it was going from camp to camp to meet with the players. Meeting number fourteen was in Tampa and number fifteen was in Clearwater Beach. In an effort to make some progress at the Clearwater meeting on the myriad issues, other than the pension contribution and other major issues that had an impact on the clubs' financial operations, we made a comprehensive proposal that covered thirty-seven different items. We put these in three categories: (1) those on which we felt we were close to agreement in principle; (2) six player demands that we asked the union to drop; (3) six club requests that we offered to drop as part of the general compromise. These proposals covered matters such as spring training reporting dates, the certification of trainers, simplification of the waiver procedure, allowances, assignments outside the United States and Canada, scheduling rules, health and safety matters, termination pay, Latin American exhibition games, September service time, a seven-game LCS, etc. These proposals at least put many things in focus and made it more difficult for the Players' Association to keep telling press and players that we were stalling.

When we moved to the Arizona spring camps and held meetings in Scottsdale and Palm Springs, the Players' Association took a very negative position about our financial claims and about moderating its one-third Benefit Plan demand, but we did make progress on the seven-game LCS. We needed an immediate decision on this in order to enable the networks to plan their schedules and we, at last, with the help of the Angels players who were attending those meetings (Bob Boone, Doug DeCinces, Reggie Jackson, etc.) were able to work something out that bypassed for the moment the question of whether the players got TV revenue from the games, but that enabled us to go ahead with the seven-game format. This was good progress, but they were still not giving ground on the major economic issues. They wanted to know what we were proposing to "cure our claimed economic problems." Our answer was that we wanted to convince them that a problem did exist and then work out something, in partnership, across the table, to ameliorate club losses. We were not asking to roll back salaries, or even put a cap on them, but simply asking them to assist us in constructing a system that would slow down the excessive annual increase in player costs. I tried to convince them that we were not interested in trying to make money for owners but were more concerned with the health and the welfare of the game itself and the ability of our smaller cities such as Milwaukee, Cincinnati, Seattle, and Kansas City to support major league baseball. The way I saw it, this was important for the players of the future, as well as for the public and the game itself.

Unfortunately, it was soon apparent that the Players' Association was not interested in an objective analysis of the teams' financial figures. Its countless requests for information transcended what was needed to ascertain the economics of the club operations and began to lean more toward a search for material it could find fault with. A few of the clubs had complicated corporate structures and operations and the association focused more on this than on the overall picture. It hired Roger Noll of the Brookings Institute as a consultant. It made sense to hire an impartial economic consultant who would look at the statements realistically and advise the association as to whether there was, or was not, a serious problem. But Noll was a man with a past record of consistently going against baseball management. Before he even saw the figures he was making public statements denigrating them. He was hired for one purpose and that was to help cast doubt on the club figures and give credence to a public attack upon them. Actually, the figures were reliable. They had all been audited by Big Eight accounting firms and followed standard accounting practices, just like any other American business. Eventually we were forced to hire our own expert to answer the attacks and we asked Professor George Shorter of New York University to study the statements and advise us if there was anything in them that should be altered in order to portray the situation fairly. We adjusted our figures to eliminate depreciation taken on player contracts when a club was purchased by new ownership and made a few other changes to recognize complaints the association had put forward. Even after that, the 1983 figures (the latest we had) showed baseball losing an aggregate of over $43,000,000. Although the union would never admit the validity of our figures publicly there was no way it could have worked with them and not understood that genuine problems existed, so the use of the financial figures, without question, did accomplish its purpose. Difficult problems were created for some of our clubs, but overall it was an essential move and our most important decision of the negotiations.

When we were unable to get the Players' Association to assist us in constructing a new system designed to slow down the increase in club operating costs, we put together our own plan. Commissioner Stern and other officials of the NBA were helpful to us in sharing their experiences in this area. We devised a plan for baseball based on the average 1985 club payroll—which came out to approximately $10.7 million for twenty-five players per club. Under our new plan, the relationship of a team's actual payroll at any time to the established "Annual Payroll Level" would then determine the rules and procedures governing the operations of that team. There were no limitations on what a team could give its own players even if that put it further over the level, but teams over the level could not acquire other players (free agents or acquisitions by trade) if it put them further over the level. Teams over the level, if the rule was adopted, would be given time to adjust to the level. The level would be adjusted annually and changed in response to increased attendance or the gross income of baseball overall. It was, in effect, a partnership, giving the players as a group a certain percentage of baseball's income. The "Baseball Payroll Plan" also included sections dealing with free agency and salary arbitration. For the players, free agency would be liberalized by eliminating the draft and professional player compensation. For the clubs, salary arbitration would be restricted by changing the eligibility requirement from two years' service to three and putting a cap on arbitrators' awards by limiting them to a 100 percent increase. We incorporated our multi-issue proposal given the players in Clearwater with this; offered to raise the minimum salary from $40,000 to $60,000; and presented it to the Players' Association as a "Comprehensive Proposal For A New Basic Agreement."

It was greeted by the other side with a remarkable lack of enthusiasm—in fact, rather with belligerency and rudeness. At this time, Ueberroth was trying to speak with the players on each team and was going into the clubhouses to talk to them as a group. Primarily about drugs. He did shock us, however (one of his surprises), by telling the players not to worry about the salary plan. Marvin and Don asked us how we expected them to consider our proposal when even the commissioner was opposed to it. When Peter told the press he thought the plan impractical, I responded publicly that, "I sharply disagree with the commissioner." I don't think he minded my statement and respected my independence. Moreover, it was his own wish to take a middle position and represent the fans (and to the extent possible, the players), as well as the owners. For all practical purposes, the commissioner's opposition ended the Payroll Plan, though I do not think the association would have accepted it in any event. It is unfortunate because the basic philosophy of an economic partnership of players and clubs is a good one. In any event, the proposal served a purpose to a degree by surfacing important positions on free agency, salary arbitration, and the minimum salary.

The 1985 All-Star Game was played in Minneapolis on July 16th. The union used the three off days in the regular schedule to meet with its Executive Committee of players and on July 15th, it announced publicly that if there was no agreement by August 6th, the players would go on strike at that time. When we all returned to New York, we suggested to them that we hold informal, small, away-from-

the-table meetings to see if we could not break the logjam of unresolved issues. The first was held at our East Side apartment on July
22nd. Marvin and Don were there for the union and Barry, Lou
Hoynes, and myself for our side. We tried another "partnership-type"
approach, but got nowhere with it. Other non-formal meetings of the
same group were held in the ensuing days at our apartment, Marvin's
apartment, and an office in the Helmsley Building. Both sides were
now down to last offers on the major issues. We offered a 100 percent
increase in the pension contribution (still far short of the one-third
formula the clubs had never agreed to) and asked for significant
changes in three areas of salary arbitration (one year less eligibility, a
100 percent cap on increases, and some language and procedural
changes). They were demanding some restrictions on the rights of the
original club to re-sign its free agents—a change aimed at eliminating
what they felt was "concerted behavior" by the clubs in signing free
agents. During this time, starting August 1st, we were having daily
meetings with our PRC Executive Committee (all the members of
which took up temporary residence in New York City) with Peter
Ueberroth sitting in on portions of these meetings.

Two more regular meetings took place, these at the offices of
Willkie, Farr, and Gallagher (National League counsel) on August 3
and 4. We were getting some things settled. The tough nuts remained
to be agreed upon, but at the meeting on the third they finally
indicated that they would come off their one-third formula for the
pension contribution. That was a big step for, without compromise
there, there would surely have been a major strike. Once the Players'
Association was willing to make meaningful compromises in this key
area, in my mind, there was no justification for another long strike
that would be damaging to baseball. And Peter was warning us that he
would not tolerate it—in fact we had to plead with him to stay out of
the proceedings and let us go all the way, even including the start of
the strike, to gain whatever we could in the final bargaining. We went
away from the table to try to resolve the last stormy issues and at a
meeeting at Marvin's apartment on decision date, August 6th, I
thought they were about to grant us the relief we needed in salary
arbitration that would have put us over the hump—but then there was
a phone call, from whom I can only guess—and the optimism of the
moment evaporated. We met twice more that night, at the Helmsley
Building and at our apartment. The time had come to make whatever
compromises had to be made and wrap things up for good. If we
could finish on August 7th we could get the players back to their clubs
quickly and any scheduled games not played could be made up. We
told the association we were ready to meet in the morning with the
anticipation of making a deal.

The association brought several players with them on the 7th. Barry, Lou, and I represented the clubs. It was our 43rd formal bargaining session. There wasn't too much left to bargain about. We got about half of what we wanted in salary arbitration; an extra year of eligibility and some improvement in language, but no cap. We agreed on an approximate 100 percent increase in the Benefit Plan contribution (about $32.5 million per annum or about one-half of what the one-third formula would have required). We agreed there would be dates limiting the original clubs' right to re-sign free agents. Most of the other issues had already been agreed to—at least in principle. We let Don and Barry sit down together and draw up a general memorandum of understanding. Peter Ueberroth joined us and then announced a late afternoon press conference to tell the baseball world that the two-day strike was over. It was a great feeling. We had not solved baseball's financial problems it is true, but for the first time in our labor history we had made some gains for baseball*; we had avoided a major strike; had hopefully made some progress in our relationship with the union; and had five years ahead (the longest agreement yet negotiated) without worrying about negotiating a new Basic Agreement. My job was accomplished and although I certainly wasn't completely satisfied with the results, I was satisfied that we had done our best and achieved all that we could without subjecting baseball to another long and crippling strike.

Before a week passed I wrote the commissioner and Bud Selig, chairman of the PRC, tendering my resignation, effective at the end of the year, and strongly urging them to make Barry Rona head of the PRC in my place. Fortunately this was subsequently done. There was a major league meeting in St. Louis to ratify the agreement and then the annual meeting in San Diego in December before my term was officially up. There was another major league meeting in Dallas in early January to which they insisted I come and on the night before the meeting I was honored with a special dinner. I was moved by much that went on that night but particularly with the commissioner's announcement that a $100,000 scholarship had been set up at Swarthmore College in my name. That scholarship, plus the American League's establishment of the Most Valuable Player Award in the League Championship Series in my name, are honors of permanence that mean very much to me. And so my baseball career finally came to an end. Before leaving I wrote the clubs urging them to accomplish on

---

*Chiefly, the abandonment of the Players' Association claim to one-third of the national television revenue, one less year of salary arbitration, and a seven-game League Championship Series.

their own, by their own individual financial discipline, the fiscal responsibility necessary to keep baseball viable. Surprisingly, in some
areas, they seem to have heeded my advice.

14

Post-Game—Retirement and Looking Back

Now that my forty-two years in baseball are behind me, am I glad that I chose this path, or should I have gone to Law School or Graduate Business School as my father urged? Thankfully, I have no regrets at all. It has been an extremely interesting and a reasonably rewarding way of spending one's life. The work varied with the season of the year and was partly office work, partly out of doors. It was generally enjoyable and almost always interesting—in fact absorbing. It was never boring

There were a few drawbacks of course. As far as I know, no one works in the Garden of Eden. The hours were demanding, especially during the season. Night games on top of regular office hours could make it a tough grind and weekends didn't necessarily mean time off. "True," some of my uninformed friends would occasionally say, "but the season only runs from April to October." Yet work in professional baseball goes on twelve months a year and is sometimes more demanding in the off-season than during the season itself.

In the off-season, at the club level, there are season schedules to work on; working agreements with National Association clubs to be finalized; organization decisions about the scouting staff and minor league managers and coaches to be made. And all of the people have to be signed to yearly contracts. Efforts to improve the team at the major league level are continuous and involve the study of hundreds of reports on teams and individual players, major league and minor, within and outside of your own organization. The major league players must be signed to contracts—each negotiation a difficult one with a demanding agent. If any of the players go to salary arbitration, the case must be prepared and argued as if it were a case before the United States Supreme Court. Fall Instructional Leagues go on in Florida and Arizona and winter baseball in the Caribbean. And there are myriad other things to be done of a non-baseball, but related, nature. Each department has its agenda. Financial matters and the budget, a season ticket sale, broadcasting arrangements, publications, promotions, maintenance of the stadium, union contracts, travel and hotel arrangements, uniforms and equipment, public appearances, preparations for spring training, and countless other tasks necessary to the playing of the game on the field. In addition, there are numerous off-season meetings for baseball executives at various locations. November, December, and January—the only months the team is not playing—can be very busy.

But it is not simply because of the time required that a job in baseball can dominate your life. The problem is also that you get so caught up in it emotionally that if you are not careful you will not maintain your interest in other matters or develop new interests or even devote the proper amount of time to your family. I don't think I neglected my family, although we didn't have many dinners together when the team was home and there were many holidays when most fathers were home and I was at work.

On the other hand, my family was able to be more a part of my work and share its ups and downs than the wives and children of most fathers. And there were offsetting plusses: times when the family could be with me (such as spring training); trips to minor league cities; and the games themselves. The only time that Jane and I actually got away from baseball completely was for a week or so in the fall. We would jump in the car and head for one of our favorite inns in New England (usually Maine) and enjoy the foliage and the changing of the seasons.

My boys spent a lot of time around the ballpark and in my office and waiting for me after games.* When they were older, at one time or another, they worked part of the summer for the baseball team or the concessionaire. Lee worked in the visiting clubhouse at Baltimore, helping the clubhouse man. Bruce and Andy both worked for the concession department in New York, deep in the bowels of the stadium, checking vendors out and in and balancing their receipts. Also each boy—through their uncle, who at that time was sports director for CBS—worked for a professional football team at their pre-season camp, helping the equipment man and doing odd jobs. Lee worked for the Colts, Al for the Cowboys, Bruce for the Falcons, and Andy for the Vikings. (Myself—I'm a rabid Giants fan.)

---

*Generally when I came out after a game there were a gang of kids waiting to get the players' autographs and especially in my younger days I would be mobbed. Someone at the back of the group would yell, "Who is it?" and then one of the kids who had gotten my autograph would exclaim in disgust, "Oh, he's nobody." But you couldn't not sign; they wouldn't believe it if you tried to tell them you were nobody; plus we were always urging the players to be patient and sign. I could hardly refuse to do so myself.

Marian was clearly Dad's favorite and he was always very proud of her. And well he should have been. After getting a graduate degree at Columbia and working for a while at New York Hospital where she met her husband-to-be,* she had a long and illustrious career at Time-Life Inc. She started with *Time* and ultimately became chief of research at *Life*. In that position she hired most of the bright young people coming to work for the magazine, including people who ultimately occupied top spots on the editorial staff. Bill, after his years in baseball, became sports director for CBS and was instrumental in starting the telecasts of NFL games. After a long term at CBS, he went to Atlanta to become sports director for Ted Turner's Cable News Network.

While with Baltimore, Jane and the boys and I could also get up to Bel Air to see my father. After he left the Yankees, Dad decided to purchase an old dairy farm and to breed cattle in Harford County, north of Baltimore, near Bel Air. The place was badly run down but the site and the surrounding rolling country were beautiful. My father's greatest satisfaction came from building and improving things, whether a baseball team or a neglected Maryland farm. When the house, guest house, and barns were completed and a natural pool installed, he planned a golf course around the center of his property and bought up as much of the land adjoining the outside of the plotted course as was available. He then built the golf course and convinced area residents to buy it and inaugurate a private club. Today it is the Bel Air Country Club.

Cattle didn't really fit into Dad's character and it wasn't long before he had switched to horses and was breeding and selling at Keeneland and Saratoga. True to form, it was not long before he set sales records at the latter. His children soon found themselves involved in horse syndicates—at first at no cost, later at cost (and you couldn't refuse). By now he also had several corporations: one owned the land, one operated the farm, another was involved in his other enterprises. And we were always on the boards. We all served reluctantly, as we knew nothing of what went on and worried about our legal responsibilities (and well we should have because eventually we

---

*Marian married Walsh McDermott, who was a professor of medicine at Cornell and later a top advisor at the Robert Wood Johnson Foundation in Princeton. Walsh was a bright and dedicated man who served as editor of a top medical textbook and who, earlier in his career, had done extensive research on tuberculosis on the Navajo Reservation in Arizona. They had a great life together in Manhattan and at their home outside the city in Pawling, N.Y. in Dutchess County, until Walsh's death in 1981.

were confronted with financial obligations). My father also got involved with the racetrack at Bowie and couldn't resist racing a few horses of his own. Some of them did quite well. He gave Marian, Bill, and me each a horse—or at least put it in our names. Bill's horse never got to the track but Marian's did quite well. Mine, named "Once a Dodger," had trouble getting out of the gate, but finally won a race at Rockingham and was claimed. And the IRS kept wanting to know why I hadn't declared the purse or claiming prize, neither of which I saw.

I often wondered if my father didn't have some regrets that he left baseball as early as he did; or regretted the incidents that led to his leaving the Red Birds, the Reds, and the Yankees. If he did, he never related them to me. He was a very proud man and he was not about to publicly admit mistakes or discuss them with his children. More than that, he was not the kind of man who looked back on past happenings. Instead, even at an advanced age, he was always looking forward. He seldom reminisced with us about his past life (even an episode like the attempt to capture the Kaiser). It was the future, not the past, that interested him. He would rather talk about his hopes for one of his yearling horses, or tell me who should be playing right field for the Orioles.

While it is true that I did not have a summer vacation during my years in baseball, and didn't really take much time off at any time of the year, there were things that more than made up for it. The annual baseball meetings, which come in early December, take you to some glamorous spots—Mexico, Hawaii, Florida, California, New Orleans—and the general managers always picked a pleasant fall locale—Scottsdale, Casa Grande, Ligonier, or Sarasota—for their meeting. And then there was the weekend at Cooperstown, right in the middle of the season, for the Hall of Fame ceremonies, a delightful and meaningful event. One of the nice things about being a league president is that you become a member of the Baseball Hall of Fame Board of Directors, and I have remained on the board after my time with the American League was concluded. Financed by admissions to the museum and to the annual exhibition game (in which the American League holds a twenty-four to sixteen edge over the National League) and by contributions, mostly from baseball people and the Clark Foundation, the museum houses a wonderful collection of baseball memorabilia. The induction ceremonies, with two or three baseball greats being inducted each year, and with outstanding representatives of the press and broadcasting media also being recognized, are truly a highlight of the year and a moving experience. In 1978, three years after his death, my father was inducted. Dad had always maintained that the Hall of Fame should be for players only and that if elected he would not agree to be inducted. I think, in part, he believed that but also, in part, I think it was a defense mechanism to insulate himself from the disappointment of not being elected. He was passed over a few times and there were legitimate arguments against inducting him. He had actually worked in the major leagues a scant ten years and ten years' service was supposed to be a requirement. Plus, some people questioned some aspects of his activities. Rumor had it that Warren Giles led the opposition to his election. If that is true it is a little ironic that Dad's plaque at Cooperstown and Warren's hang right next to one another.

In any event, our family was there in mass for the ceremonies— one wife, four children, two sons-in-law, four grandchildren, and two great grandchildren. We were all very proud. My brother and I received the plaque for Dad and while we did not attempt to white-wash all his various activities while working in baseball our feelings about him and his accomplishments were very apparent. The plaque reads:

Leland Stanford MacPhail
"LARRY"

Dynamic, innovative executive made his mark as progressive head of three clubs—Cincinnati Reds, Brooklyn Dodgers and New York Yankees—from 1933 to 1947, won championships in both Leagues— with Dodgers in 1941 and Yankees in 1947. Pioneered night ball at Cincinnati in 1935. Also installed lights at Ebbets Field and Yankee Stadium. Originated plane travel by playing personnel and idea of stadium club. Helped set up employee and player pension plans.

In my case, it is now time to find out how well I can adjust to retirement. Fortunately I have my wife Gwen to share it with. So far the news is good. It has its ups and downs—like most things in this world—but I have been thoroughly enjoying the time and the leisure. Although my interest in baseball is as keen as ever (especially in the Minnesota Twins with my son Andy working there),* I now have more opportunity to pursue other interests. From my earliest years, I have been interested in American History. When I agreed to go to Deer-field Academy to teach in 1943, it was because I thought I was going to teach American History (but ended up teaching Math). I am proud of

---

*I get as worked up about the Twins today as I used to about the Yankees or Orioles. It is a perfect retirement situation for me because I live their ups and downs but don't have the responsibility for them. And I tell Andy how lucky he has been to spend the first years of his baseball life with the Cubs, who played all day games, and then work for the Astros and Twins, who play in domes, where you don't have the headaches of deciding whether to call games for rain.

my collection of American History books. I have a biography of every American President—several of most. I also have a picture of each president, since Taft started the custom, throwing out the first ball on the Opening Day of a baseball season.

I have always been interested in classical music, and I thank my father for this. As children, the house often resounded with classical music on records—and he drew us into that world with his enthusiastic remarks about different works. Plus he began to take us to the concert hall in our early teen years. His greatest interest was in the conductor and, not surprisingly, he liked the dramatic ones. So I grew up loving music, mainly Tchaikovsky at first because he was my father's favorite. When I met Jane, she converted me to Brahms, and during our college years we made several trips from Swarthmore to Philadelphia for symphony concerts. (At the Baltimore-Philadelphia World Series in 1983 I caught a Philadelphia Symphony concert. It played Tchaikovsky's Third Symphony and the music and the hall brought back many memories.) Music has long been an essential part of my life.

I guess I feel a little like Joseph Addison (of Addison and Steele and the *Spectator*) who wrote, "Music, the greatest good that mortals know and all of heaven we have below." Some people have expressed surprise that music and baseball can be one's shared loves. I don't think it is surprising. Eugene Istomin, the noted pianist, is a close personal friend of mine. One of the reasons we are friends is that his vocation is music and his avocation is baseball, while my vocation was baseball and my avocation is music. Eugene thinks there is a natural bond between them. He expressed it thus:

What can the greatest of the performing arts and the king of spectator sports have in common? Supreme efforts effected in millimeters in the space of seconds and milliseconds. Both demand a fusion of intensity with finesse. Both are played under the pressure that excellence requires. The mastery comes from the art of channeling the adrenaline that is the offspring of do or die. That's where they meet. Can you compare a Casals, Rachmaninoff, or a Heifetz to a Ruth, Hubbell, or a Gehringer? Yes—the explosion of the marvelous action timed through the gasp and the roar makes baseball to sports what music is to the arts. The ultimate!

When I met Gwen, I found that she was not indoctrinated to music, but loved art. It seemed to me that if I was going to expect her to go to concerts with me, I was going to have to learn something about art. I started going to museums and reading about art, and as a result I got hooked on it.* I have my favorites, but I have a fairly open mind with respect to both music and art and go to many concerts and museums and galleries. In fact, in my later years in baseball I tried to see if I could get to an art museum and hear a symphony concert in every city in the American League. It was easy to use an extra hour or two to go to an art museum and I accomplished this in all fourteen cities. The concerts, as they were generally at night and required more time, were tougher and when I retired I was still missing Chicago, Dallas, Los Angeles, and Seattle. Now maybe I can pick up those missing cities.

So American History, art, and music have been important to me and combined with my interest in sports—football and golf in addition to baseball—have kept my mind active and my days interesting.‡ It is nice having time to do some of the things you always wished to do. One of my first was to return to Columbus with my brother to see an Ohio State-Michigan football game. (I for the Wolverines, Bill for the Buckeyes.) I now might even be able to make it to the Highland Games at Grandfather's Mt. in North Carolina with my son Bruce. And, of late, we have been taking a summer trip with a group each year—so far, on a private train in Scotland and on a barge in France. We have a great group, mostly baseball people who are also making up for those missed summer vacations. And living in New York City means that just about anything you wish to do is right at hand: art museums, the theater, concerts, ballet, and sporting events (for me baseball at Yankee Stadium or Shea; the Giants at the Meadowlands in the fall; an occasional outing at Belmont or Aqueduct or a Rangers' game at the Garden, etc.), or just walking down Fifth Avenue and people-watching, or taking a stroll through Central Park. Plus, it goes without saying that there are hundreds of outstanding restaurants throughout Manhattan. Recently, my wife Gwen and her daughters found a little French restaurant they prized. Gwen raved about the continental atmosphere and could hardly wait to get me there. As we were leaving, the owner came after me, "Mr. MacPhail, Mr. Mac-Phail," he called. We stopped and he said, "You don't remember me. I was in charge of the security guards at Shea Stadium." So even in retirement you can't get away from baseball, even if you wanted to.

My working days behind me, it is possible to look at baseball from a semi-detached viewpoint. Quite naturally, I have many opinions. Here is a quick rundown on just a few of them, given not because I think my

---

*If you like both art and baseball, pick up a copy of *Diamonds are Forever*, published by Chronicle Books in conjunction with the Smithsonian Institute.

‡One of my Florida golfing partners is Dom DiMaggio.

views infallible, but simply because the story of "My Nine Innings" would be incomplete without my views on these important subjects.

Designated hitter. I am basically a purist at heart when it comes to baseball. We have a great game, which somehow just fell into a perfect ratio of distances and timing. The sixty feet six inches from mound to plate; the ninety feet between bases. It all evolves into a proper confrontation between pitcher and hitter and the right distances between home and first and base to base. When a ball is fielded and fielded properly a player is just out; when it isn't, and there is some small flaw involved, it turns out he is just safe. On the other hand, few things in the world are so perfect that some small changes cannot be made to improve them. Even the United States Constitution, designed by our Founding Fathers some 200 years ago, provides for Constitutional Amendments—and we have had twenty-six of them.

When the game of baseball came into being, circumstances did not exist that made pitchers futile hitters. Somehow, over the years, circumstances have evolved that have brought professional pitchers to that status. Most pitchers simply can't hit, as 1986 National League regular season (.143) and the recent World Series figures (.111) prove. Now what excitement is there in seeing a pitcher go up and strike out (as they did 1,594 times [more than once every three at bats] in the National League in 1986)? Part of the fun of baseball is scoring—or at least the threat of scoring—and when one inning out of every three is handicapped by having the pitcher hit, it detracts from the action of the game.

The designated hitter rule, first suggested many years ago by Connie Mack, actually came into being during a period when the defense was gaining the ascendancy over the offense. Pitchers were throwing harder and coming up with varied pitches. The relief pitcher had become a critical factor in the game. Improved gloves and the improved abilities of defensive players were taking hits away from the offense. In the National League this was counter-balanced to some extent by artificial turf but the American League had less artificial turf. The American League, therefore, turned to the designated hitter rule. It has helped the offense, kept colorful stars in the game for a longer period of time, and has been accepted by the fans.* The people who don't like the DH rule are the purists and they make certain their voices are heard. The complaint—other than that any changes are bad—is that it subtracts from the strategy of the game. But the difficult decisions affecting the removal of the pitcher are not

---

*Cumulative batting average of all American League players for the five years prior to the Designated Hitter Rule—.242. Average for the first five years following its adoption—.262.

whether to pinch hit for him when you are behind, but whether to remove him for a reliever in the late innings. This applies as much—and even more often—in the American League as it does in the National.

People lament that baseball should not be played under different sets of rules. If that is so, then the National League should join the American League, ninety-five percent of the minor leagues, the colleges, the high schools, the American Legion, etc., all of which use the designated hitter. That is probably too much to expect. I am not sure how harmful it is to have this debate going on in baseball, but if there is some compelling reason that everyone should play under the same rules, then a compromise rule should—and could—be devised. At one time Chub Feeney was for this, and we discussed a compromise that would have really added strategy to the game. I tried to get him to join me in recommending this to the Executive Council but after thinking about it further he decided not to do so.* Someday baseball will probably come to this.

Home runs and the ball. As this is being written in the middle of the 1987 season, there is much discussion about the liveliness of the ball and the increase in the number of home runs. There is no question that home run production is up at this point, and significantly so. The question is whether or not it is a phenomenon of the games to date or is going to continue. Every few years, in recent times, we seem to go through this. There is much publicity and then, as home run production levels off, it subsides. Perhaps it will level off to some extent in 1987, but at this point it appears the number of home runs is clearly going to be up for the season.‡ This development is going to be interesting to watch. In an article in *The New York Times* on July 12, 1987, Leonard Koppett, a very astute student of baseball statistics, analyzed scoring and home runs in the major leagues throughout history. He pointed out that each time there has been a significant change in the numbers there has been an apparent reason for it (e.g., an intended change in the ball, either deadening it or making it more lively; the spit ball outlawed; the mound lowered; the strike zone altered). In 1987 it appears there will be a significant change, but we are still groping for the reasons.

For decades major league baseballs were made by Spalding, at its plant in Chicopee, Massachusetts. When I was league president,

---

*Chub and I did work together to eliminate many other procedures that were different in the two leagues such as the strike zone; the outside umpires' protectors; where the pitcher took his sign with men on base; where the second base umpire positioned himself with men on; etc.

‡Final 1987 figures for the two leagues combined showed home runs up by 17%.

Spalding came to us and said it could no longer get the proper horsehide and asked us to agree to a change in the specifications to substitute cowhide. This we did, and the change was made throughout all baseball without controversy. Subsequently, production of the ball became economically unfavorable for Spalding so, as its contract neared conclusion, at its instigation, we asked for bids from other companies and awarded a ten-year contract starting in 1976 to Rawlings. The Official Baseball Playing Rules and the contract with the baseball manufacturer set forth the specifications for the baseball—the center, the type of yarn, windings, the cover, stitching, weight, and circumference. We found that the Spalding ball, in the last year or two of the contract, varied from some of those specifications and was probably deader than it should have been, and the new Rawlings ball proved to be a little livelier than the Spalding ball. We felt that this was the result of getting better compliance with the specifications and we welcomed the change. After Rawlings took over we amended the specifications slightly to try to provide more standardization and added a formula called the "coefficient of restitution," which relates to a test of the ball's resilience. Actually, though, no two balls are exactly the same, as in part the balls are handmade. It seems hard to believe but all the baseball manufacturers maintain that it is not possible (or practical) to have the ball machine-stitched. Nor is it economically practical to have the ball finished in the United States. The material is therefore sent to Haiti, where the core is wrapped and the covers then sewn by hand. As they come off the end of the assembly line, the balls are checked for size, weight, and blemishes, and those qualifying are marked with the major league label and league president's signature. Still, there is enough difference in stitching and permitted size and weight (one-quarter inch in circumference and one-quarter ounce in weight) to make each ball slightly different from the others.

In my opinion it is doubtful that the manufacturing process, with a resulting increase in the liveliness of the ball, is the major cause for the fairly dramatic increase in home runs and scoring. There have been no instructions from the league or commissioner's office to change the ball. The manufacturer claims there is no change in its methods or material, and baseball has confidence in Rawlings. Chub Feeney and I made a trip to Haiti one spring to view the process and we were impressed with the plant, the people working there, and the care used in producing the ball. The conditions under which balls are stored can affect the liveliness of the ball. It is not logical to assume, however, that all clubs would change their storage methods in the same manner at the same time, so unless Rawlings itself has done so, this cannot be the answer.

There has been a general increase in home runs in modern day baseball, due to several factors. First, the hitters are bigger and stronger and they are also concentrating on muscle building. (It was not too many years ago that this was strongly discouraged. It was felt that this would make the player too tight and he would not be able to get around on an inside fast ball.) The second factor is the bat. The new thin-handled bats are designed for power. They sacrifice contact for distance. And third, hitters are able to dig in at the plate more as brush back and bean ball pitches are no longer condoned. Despite these changes, however, the home run leaders of the last five years (through 1986) do not equal the output of their counterparts of fifty years ago (Klein, Ott, Foxx, Gehrig, etc.) Also, after a major increase in home runs in the years following World War II, home run production has been relatively stable. Since playing 162 games, the per-team average in the National League (used as an example to avoid the increase due to the DH) was 132 in 1965, 123 in 1975, and 127 in 1986. In 1987, however, as we reach September, it would appear the per-team average could reach 140 or 150.

Recently, to some extent, the focus of the controversy has shifted somewhat from the ball to the bat and the illegal practice of "corking" the bat. Accusations started flying after a bat that was illegally tampered with was uncovered in a game at Houston. The subject of illegal bats, like the subject of the ball's liveliness, comes up periodically. In 1982 the Yankees were convinced that Reggie Jackson's bat was illegal. George Steinbrenner wanted the league to go into the visitor's clubhouse when the Angels were in New York, commandeer and test all their bats. This I refused to do, but I did say that any time they officially protested a game we would test the bat in question. Reggie did not get a hit that night so they didn't protest, the Angels left New York, and the controversy faded away. In 1987 the commissioner announced that each team could challenge a bat once in a game. This approach was scoffed at by some managers and players, but baseball may have to find some solution to the problem. At one point I asked Hillerich and Bradsby, the bat manufacturers, to make tests for me on the effect of a corked bat on the ball. Does it propel the ball further than a regular bat? Hillerich and Bradsby reported to me that its tests indicated that cork in the bat did not alter the way in which the bat drove the ball. It did point out that a corked center would permit a player to use a slightly bigger bat without making it heavier to swing. How much advantage this gives the hitter I do not know, but it would not appear to be significant enough (or the practice prevalent enough) to account for the 1987 increase in home runs.

Now we must consider another part of the equation—the pitching. Bad pitches often result in home runs. It is possible that younger, harder throwing, but less control-oriented pitchers are contributing to the phenomenon. It does seem that all clubs are short pitching. I heard Vin Scully say on a broadcast in 1987 that there were 140 pitchers pitching in the major leagues at that time who either had previously been released by some other major league club or who had less than two years of major league experience. It is very possible that the increase in today's offensive figures relates primarily to a temporary low point in the caliber of major league pitching.

Whatever the reason for the increase in home runs, I think it is extremely important that baseball develop a means of scientifically testing the resilience of the ball. At present, the only real tests are those conducted by the manufacturer itself. This is not satisfactory. While league president I tried to work something out in this area. I contacted the Federal Government's Bureau of Standards and numerous universities. We did get help from the University of Missouri School of Mines at Rolla, Mo., but this was through Rawlings. I guess there were too many other things laying claim to my time that kept me from finding a solution. But that is not a valid excuse. Baseball should be able to know absolutely that the home run increase is not the result of a change in the ball, and I would hope that baseball will do whatever is required to provide a reliable system for testing the baseball.

Yesterday and today. Young Americans today are probably stronger and healthier than their counterparts of four or five decades ago. Improved diet and strides in medical knowledge have helped bring about this improvement. It is only natural, therefore, that young men coming into professional baseball and ultimately reaching the majors are, overall, a little bigger and stronger than the men who played in the thirties and forties. We see records broken in all sports—athletes are running faster, swimming faster, jumping farther, etc. It is not surprising, therefore, that today's major league player can run faster and throw harder than his predecessor. Of course, there are many individual exceptions at both ends of the spectrum, and I don't think we are talking about any astounding percentage change—ten percent at the most, or perhaps five percent would be more realistic. (In either case it is only a wild unsubstantiated guess on my part.) I do, however, think it is a true and safe statement that today's player has slightly better physical tools than the player of yesterday. The use of weights has aided him in further developing his abilities. He also has better tools—gloves that enable catches (both infield and outfield) to be made that never could have been made with the old gloves; bats designed for power; better shoes and uniforms; better lighting; etc.

I think it is also true that the modern player takes better care of himself physically than the prewar and early postwar player did (the small number who have experimented with drugs excepted). This is particularly true in the off-season. Gone are the days when players commonly reported ten or fifteen pounds over their optimum playing weight and spent spring training trying to shed the excess. Today's players are more apt to come to spring training after working out for some time in advance of the reporting date. I also think today's players are probably better educated than those of yesterday. Most players were signed after graduation from high school and not too many went on to get a college education. Today, a good percentage of professional players are signed from colleges or junior colleges and most have had some college education. Moreover, improved salaries make it possible for more young men to continue their college education once they have signed. How much education can augment baseball ability can, of course, be disputed, but I personally think it can be a definite plus.

These qualities—more rough physical ability, better conditions, and more education—all contribute to better baseball. On the other hand I think we have to conclude that today's players as a group are not as dedicated to the game as the players of the thirties, forties, and fifties. Earlier players, for the most part, devoted their lives to the game of baseball. Next to their families, it was clearly their first interest. The player today has more interests outside baseball—which isn't necessarily bad for him as an individual but which can slightly dampen the intensity of his play. It has also been my impression that the "older players" were a little more team-oriented and less individually-oriented than many of the players of today. The change in the economics of the game has contributed greatly to this, particularly the fact that all salary information is publicized. Today, the player is too concerned with making sure that he is getting what he considers his fair share of the pie, and then with how his money is being invested. Agents get into the mix. These are natural reactions to circumstances that exist and one cannot really blame the player, but I think one must also concede that these things don't always necessarily contribute to a one-dimensional, completely dedicated attitude on the field. Certainly, too, the long-term contract has played a major role in this. No player consciously lets down because he has a long-term contract but, on the other hand, that extra incentive is not still there. Figures clearly show that long-term contracts result in more time on the disabled list and, to some extent, indicate that performance itself is also affected.

Today's major league player also comes up to the major league with less professional experience than was the case in the past. In earlier days, teams had farm systems with more than twenty minor league teams. Many players at the Triple-A and even AA level were ex-major league players or career minor league players. As a result, a young prospect gained valuable experience playing with and against this type of veteran player, as he spent five or maybe even six years in the minors. When he came up he "knew how to play." Today, because of the operating costs, major league farm systems generally consist of from four to six teams, and these teams, for the most part, are made up of young prospects. The players miss the learning experience of playing against veterans and, in addition, come up to the majors a little sooner. Today, young players are getting the training and experience in the majors that players used to get in the minor leagues.

There are environmental and psychological factors that could also have some bearing on whether today's or yesterday's player as a class is better. I think the press today puts more pressure on a player. Certainly, the writers are also less shielding than they used to be. In earlier days the team and writer both considered the writer as almost part of the team. Television has added another new dimension. At the same time, the relationship between the player and his club has radically changed. By this, I do not mean with his fellow players or even with his manager, but with the organization, the general manager, and the owner. And perhaps with the city itself. Free agency, the Players' Association, and agents have all contributed to this and I think there has been a definite diminution in loyalty to the organization which used to exist in baseball. Whether this affects the game on the field to any degree I am not sure, but I am inclined to believe that to some extent it does. Finally, one must also bear in mind that in the earlier days with which we are making a comparison, there were eight teams in each league (approximately 400 players), and today there are twenty-six teams (approximately 624 players). This certainly is a critical difference—not so much with respect to the stars, but with respect to the extra players on a team's roster.

Those are the areas in which differences between the game today and the game of yesterday exist. Which group provided the best baseball? Most fans who have watched the game in both eras would probably say, as older people generally do, that "the old days were best." As far as I am concerned, I think baseball was great then and it is still great today. Everything changes and all changes are not for the best, but many (most?) of them are. For me, the 1986 World Series was just as exciting as the 1947 World Series, and vice versa.

Drugs. When drugs first slipped into professional baseball, the people responsible for running the game were pretty naive and uninformed about the whole subject. Rumors were generally met with disbelief and drug usage occurred without clubs being aware of it. Even the managers and coaches, who work most closely with the players and were together with them in clubhouses, on the field, and on the road, were slow to recognize problems. For the most part, the managers and coaches came from a different age and environment and were not quickly alert to danger signals. When the seriousness of the problem was recognized, baseball's official reaction was that people with drug problems should be helped medically but should also be eliminated from the game—preferably permanently. This, of course, was not an obtainable objective, but both recent commissioners were clearly dedicated to attacking the problem as forcefully as possible. They wanted baseball to play a leadership role in completely eliminating drugs from our society; commendable, but difficult to accomplish.

The present concern over AIDS has, to some extent, taken the spotlight off drug problems in our society, and possibly moderated slightly the general public's perception of the drug problem. The drug problem, unfortunately, is still with us and as serious as ever, but perhaps there is a realization that it is not something that can be completely obliterated with one all-out attack. There is an understanding that we probably cannot completely eliminate drugs of all kinds from all levels of baseball and that instead we will have to pursue a long time program of education, prevention, and rehabilitation.

I don't think anyone is reliably certain of the extent of drug usage in professional baseball today. I have a feeling that there is very little usage of hard drugs among major league players, but I have no concrete reasons for that feeling, other than it is what I want to believe. As stated many times herein, I think the proper approach to tackling the drug problem is through a Joint Drug Program. A Joint Program (clubs and Players' Association) could probably obtain an immediate and fairly accurate appraisal of the dimensions of the problem and, in my opinion at least, is also the only effective means of attacking the problem. Any failures under the program would serve to spur the representatives of the players to further efforts to eradicate the problem. When a solution to the deadlock over testing is found, and I am convinced that it will be, baseball will reinstate a Joint Drug Program and get on with the objective of eliminating drug use, should it exist, and rehabilitating drug users.

Selection of All-Star team. There has been a longstanding disagreement, which again came to the fore in 1987, as to the proper means of selecting the teams for the All-Star Game. The game was originated by Arch Ward of the Chicago *Tribune,* and originally the teams were elected by votes cast with the *Tribune.* Eventually votes were cast nationwide, primarily at the ballparks, but it was obvious from the beginning that players playing in large cities or on teams that drew well had the edge. There is no restriction on the number of times a person can vote, nor would it be possible in practice to impose such a restriction. In 1957 Cincinnati mounted an aggressive campaign to elect members of its pennant-contending Reds to the team and practically the entire team was elected. This led to a change in the voting procedures with only the managers casting ballots. This was an effective method and there were few disputes as to the legitimacy of the lineups.

On the other hand, one of the things that made the baseball All-Star Game by far the most popular and interesting of the All-Star Games was the participation of the public in the selection of the teams. Fans enjoy voting and such voting gives them the feeling that it is their game and engenders interest in the game. In 1969 Bowie Kuhn decided that the vote should be returned to the fans, and the fans have elected the eight starters for each league (exclusive of the pitcher) since 1970.

Which system is better? There have been problems with fan voting in recent years and the old flaws still exist. Obviously the fans are not as knowledgeable as the managers and not as informed as to who is having a good year, who is injured, etc. As a result, they are inclined to vote for established name players over younger players having outstanding seasons. But what makes up a true all star? Is it a player having a great first half of the current season or is it a well-established name player who has excelled for many seasons? I am inclined to think it should be (within acceptable limits) the latter and that the type players generally selected by the fans are the players that should be showcased in the All-Star Game. Is this fair to the players that are having better years but are passed over? The fans select only eight players for each team. The managers and the leagues pick the balance of the squad, so deserving players will be chosen. And if they are young players just emerging into stardom their time of national recognition is still ahead of them. So my vote is to continue fan participation and maintain the public voting for the teams.

Replays and electronic calls. In recent years, since the advent of television and the advancement of electronic devices, it is frequently proposed that baseball use these modern inventions to eliminate erroneous calls by umpires. I am strongly opposed to such a move for two reasons. First I think umpires are an integral part of the game and to downplay their role in any manner would be taking some of the color and tradition out of the game. Second, at least at this point in time, the real objective could not be achieved. I simply do not think it is practical. I presume there are two possible approaches: by running conventional TV replays and by some sort of electronic device that would automatically register a decision. I don't think either would work.

Consider the following, first as to replays: football, of course, is using replays to a very limited extent, but in football the ball is generally dead after the play in question. (Did he fumble or didn't he?

Did he catch the pass or didn't he? Did he step out of bounds?) In baseball, the ball is often alive following controversial plays. Did an outfielder trap the ball? Baserunners can't wait for people to study replays before they make a decision to run or return to their base. They must rely on the immediate call of the umpire. There are many plays in baseball for which this is true. So we must restrict the use of the camera to certain plays—the call at first base, or at second, third, or home. Even on these plays, much depends on the angle of the camera or whether the camera view is blocked. A good umpire will keep from being blocked.

As league president I viewed many tapes sent to me by teams attempting to show erroneous calls by umpires. For the most part the plays were so close that one could not tell whether the umpire had erred or not. In those cases, you surely would not (just as football does not) overrule the umpire. Therefore, all you are ensuring against is the obvious mis-call and mis-calls, in my judgment, are too few to warrant any such drastic interference with the historic procedure of our game. Certainly you could not use the TV picture on ball and strike calls. Here time would not permit slow motion replays and it would simply be a case of taking the judgment of someone in the press box viewing on TV over the judgment of an umpire immediately behind the plate. Having witnessed how often the TV announcers are wrong under such circumstances does not give one confidence that viewing through a camera with an angled view is too dependable. Moreover, if the home plate umpire was overruled from the press box on many occasions, it would utterly destroy his effectiveness.

Next, consider an electronic device for calling balls and strikes. A strike is determined in part by the players' height and stance. Who is going to adjust the device for each hitter that comes to the plate? This adjustment would be subject to as much dispute as the actual ball or strike call. And as to whether the ball did or did not pass over the plate—how is this to be triggered? It cannot simply be triggered by an object crossing the plate because the bat or catcher's glove would have the same effect. Would it be some special device in or on the ball? Might this not affect the ball? And could we be sure the amount was proper, or the device working? Could it be tampered with? Could someone use a like material on a catcher's glove in a key situation? All of these questions lead me to believe that the procedure—undesirable in and of itself—is also not practical.

At the very best, replay equipment might be used to correct obvious errors on calls at the bases or on the foul lines. There is no real evidence of any pressing need for such. (Better to replace an umpire who errs too often.) In short, if it doesn't need fixing, why try to fix it and, at the same time, detract from an historic part of baseball—the role of the umpire.

Ballparks. We have a great variety of parks in baseball today, from historic old Fenway Park, Wrigley Field, Comiskey Park, and Tiger Stadium; to the new, uniform-shaped stadia in Pittsburgh, St. Louis, Cincinnati, Atlanta, Philadelphia, and San Diego; to domes in Houston, Seattle, and Minnesota. Just what kind of stadium is best for major league baseball?

In my opinion, the stadium in Kansas City comes closest to serving as the model I would like to see used when new stadia are built (but with natural grass). For financial reasons professional baseball and football often must share a facility, but this is certainly not ideal. It does not provide the best playing conditions, nor the best viewing conditions, for either sport. Unfortunately, sixteen of our teams are playing under these conditions today. But if we are talking about an "ideal" stadium, clearly it would be one built specifically for baseball.

The second major qualification is that it not be too large. The mammoth size of Cleveland Stadium is a handicap to baseball in Cleveland and the increased seating at the Angels' stadium in Anaheim for the Rams has made it less attractive for baseball. The third major qualification is proper access and parking. Some teams, notably Boston and the Cubs, have done well in spite of this lack, but both have good public transportation, limited capacity, and especially loyal fans. If they had larger capacities, the limited parking would probably affect their ability to fill their parks.

In addition to Kansas City, in my opinion, the best stadia for baseball are Yankee Stadium and Dodger Stadium, but I also love the historic, old parks such as Wrigley, Fenway, and Tiger Stadium. Comiskey Park is that type of facility but, sadly, age seems to be catching up to it and hopefully the White Sox will soon have a new place to play.

As time goes by we will have other new parks—Toronto in the near future, perhaps Chicago and Baltimore next, and hopefully, San Francisco and Cleveland, as well as the expansion cities, should expansion someday come. Let us hope that all these cities will be able to find a solution for the financial necessities that dictate the building of dual-purpose stadia. The dome certainly allows a city to get maximum use out of its facility. Domes make sense in rainy Seattle, or with the frigid spring and early fall of Minneapolis, or in the heat and humidity of Houston. I cannot bring myself, however, to regard domes as ideal baseball stadia. The solution—someday—will be the removable roof. Toronto is pursuing that approach. Another factor relating to stadium desirability is location. Here, I think either a good downtown location (i.e., Cincinnati, St. Louis, or Minnesota), or a good suburban location with good roads and parking, is acceptable.

I hate to see cities invest millions in structures that are not properly adaptable to baseball (such as New Orleans and Indianapolis). In my mind, the ballpark—the ability to reach it, the ease of access and egress, and the atmosphere within—has a great deal to do with the drawing power of the team. Almost any city will draw when its team is in the thick of the pennant race, but even then attendance can be disappointing if the park is not inviting. And baseball, even with a team down in the race, can be attractive as family entertainment in the right stadium.

Expansion. When will expansion come? The Players' Association has recently made several self-serving appearances before congressional committees urging that pressure be put on the clubs to expand. Obviously, it is interested in more jobs for its people, even at the cost of inferior play. The clubs must be concerned about the quality of the product presented to the public and about the economic health of the game overall. I think expansion will come when baseball feels a clear, moral obligation to expand. When will that be? Only when there are at least two metropolitan areas that meet the criteria that have been set forth by baseball. In addition to a proper market, the criteria primarily requires good, locally oriented ownership with adequate financing; an area government (state, county, city) with an understanding of baseball's role in the community and willingness to cooperate to make the operation of a major league franchise in that area practical; and a good baseball stadium with adequate parking.

One must understand that there is virtually no reason for baseball to expand other than for the moral reason of providing major league baseball to an area definitely anxious to have it and able to support it. There are absolutely no plusses for the existing clubs from expansion. First, their schedules are altered so that they may play games with the expansion teams and as a result they play fewer games with their historical rivals (e.g., Yankees vs. Red Sox). Second, without increasing the revenues from national network television, the number of clubs sharing same is eventually increased. Third, the existing teams must give up players to the expansion teams, many of whom are players they have developed at considerable expense and whom they do not wish to lose. Fourth, to some extent, the overall quality of play in major league baseball is diluted. When there were sixteen teams they were represented by the best 400 players in the world. Today, with twenty-six teams (even with twenty-four instead of twenty-five active players) there must be 624 players and expansion of even two more franchises would bring the number of players needed to 672. Pension costs, of course increase proportionately, but of more concern is the increased demand for and the greater inability to get good talent, the added economic competition resulting therefrom, and the accompanying fear that the overall quality of play would suffer. Hopefully, however, an increasing population, with more boys playing baseball and with better amateur programs, could take care of this concern.

The generally accepted blueprint calls for the National League to expand first by two teams, thus evening the two leagues at fourteen teams each. Unfortunately, a fourteen-team league is more unwieldy and more difficult to schedule for than a twelve-team league, thus creating another negative against expansion. The second stage would probably come several years later and encompass four additional teams, two in each league, creating two sixteen-team leagues. Here again there are complications. Does a sixteen-team league consist of two eight-team divisions or four four-team divisions? Eight teams is more than is desirable in one division and four teams is too few. Four team divisions would also increase post-season playoffs, which many people would consider undesirable. Or perhaps you would try to realign baseball geographically with changes in the leagues. Possibly three leagues instead of two. Now you are tampering with the historical pattern of the game and the magic of the League Championships and the World Series. No city is going to want to leave the American or National League for a new league. So when clubs are added, so are the complications and the tendency is—in view of the economical and artistic negatives—not to try to fix something that doesn't need fixing. That is why I say a clear, moral obligation must exist before baseball will elect to expand.

Should there be expansion, what cities are the best bets to get franchises?* In my view, Denver and a franchise in Florida would be the first two. How about Washington? Here is another expansion problem. To expand without including Washington would risk governmental displeasure and possible interference. On the other hand, to put a team in Washington risks creating another Oakland Bay area problem, where the market is really not big enough for two teams. This is another casualty of the great increase in player costs—overall operating costs have become so inflated that teams need larger, and preferably exclusive, operating areas. In any event, if Denver, Florida, and Washington are the best bets for the first phase of expansion, one of those areas plus one more Florida locale and Phoenix and Vancouver are probably second phase potentials. That would leave Buffalo, Columbus, Indianapolis, Louisville, Memphis, and New Orleans as dark horses. Some of those markets are good, but the problem is

---

*Any opinions expressed here are purely off the top of my head and do not necessarily reflect the present-day thinking of baseball.

that they are too close to and would hurt existing franchises. Every aspect of expansion causes problems—but someday it must come. The fact that baseball recognizes the problems does not mean it will not move responsibly when the time comes.

Economy of baseball. People are inclined to shrug off the reported operating losses of major league baseball teams. They feel the owners are all multimillionaires who can afford to lose millions or that they have tax write-offs that make up for a good part of the losses. There is some truth to these beliefs. On the other hand, not all the owners are on the Fortune 500 list, and repeated and increasing losses will eventually force some good owners out of the game. Moreover, no one, no matter how wealthy, likes to lose money continuously—and will there be others to replace them when they finally tire of the experience?

I have always felt—and I tried very hard to convince the Players' Association—that it was very important that baseball be able to stand on its own economically. If, over a long period, it cannot, it seems to me the consequences will be unfortunate for everyone concerned including the fans and the players themselves. My concern would be that smaller cities, with smaller broadcast markets, would not be able to stand continuing losses and eventually either could not compete on the field with the larger market cities or could not adequately support their team and would lose their franchise. My other concern is that baseball ownership would eventually consist primarily of entities that were in the game not for the game itself, but for other interests (e.g., broadcast), and that decisions would be made, not on the basis of what was best for baseball, but for what was best for their other enterprises. And as operating costs continue to escalate, more and more of it would be passed on to the fans. I don't think we should have large increases in ticket prices—or that Cleveland should lose its franchise—in order to sustain a continuing increase in the *average* player salary, which has already climbed from $52,000 in 1976 to $413,000 in 1986.

A dangerous by-product of the inflation in player costs has been the proliferation of long-term contracts. Before this decade one-year contracts had been traditional in baseball, but three- to five-year contracts have become common in the eighties. One club was even signing players to lifetime contracts. Much of the blame for this has to rest with the owners themselves. As a result of these long-term contracts, the clubs collectively owed more than $40 million in 1984 to players who were released and not even playing anymore. (This does not include previously earned money owed to players under deferred contracts.) In addition, time on the Disabled List has climbed steadily in direct proportion to the long-term contracts, further escalating total payrolls.

Collectively, the clubs were operating at about the break-even level when free agency came about in 1976. For two or three years, the impact was moderate, but throughout the 1980s operating costs have increased at a staggering rate and the great bulk of the increase has come from player costs. An accomplice to free agency in hiking player salaries has been the salary arbitration procedure. The number of players filing annually increased from fifty-three in 1974 to 160 in 1986* and the percentage salary increase received by these players increased from an average of twenty-seven percent in 1974 to sixty percent in 1986. During the last negotiations the Players' Association was given operating figures for 1983 which showed that eighteen of twenty-six teams lost money and that the industry collectively lost $60,236,394. When the Players' Association objected to the inclusion of player depreciation costs, we subtracted initial roster depreciation, but the aggregate loss figure was still $43,763,741. In 1983, only three teams made over $1,000,000, while seven teams lost over $1,000,000 and one team lost $12,905,000.‡

One hope that sustained several of the clubs over the early 1980s was that a new national network broadcast package to commence in 1983 would be significantly higher—and it was. The other hope was that pay TV would prove to be another major source of income for them, but this has not borne fruit (in fact many of the teams that have put pay TV broadcast packages together have lost money on them). In addition, recent indications are that the next over-the-air, national TV contract may not be as lucrative as the last one. Given their high operating budgets, any major loss in TV revenues, local or national, would be catastrophic for the clubs and would have to bring about some very painful economic readjustments.

Players' Association. In a sense, the Players' Association is an anomaly. It was an association of team representatives, not truly a union, until Marvin Miller took over. Then it became a union, but not a labor union in the traditional sense. In the first place, the Players' Association does not negotiate individual player's salaries. It negotiates all working conditions that players have in common, leaving the individual salaries to be negotiated between player and club. Also, it does not represent "labor." You cannot categorize baseball players who work five hours a day, eight months a year at an average salary of $413,000 per annum and a pension (ten-year service at age 60) of $90,000 per

---

*Even though fewer players were eligible to elect salary arbitration in 1986.

‡It is my understanding that increased attendance, the national television package negotiated in 1983, the decrease in monies owed players no longer in the game and improved promotional revenues generated by Ueberroth, have improved the overall picture in the last half of the 1980s.

year for life, as laborers. Nor are the economic circumstances determining the salaries teams will pay subject to the normal laws of supply and demand. Ownership is more likely to succumb to the pressures of the media and their own intense desire to win in deciding what salaries they will pay, even though those salaries are insane from an economic point of view, than follow reasonable financial dictates. So the Players' Association has operated under a unique set of circumstances and, in reality, became whatever Marvin Miller wanted it to become. Throughout the past decade Marvin has clearly been the dominant figure in this area, and though he has retired his teachings are firmly established with the present officers of the association and the older player representatives.

Miller came to baseball from the Steelworkers Union by chance (see Chapter 8). He is a very intelligent, honest, hard-working, doctrinaire labor zealot. His sole concern was in getting the most he possibly could for his members. He did a remarkable job for them and their early gains of free agency, increased minimum salaries, and improved pensions were deserved. I think it is also only fair to point out that although it is generally baseball players' salaries that are pointed to as outrageous, salaries in other areas of sports and entertainment are also extremely high. On the negative side, Miller had no concern for baseball as an institution or for the long-term welfare of the game. He was not interested in constructing a partnership or cultivating good relationships between players and clubs. He was not concerned with trying to see that all participants in the game—players, management, and fans—shared fairly in its ample rewards.

The fact that the association does not negotiate individual player salaries actually works to the disadvantage of the clubs. The present system places them in double jeopardy. The association takes a very tough stand in the areas in which it negotiates, bringing about conditions which lead to a great upsurge in salaries. Then the agents take over from there, battling for the highest possible figures in the arena prepared by the Players' Association, and the rivalry between agents and union—both trying to convince their clients that they are the most important element in the mix—adds to the difficulties. Then, to compound it all, the salaries are negotiated in a climate in which the fans and the media apply the maximum pressures on management to sign their own players to prevent their opting for free agency and to sign other teams' free agents. It is no wonder that out of all of this a pattern of player contracts has emerged that is financially insane. After years of suffering through this, with conditions getting worse each year, the clubs—one by one—have finally, gradually, invoked some self-discipline. This development has led the Players' Association to file grievances claiming a violation of a clause that prevents teams from "acting in concert" with respect to free agents.*

I have always believed that the best interests of the game itself would be served by a good working relationship between the Players' Association and the clubs. I believe the players themselves as a group would favor this. I also believe Don Fehr, under the proper circumstances, would not be opposed to such a relationship. I believe our joint negotiation of a Drug Program in 1984 is an example of what can be accomplished when the two sides are willing to work together and compromise. With a little more cooperative approach in the area of testing, that program would probably still be in existence today and might have accomplished much. Subsequent to that, I think our 1984–85 Basic Agreement negotiations made progress in the direction of cooperation, with the Players' Association making meaningful compromises in several areas. At the present time, however, current developments have again separated the parties. It is my hope that eventually things will get back on track.

And so I come to the end of this volume. Some of us must have projects to work on. For me, this was such an exercise; I have enjoyed reliving "my nine innings." There were disappointments during those innings, as I have related, but also so many pleasant satisfactions. Perhaps my greatest disappointment was not being able to win a pennant with the Yankees after my return as general manager, but the toughest part of the job for me while with a club was simply losing. Every loss was tough to take. Some were tougher than others; blowing late inning leads could tear you apart. After years in the game it would seem one would get used to it—take what came a little more philosophically—but for me that was certainly not the case. It actually got more nerve-racking as time went on. Strangely the thrill of winning, as nice as it was, didn't quite seem to match the bitterness of defeat. I guess one looked upon winning as the expected and the natural; losing was a detour to disaster. Even so, the good things easily exceeded the not so good: the yearly improvement our teams showed at both Baltimore and New York; youngsters developing from high school signees to major league stars; the enjoyment of the crowds at the games; and a few achievements in the league and PRC offices. Most gratifying of all, however, was the relationship with the people in and around the game—scouts, minor league managers, major league and minor league executives, players, members of the press and broadcast media, and all the people who worked with me in the

---

*An arbitrator has ruled in the players' favor. No penalty has as yet been determined. This can create a very serious problem for the clubs.

various baseball offices. They are the salt of the earth and I was fortunate to spend my working life with them.

I began to recount this tale in Chapter 1 on a balmy Florida day in March. My son Andy and I were going to a Twin-Yankee exhibition game in Ft. Lauderdale. Now it is September. It is still warm but there is a hint of fall in the air. And that means the baseball season and the pennant races are coming down the stretch. As this is written, four teams in one division, and three teams in the other three divisions still have a chance to win. There is special excitement in 12 of our cities.

What is going to happen? The remaining schedule would seem to give a slight edge to some of those teams. But there are so many unknowns. Will a serious injury to a key regular on any of the leaders knock them out of the race the way Freddy Fitzsimmons' injury did the Dodgers in the 1941 World Series? Will some favorite turn cold at the very end and blow it all—the way Gene Mauch's Phillies did in 1964? Or will some team get very hot, go on a tear, and put together a winning streak that wins a division championship—the way the Cardinals did in 1942; or the Cubs did in 1938; or the Yankees in 1964? Can any division winner defy the jinx and win again in 1987? Will the weather help or hurt one team—the way it helped the Yankees in the 1962 World Series against the Giants? Will the great enthusiasm of the fans in some city provide that little extra support that might make the difference? Will there be heroes—like Dave Henderson of the Red Sox in the 1986 ALCS? Or goats—like poor Bill Buckner in the 1986 World Series? Will the breaks make—or destroy—some team's chances of winning? And will one or more of the races go down to the last series, or the last day, as they have so often—as, for example, in 1967 when the Red Sox, White Sox, Twins, and Tigers all were in the scramble to the very end. Or maybe end in a dead-tie, as they have on six different occasions (Cards and Dodgers in '46; Indians and Red Sox in '48; Giants and Dodgers in '51 and '62; Dodgers and Braves in '59; Yankees and Red Sox in '78; and Astros and Dodgers in '80).

At some point, we will be down to four teams, and then to two, and finally it will be history and one team will have won it all. That is what baseball is all about. But there is more than that for, best of all, there is always next year. This year's winners will be trying to find a way of avoiding the catastrophes that in recent years have plagued winners. And the also-rans will be making changes; trying to fill holes, add punch, augment pitching staffs, to be ready for the brand new season that gives everyone a rebirth and a fresh new chance to start all even. For the people working in baseball the 1987 season will have ended another chapter in their nine innings—but a new, and maybe brighter one, will soon commence. That story has ended for me. I have had "my nine innings," and even an extra one, but I can still be an avid and enthusiastic observer, and as long as I am around, baseball will be an important part of my life.

Epilogue

October, 1987

As the country knows, and Minnesota will never forget, the Twins—battling down to the wire—won the 1987 American League West by two games. Skeptics wondered about a team that couldn't win on the road, finished only five games over .500, and represented what some people considered the weakest of baseball's four divisions. They overlooked the fact that the Twins were the first team to clinch their division title and were ten games over .500 when they did so. They may also have underestimated the American League West and had no way of knowing the effect the Twins so-called "tenth man" (an extremely enthusiastic "homer hankie" waving crowd in a noisy dome) was to have. The Twins rested their short-handed pitching staff before the season ended and benefitted from the off-days in the postseason schedule and from the fact that both the League Championship Series and the World Series opened in Minnesota. They won the first two games against Detroit at home and then belied their road record by winning two of three in Detroit. When they deplaned on their return home they were met by a huge outpouring of fans at the Metrodome. The decibel count in the dome continued to mount as they won the first two games of the World Series in Minnesota, but the bubble appeared to have broken when they lost three straight in St. Louis. The big game was game number six in Minnesota, with Cardinal ace John Tudor going against rookie Les Straker. Down 5–2, the Twins came back on home runs by Don Baylor and Kent Hrbek to win 11–5, and Frank Viola clinched matters with a 4–2 win in game seven. Needless to say, I saw each game of both series and, though only an onlooker, the Twins' victory probably provided me with one of the top thrills of my baseball life. In addition to the great satisfaction I received from seeing Andy's team win the World Championship, it was a pleasure to witness the tremendous excitement and enthusiasm in the

Twin Cities area and the support the fans gave their team. It was a testimonial, not just to the Twins, but to baseball itself.

Spring, 1988

The 1988 season opened with new interpretations by the leagues and the Playing Rules Committee with respect to the strike zone and balks. In an irrational—but sensible—approach to the problem of getting umpires to call more strikes in the upper part of the strike zone, the strike zone—by rule—was lowered. This move caused very few problems on the field and appears to have had some positive effect. In a rational—but not sensible—approach to balks, one section of the balk rule was strictly enforced as written.* In my opinion, this was not a sensible approach for two reasons. First, it needlessly disrupted the game and, with a 161% increase in the number of balk calls, caused the outcome of several games to be affected by a technicality.

Second, it moved the balance of the game in the wrong direction. With baserunners achieving superiority over the defensive pitcher-catcher combination, the number of stolen bases and the percentage of successful steals had been steadily mounting. (About ten years ago, in 1977, approximately 35% of runners in the National League and 39% of runners in the American League were thrown out trying to steal. Five years later (1982) the approximate figures were down to 32% and 36%. In 1987 the percentages were 29% and 31%. In 1988 the percentages remained about the same, but the true effect of the rule tightening may not manifest itself immediately. It certainly is not going to reverse the trend and, if it doesn't, why put everyone through all this turmoil?) The stolen base is one of the most exciting plays in baseball, but not when the outcome is predictable and suspense has been eliminated. It was commendable to try to establish uniformity between the leagues (the National League interpretation of section (m) of the rule was somewhat stricter than that of the American League, in which a change of direction of the pitcher's hands was considered a "stop"), and it was commendable to make play on the field conform to the rule as written. What the committee should have done, in my opinion, was reword the rule to define the balk less strictly.

Summer, 1988

Another intriguing development in 1988 was the decrease in home

---

*Section (m) of the Rule states it is a balk when: "The pitcher delivers the pitch from a set position without coming to a stop."

run production in the major leagues (see Chapter 14). The 17% increase in home runs in 1987 which so concerned everyone turned into a 28% decrease in 1988. (This amounted to a 16% decrease in home runs from 1986 to 1988.) Major league home run production appears to be as volatile as the stock market, and changes create doubts. No one has the answer to the riddle. One player even accused management of deadening the ball to reduce home runs and averages and thereby salaries. (He seems to have overlooked the fact that pitchers also get paid based on results.) So, once again, the variations only reinforce my conviction that baseball needs a reliable, independent testing system to measure the liveliness of the ball. If the ball is the same, at least we will know that the differences relate to happenings on the playing field.

The 1988 season witnessed the first night game at Wrigley Field, a change that had to come. One can only escape reality so long, and if the historic old park was going to continue as the Cubs' home, it was the only course to follow. One can regret the change, just as the loss of many nostalgic things are regretted, but perhaps it can be viewed as a necessity rather than a tragedy. There is an old proverb that says, "wisdom is to make virtue out of necessity." And 1988 also taught us traditionalists that when the heat stays over 90 degrees for days on end, a dome is not necessarily a bad place to play—or watch—a game.

In 1988 baseball lost an exceptionally fine man who had served the game well for thirty-four years. In June, Bob Fishel succumbed to the asthmatic condition that had plagued him in the late years of his life. He was mourned by the countless friends he had in the game and many of his friends in the press wrote fine tributes about him. Leonard Koppett, writing in *The New York Times,* said, "He not only managed to balance complete loyalty to employer with utter truthfulness to journalists, but he also provided guidance and assistance to anyone with a problem on either side of the fence. He was obsessed with fairness, accuracy, honesty and ethics." I first met Bob in 1954 when he joined the Yankees, and we were close friends for the remaining thirty-four years of his life, working together for twelve years with the Yankees and for his twelve years with the American League. He was a prince among men and I will miss him very much. Along with my family, this book is dedicated to his memory.*

---

*Sadly, baseball lost some other people in 1988 with whom I was very close: Gene Martin, with whom I had worked in New York in the fifties; Johnny Johnson, another former Yankee compatriot and long-time president of the National Association; Edward Bennett Williams, owner of the Orioles; and Joe Reichler, whom I had persuaded in 1966 to leave AP and join the Commissioner's office.

September, 1988

As the close of the season approached, Peter Ueberroth announced
that he did not wish to continue as commissioner for a second five-
year term, and that if a successor was named prior to the end of his
term (January 1, 1990), he would remain only as long as necessary to
assist in an effective and orderly transfer of his responsibilities. In
September the clubs unanimously selected A. Bartlett Giamatti, the
president of the National League and former president of Yale, to
succeed Ueberroth. April 1, 1989 was designated as the date the
change is to become effective. Thus, Peter Ueberroth's stewardship as
the sixth commissioner of baseball will soon terminate. People have
found it difficult to assess Ueberroth's mark on the game as his period
in office has been so short. It is unfortunate that he did not seem to
have the deep attachment to the game itself that would have motivated
him to stay on. It is probable that he never envisioned his role in
baseball as more than a temporary one.

   A man of great personal charm, with unique business abilities, he
contributed a great deal to the improvement of baseball's economics,
particularly in the area of the clubs' collective income. He also assisted
the clubs in marketing the game and focused their attention on
presenting it in a proper family atmosphere in their stadiums. This
contributed to some extent to record-breaking attendance levels that
were reached in both 1987 and 1988. A strong leader, he was at times
impatient with baseball's slightly clumsy, but democratic, ways of pro-
ceeding and, on occasion, this estranged him from some of the club
owners—particularly those who took part in and enjoyed leadership
roles in baseball's administration. He came into baseball from the
Olympics, where it had been possible to deal with drug problems in a
somewhat dictatorial way, and the same approach led to a confrontation with baseball's Players' Association. I personally thought his influence in bringing about the demise of the Joint Drug Program was ill-
advised and yet, on the surface at least, drugs do not seem to be quite
so serious a problem in baseball today as in other major sports. With
the collusion charges associated with free agency however, his time in
office has witnessed a worsening of the relationship between clubs and
players. This is something that his successor will have to address.

   What kind of commissioner will Bart Giamatti be? He certainly
has the necessary intelligence and administrative experience. In addition, he has a deep love for the game. Hopefully, this will provide
long-term stability in that important office. Bart must undergo an
immediate and very difficult test in his handling of the results of the
collusion cases lost by the owners and in the collective bargaining
required to reach accord on a new Basic Agreement with the Players'

Association. The present five-year Basic Agreement expires at the close of the 1989 season. I feel that Bart will strive to achieve a better relationship with the Players' Association and I also feel that his contacts with the owners will be more positive than Peter's. One is sorry to see a man of Peter Ueberroth's abilities leave, and from a personal standpoint no one could have been more considerate to me, but I am confident that our game will be in good hands with Bart in charge.*

October, 1988

And what of the pennant races?

Once again, the preceding year's division winners could not repeat. (No team has won its division two years in a row since the Dodgers and Yankees in 1977–1978.) The World Champion Twins played over .500 on the road, made fewer errors than any team in history, and were one of four teams to win ninety games, but could not match the red hot Athletics. The National League champion Cardinals got off to a terrible start and finished fifth. The San Francisco Giants could not keep pace with the resurgent Dodgers and in the one real down-to-the-wire division race the Tigers fell to the Red Sox. Jose Canseco became the first forty home run, forty stolen base player in history; Tom Browning pitched a perfect game; and Orel Hersheiser pitched fifty-nine consecutive scoreless innings to break Don Drysdale's record. Even though only one division race was tight, baseball had another banner year at the gate, with an average attendance of over two million per team.

The A's swept the Red Sox, but the National League Championship Series was a real donnybrook with the underdog Dodgers winning in seven. (The Mets led in the ninth inning of game four by two with Gooden pitching and a 3–1 lead almost in hand, but Scoscia's home run tied the score and the Dodgers went on to win on Kirk Gibson's homer in the 12th.) In the course of the series, Bart Giamatti had to make a ruling when pitcher Jay Howell of the Dodgers was caught with pine tar on his glove. It was a tough decision, and I thought his ruling of a three-game suspension, reduced to two after a hearing, was strict but responsible. I was asked by media people to relate it to the Brett pine-tar incident, but it really wasn't comparable as the pine tar in that case, being applied to the bat, did not affect performance as it may have when applied to the ball. In any event, I was thankful that I had not had to make the Brett ruling during a

---

*After all, it was I, with Chub Feeney's second, that recommended Bart to Bud Selig's Commissioner Search Committee in 1984.

post-season series. (When I had to rule on a possible suspension of Richard Dotson in the 1983 League Championship Series, I deferred any suspension to the 1984 season.)

The A's were odds-on favorites to win the World Series just as the Mets were favored to win the NLCS, but once again a gutty Dodger team, led by Tommy Lasorda, overcame injuries and surprised the baseball world by winning in five games.* Kirk Gibson's dramatic ninth inning home run won the opener and Orel Hersheiser was simply unbeatable in his two starts. How can a team that looks as superior on paper as the A's lose? Too long a layoff after the Red Sox series? Too inexperienced? A case of outstanding pitching stopping good hitting? Or simply a down streak at the wrong time for the A's combined with a Dodger team that would not lose? Who knows? That is what makes baseball the intriguing game it is.

December, 1988

Peter Ueberroth's final contribution to Baseball was a new network television contract. With his broadcasting department, headed by Bryan Burns, working under his direction, he formulated a one network over the air program for the World Series, League Championship Series, and All-Star game, plus a limited number of regular season games. This he augmented with a cable network for additional regular season games. CBS was the top bidder for the regular network program, agreeing to pay $1.1 billion for four years, an appreciable increase over the previous contracts with ABC and NBC ($1.25 billion over six years). I am happy for the clubs as this is an essential part of their income and television revenues depend to some extent on extraneous factors and can be volatile. I was sorry, however, that NBC lost its baseball connection, as it has had a close relationship with the game for many years and has made a significant contribution to the promotion of the sport. ESPN was the top bidder for the cable portion, bidding $400 million for 175 games a year for four years. Apportioning games to the cable sector makes sense, as long as the "jewels" (World Series, League Championship Series, and All Star Game) remain on free TV.

Shortly before the conclusion of the national package deal, the Yankees announced that they had sold their games, starting in 1991 on an exclusive basis, to MSG (Madison Square Garden Cable Network) for $500 million for 12 years. (Hopefully some of those games will end up on regular free television.) Not many metropolitan areas can come close to New York in television revenue, but improved local

---

*Surprisingly, over one-third (nine) of the Dodgers team had been acquired from American League clubs within the last year or so.

packages, plus the national contracts, plus record-breaking attendance years, should put Baseball in a strong financial position. It is
well that this is so, for following the close of the 1988 season the teams
again entered into extravagant player contracts. I am all for the
players, individually and collectively, receiving their share of income
from the sport, but I still feel—perhaps more so than ever—that it is
imperative that a system (fair to the players) be devised that regulates
signings and maintains fair competition among the teams.

The 1990 labor negotiations loom ahead even more significantly.
Obviously, in view of the change in Baseball's economics, the Players'
Association is going to be harder to convince that any major altera-
tions in procedures are necessary and, not unreasonably, is going to
be skeptical of any program that could significantly reduce player
income. This makes the task ahead even more difficult. And the
skirmishing has already begun, with the clubs apparently trying to
position themselves for a possible lockout prior to spring training in
1990, if that is required to protect their bargaining position.

1989

What about the collusion cases? There are three. One based on the
clubs' activities with respect to 1985 free agents; one relating to 1986
free agents; and one concerning 1987 free agents. The first two have
been ruled upon by arbitrators (Thomas Roberts in 1985 and George
Nicolau in 1986). In both cases, they ruled that the clubs had violated a
provision of the Basic Agreement with the Players' Association which
provides that, with respect to free agents, both players and clubs must
act individually and not in concert with other players or clubs. This
provision was made a part of the 1981 agreement at the suggestion of
the clubs, as they were concerned about the attempt by Don Drysdale
and Sandy Koufax to negotiate their contracts jointly with the
Dodgers and by the fact that the entire infield of one team was
represented by the same agent.

The clubs do not concur that they acted improperly, but decisions
that they did have been made by two impartial, professional arbitrators after all the facts had been examined.* Both decisions gave a
second chance for free agency to a limited number of players who had
resigned with their original clubs and had not had a subsequent free
agency opportunity. (Kirk Gibson was one of the 1985 group and
signed with the Dodgers.) The clubs have no alternative but to comply
and, further, to conduct their future affairs in a manner compliant

---

*It is very possible that the 1985 ruling would not have gone against the
clubs if the 1986 non-signings had not occurred prior to Roberts' decision.

with these decisions. Final penalties have not yet been imposed by the arbitrators. Hopefully, while further penalties may be financially costly to ownership, they will not be framed in a manner that will disrupt the abilities of the clubs to put together their teams for the coming season or affect the game on the field in any way.

What exactly did the clubs do that led to these adverse decisions? To the best of my knowledge, and I was pretty well aware of everything that went on through 1985, there was never any agreement between them governing their relations with free agents. What I believe did happen was that the clubs, aware of their deteriorating finances as a result of the publication of financial figures in the 1984–85 negotiations and learning from their own disastrous experiences with free agent signings, finally listened to the advice that they had been receiving from their central offices (the Player Relations Office, the League Offices, and the Commissioners' Office) urging them not to make bad economic decisions in signing their players. In their intense desire to win clubs had been signing free agents, or their own players who had the option of becoming free agents, to contracts that were not only for unrealistic amounts, but for multi-year periods. As a result, any rational salary structure for the rest of their team was disrupted. Moreover, they often had to release players with large, long-term contracts and pay them for several seasons following their release. (In 1983, not including earned deferred salary, major league clubs paid over $40,000,000 in salary to players released and no longer playing.) Such signings resulted in eighteen of twenty-six teams operating at a deficit in 1983, and an industry loss of over $60,000,000. It was this kind of questionable economic behavior that baseball's central offices were advising against. The arbitrators, in their decisions, stated there was no prohibition against such advice being given. (Was there a prohibition against such advice being *heeded?*) However the arbitrators felt that the pattern of free agent signings had changed so drastically that there had to be some common understanding among the clubs to "accomplish such a universal effect" and that "there was a patent pattern of uniform behavior, a uniformity simply unexplainable by the rubric of financial responsibility or by any other factors."

I believe, in part, that the clubs were motivated by what they came to understand was best for the game itself. In this, they made their own individual decisions and were not bound by any agreement to act in concert. Perhaps, on occasion, peer pressure may have been exerted and, if so, this would have constituted a violation. But they saw severe economic problems threatening the game and creating doubts as to the ability of certain franchises to continue under existing conditions. Should a team have to move out of a Cleveland or a Pittsburgh, for example, to enable the *average* player salary to continue to soar beyond the $400,000 level or to enable more and more players (over seventy in 1988) to earn over $1 million a year?

If clubs are not permitted to be influenced by the advice of their central offices and as a result may not make individual decisions for the best interests of the game overall (and ultimately for their own best interests), how are they to conduct themselves with respect to free agents? Do the arbitrators' decisions require the teams to engage in economically disastrous bidding against one another? Some clubs have never signed free agents. Certainly they cannot be required to change this policy. But does it mean that other clubs are not free to adopt that same policy? Unless reason can guide their activities, there is danger that the pressures of media and fans, plus the uncertainty of what procedures are proper under the arbitrator's decisions, might result in a recommencement of ill-advised signings and a self-destructing economic cycle. Economic laws of supply and demand do not function here and cannot prevent this. It seems that it is imperative, then, that in negotiating a new Basic Agreement to commence in 1990, the clubs and players must work together to create a system that will provide free agency for the players with the opportunity to change clubs and to receive a fair market value for their services, but will also provide protection for the clubs and the game from enforced competition destructive to the game and, in the long run, not in the best interests of clubs, owners, the vast majority of players, or the public.

If some kind of control mechanism to accomplish the above is made a *sine qua non* on the part of either the clubs or players to agreeing upon a new Basic Agreement, it makes the upcoming negotiations extremely important and probably also extremely difficult. It will require a good deal of intelligent thought and ingenuity, plus a willingness on both sides to approach the problem with understanding and fairness. With the improvement over the last five years in the economic position of the game, there is enough money available to satisfy the justifiable interests of both parties. And it is well past time for the two parties to start pulling together to reach needed compromise solutions, not only to the signing of free agents, but to other problems in baseball, including safeguards against drugs. Baseball is part of our culture and those who administer it have a trust to preserve its values. What is needed is the following:

- A proper attitude on both sides directed not solely toward their own economic gains, but toward what is best for the game and what both sides can tolerate.

- An understanding of the other parties' problems and positions.
- Some very keen minds capable of putting together new solutions for old problems.
- A great deal of patience.
- The ability of each side to sell its constituents on the soundness and desirability of such an approach.

Without these the 1990 baseball season could be marred by a long and bitter work stoppage.

The Future

I believe that there are enough capable and fair people on both sides to clear the hurdles just described. I am also confident that, barring gross mismanagement, baseball's position in the minds and hearts of Americans is secure and that it will continue to be our National Pastime. The game has been part of our history and its place in our lives has been passed on from generation to generation. Its appeal is deep and stems from many facets: the openness of the game, with every part of the action clearly seen; the recognizability of the players; the contest of pitcher against batter, individual against individual; the ballet-like beauty of many of the plays; the lack of violence; the fact that (unlike most other major team sports) it is not played against the clock and a team can still win until the last man is out ("it ain't over 'til it's over"); that ability is not restricted by size (a player does not have to be seven feet tall or weigh 285 pounds); the fact that it is an everyday game with box scores and records to be followed regularly; that it is family entertainment at prices that a family can afford; and that attending a game is part excitement and part a time for socializing with companions. Of course there are many more reasons.

Many beautiful things have been written about the game of baseball, expressing its valued qualities far more ably than I am able to do. Roger Angell, in a 1972 essay, remarked:

> Within the ballpark, time moves differently, marked by no clock except the events of the game. This is the unique, unchangeable feature of baseball, and perhaps explains why this sport, for all the enormous changes it has undergone in the past decade or two, remains somehow rustic, unviolent, and introspective. Baseball's time is seamless and invisible, a bubble within which players move at exactly the same pace and rhythms as all their predecessors. . . . Since baseball time is measured only in outs, all you have to do is succeed utterly; keep hitting, keep the rally alive, and you have defeated time. You remain forever young.

I also like an editorial that ran in the *New York Times* on June 5, 1984, which said, in part,

> Baseball is one of the symbols of those things constant in American life. Not even the toxic intrusion of artificial grass and megabuck contracts can spoil the naivete and optimism that is baseball. Millions of Americans look to it for a nonviolent escape from the weariness that exists in the world beyond the centerfield wall. Baseball is constant and no matter how bad things get there is always next year. As Emily Dickinson put it, "a little madness in the spring is wholesome even for a king."

And if it lasts from March to October, well that's just fine!

Index